ANNUALS

VENIDIUM FASTUOSUM

[*Frontispiece*

ANNUALS

ROY HAY

THE GARDEN BOOK CLUB
121 CHARING CROSS ROAD,
LONDON, W.C.2

FIRST PUBLISHED BY
JOHN LANE THE BODLEY HEAD LTD.,
IN 1937
REVISED EDITION 1950
THIS SPECIAL EDITION FOR THE GARDEN BOOK CLUB 1955

PRINTED IN GREAT BRITAIN BY
LOWE AND BRYDONE (PRINTERS) LTD.,
LONDON, N.W.10

CONTENTS

ILLUSTRATIONS

Venidium fastuosum   *3 Colour Frontispiece*

Black and White

AUTHOR'S NOTE

IN MATTERS of nomenclature the *Index Kewensis* has been taken as a reference, and I have obtained much helpful information regarding the size and geographical distribution of genera from Dr. J. C. Willis's invaluable work, *Flowering Plants and Ferns*.

My thanks are due to many kind friends for numerous valuable suggestions, and I am particularly grateful to Messrs. Watkins and Simpson, Ltd., for permission to reproduce many of the illustrations in black and white and also for the loan of some blocks. To the late Dr. Fred Stoker, for his advice with regard to the arrangement; to my Father, for much help and criticism; to my Mother, for her assistance in reading the proofs, and to my wife, for her painting of *Venidium fastuosum*, I am deeply grateful.

In this second edition I have added the important new varieties which have appeared since the book was first published, but little has been done in the production of novelties during or since the war.

Haslemere   ROY HAY

In Memory

of

ALFRED WATKINS, V.M.H.

Part I

CHAPTER I

Definition, Distribution and Development

BOTANICALLY AN Annual may be defined as a plant which completes its entire life-history—from seed to seed—during the favourable season, which in some cases may last only a few weeks. During the unfavourable season it survives in the form of seeds. For the gardener an Annual is defined as a plant which is raised from seed, grows to maturity, flowers, produces seeds and dies naturally (not through the effects of frost) within the period of a year.

In this work, however, a number of plants are included which do not conform strictly to this definition, but are so conveniently flowered from seed during the first year of their life that they are suitable for culture as Annuals and in many cases are commonly treated as such. Certain Biennials and even Perennials are included in this category, many of them giving better results when grown as Annuals than when cultivated in the manner usually recommended for their particular class.

A Hardy Annual will withstand a certain amount of frost, in many instances frosts of considerable severity causing little damage.

Half-Hardy Annual is a term applied to a wide range of plants susceptible to damage by frost—the degree of susceptibility varying with different plants. The successful cultivation of this class of Annuals depends to a great extent upon climatic conditions and the position of planting in the garden.

A Tender or Greenhouse Annual is a plant requiring

warmer conditions than those generally provided by the climate of this country and it is consequently unsuitable for cultivation out of doors. In view of its comparatively limited appeal this class of Annuals is not dealt with at any length in these pages.

Nature seems to have compensated the Annuals for their short life by giving them a brilliancy of colouring unsurpassed by any other class of plants, and it is this quality combined with their easy cultivation which has won for them the important place they hold in the gardens of to-day.

Their geographical distribution is interesting, for by far the largest proportion of the most showy Annuals are to be found in the temperate and sub-tropical parts of the world, and for this reason they are specially suitable for outdoor cultivation in this country. Since their seeds are well protected against drought by a firm impervious testa, Annuals are able to live in regions with a very hot and dry climate and only a short favourable season; steppes and deserts are comparatively rich in Annuals, but they tend to disappear towards the Poles and snowy regions of mountains. California and the Mexican desert are strongholds of Annuals, and in the Death Valley they account for 42 per cent. of the vegetation. It is to North America that we owe the greatest number of our cultivated species. North America has provided us with such splendid garden plants as the Clarkias, Coreopsises, Godetias and Eschscholzias, to mention but a few, and although our flower beds and borders have gained so much from these there is reason to hope that the supply of new genera and species has not yet been exhausted.

Mexico, whence have come all the original types of the Marigolds we now grow in ever-increasing variety, has given us also one of our finest edging plants—*Ageratum conyzoides* —and *Salvia splendens*, whose modern varieties are unique among bedding plants.

The countries of South America, although not yet fully

explored botanically, have nevertheless yielded many note-worthy Annuals; the Petunias, Tropaeolums, Calceolarias, the Chilian Salpiglossis and the beautiful Schizanthus or Butterfly-flower are among those which have found favour in English gardens.

In numbers, no less than in variety of beautiful types, South Africa follows closely upon North America, and during recent years many valuable Composites—the Ursinias, Gaz-anias, Dimorphothecas, Arctotis and Venidiums—have come from there, all of them richly coloured and typical of that sunny continent. Morocco, the home of *Linaria maroccana*, promises to give us in the future even more desirable plants than she has already given. The regions of the Mediterran-ean are rich in annual species, and from Southern Europe have come such notable garden favourites as the Sweet Scabious, and *Lathyrus odoratus*, the progenitor of the mod-ern Sweet Pea.

Native to the Balkan States and Caucasia, many of the wild Papavers have given rise to highly ornamental garden forms, while from Turkestan has come that delightful and singular plant, *Statice Suworowii*.

From India, the home of the Celosias; from China and Japan, whence came *Callistephus hortensis*, the originator of the unending family of Annual Asters, upon which we rely so much for our late summer and autumn bedding; from Australia, where dwell the Helipterums and Helichrysums, those gems among the everlasting flowers—in short, from every temperate part of the world have come these charming Annuals, whose uses are legion and appeal universal.

From the moment that each one of these species has ap-peared in cultivation, its destiny has been shaped and its development watched by plant-breeders and selectors all over the world. The countless garden hybrids and varieties we know to-day have been the result in many cases of years of careful and patient breeding, of steady progress towards that ideal which is the aim of all those who labour to improve upon Nature's work.

Whether the changes which plant-breeders have been able to make in the size, habit or colours of our garden plants have always been worthy of the efforts expended upon their attainment, or whether in some cases the untouched wild forms are not in many ways as lovely, is a matter upon which opinions must differ and individual preferences decide. However, comparisons show most convincingly that in numerous instances the changes in form and the pleasing combinations of colours which are the outcome of the ceaseless watchfulness and ingenuity of specialists everywhere, have done much to enrich our gardens and provide annual subjects for almost every conceivable purpose or position.

The results which have been achieved by straightforward selection are often quite surprising. By harvesting seeds from those plants only which show a tendency, sometimes very slight, in the direction that the plant-breeder desires to follow, it is often possible during the course of a few seasons to produce strains with completely different characteristics from those possessed by the parent plant. No two individual plants are exactly similar; they may differ only imperceptibly from their parents or from each other, or they may show considerable divergence in a variety of ways, and it is only by constant selection of the best types that strains can be improved or uniformity maintained.

The objects of the plant-breeder depend upon the potentialities of the material at his disposal. Straggly, untidy subjects may be improved by selection and produce, in time, plants of upright and stately bearing, thus obviating in many instances the necessity of staking and tying unruly shoots in place. Similarly, by selection, many tall-growing plants have been slowly changed into dwarf compact types suitable for cultivation as pot plants, as edging and bedding plants, and for use as rock-garden subjects.

Greater floriferousness, the increase in the size of individual flowers, the introduction of an infinite variety of colours and shades of colour, the production of double forms, laciniated or fringed flowers, the advancing or retarding of the time of flowering to prolong the effective season, the lengthening of stems for cutting purposes—all these points receive the careful attention of plant selectors, and it is only when actual comparison is made of the original and the selected forms, such as those shown at pages 49 and 185, that the importance of their achievements can be appreciated.

Cross-fertilization between plants bearing valuable features which it is desired to combine is constantly being practised, and the results of these labours are to be found in countless gardens. This work is highly skilled and costly, and in consequence the better strains of flower seeds as well as the newest varieties must of necessity be sold at relatively higher prices than the commoner unselected strains. But invariably it will be found that by purchasing seeds only from reliable firms, and by paying a reasonable price for the best selected stocks, failures will be fewer and results far more satisfactory than if cheaper strains are obtained or varieties chosen without due discrimination. A little extra initial outlay expended upon good seeds may save disappointment when flowering time comes.

CHAPTER II

Annuals which Have Been Lost

THOSE HAVING access to a botanical library rich in plant por-
traiture cannot fail to be impressed by the number of beautiful plants, both garden hybrids and species, that from one
cause or other have gone out of cultivation. There are many
reasons to account for their loss, which may be due to changes
of fashion or to difficulties of cultivation. It will, also be
found that the loss is far greater among truly perennial
plants than among those that are only of annual duration,
which goes to show that plants which must be raised annu-
ally from seeds are more abiding; to retain them in cultivation only one condition is necessary, namely, the saving of
seeds, which the majority of annual species provide with the
greatest prodigality. The older books, however, remind us
that not a few annual plants of great garden merit have been
lost, but their portraits in colour remain to encourage those
interested in the introduction of fine plants. Those about to
be mentioned would again provide all the interest and
glamour that is attached to a new species.

Most of the genera from which our garden Annuals are
drawn provide some members which have, in our long garden
history, been grown for a brief period, and from one cause or
another have now quite disappeared.

As a group, Malvaceous plants provide many species of
great garden merit, so that the re-introduction of *Malva
mauritiana*, as figured by Sweet, is much to be desired; it
graced our borders a century ago, and writers of those days
have much to say in its favour.

At the present time Calendulas are in high favour, so that the re-introduction of *C. graminifolia* might provide a new race with elegant narrow grass-like foliage as depicted in the portraits of this old species, which is a native of the Cape.

Calotis cuneifolia, a lovely blue-flowered, Daisy-like plant, is another subject, at one time cultivated at the Physic Garden, Chelsea, which seems well worth searching for.

Another elegant plant no longer catalogued is *Angelonia salicariaefolia*; it grows to two feet in height and has large open Mimulus-like flowers of pale blue, and is found in company with the Alonsoas in South America.

From the same part of the world came *Cleome rosea*, at one time highly esteemed; now that the Spider Plant is again appearing in our public parks and gardens the re-introduction of this richly coloured and spineless species is much to be desired. *Palaua rhombifolia*, also from South America, would again be a highly appreciated Annual; it carries fine terminal clusters of rose-coloured flowers, as handsome as any modern Godetia.

Leonotis Leonurus is quite a showy greenhouse Perennial familiarly known as the Lion's Tail; it is not generally realized that this genus provides us with one or two annual species which are good border plants. *L. heterophyllus* was used for this purpose over a century ago, and we are informed that it ripened an abundance of seeds; it grows two and a half feet high, with fine branching spikes of rose-coloured flowers. It came to us from Brazil.

At the present time Nierembergias are popular and gardeners would again give *N. intermedia* a warm welcome; it would provide a new shade of colour in this lovely genus, as the flowers are of a dark coppery-red and have the same elegant and graceful habit as all their relations.

Regrettable also is the loss of *Palafoxia Hookeriana* (sometimes now referred to as *Polypteris Hookeriana*), with its magnificent heads of rose-purple flowers; although not quite an Annual it can be flowered the first year from seeds.

In Palestine is found *Ricotia Lunaria*, which may be described as a giant-flowered Virginian Stock; rose-coloured and fragrant, it was a favourite Annual and cultivated by Philip Miller when this famous gardener was in charge of the Apothecaries' Garden at Chelsea in 1832.

One recommends a member of the genus *Bidens* with some hesitation, but if *B. procera* is half as showy as its portrait in the *Botanical Register* it would be well worthy of a front place in the Annual border; it is a native of Mexico.

Dr. Lindley tells us that *Valerianella congesta* is a very beautiful Annual, that it was sent home by David Douglas in 1826, and that it flowered in the Royal Horticultural Society's Garden, is perfectly hardy and easily cultivated in the open border. It has vanished from our gardens and awaits re-introduction. At the same time Douglas sent home *Lupinus leucophyllus*, which is claimed to this day by American writers to be one of the most elegant of species, but seeds are rarely forthcoming. It is high time we had another opportunity of trying out this handsome plant.

The genus *Lesquerella*, of which there are several species in North America, would also be acceptable as front-row edging plants; the little experience we have of this genus is sufficient to prove that it is well worth growing.

In the more or less desert regions of America are found the Arctomecons. The genus consists of only two species, both very beautiful and remarkable Poppy-like plants; one has pure white flowers, the other yellow. There is a beautiful figure of *A. californicum* in Fremont's *Expedition to the Rocky Mountains and to Oregon and South California*, 1845. There is also a fine sheet of specimens at the Natural History Museum, and it is sufficient to say that there is no more lovely member of the Poppy tribe. It is astonishing that they have

never been introduced into this country or into any of the
great nurseries of the United States.

There are other fine Annuals which have had a brief spell
in cultivation and have vanished; no doubt they still survive
in their native habitats and may one day be re-discovered.

It may be convenient to mention here that the provision of
new species is not at an end. There are specimens in our
national herbaria of many desirable Annuals which we have
not yet seen as living plants. They will, no doubt, eventually
reach us from many widely separated parts of the world. The
majority of them may be only new members of genera already quite familiar to us, but there will also be new generic
names to add to our present long catalogue of garden Annuals.

The genus *Anticharis* will provide certain members
likely to succeed in the open border, and will reach us by
way of Africa and Arabia. The gentianaceous *Belmontia* and
Blackstonia may be expected to enliven our borders in the
near future, while others such as *Wormskioldia*, *Ceratotheca*,
Monsonia, will be fine additions to the many richly
coloured subjects in our conservatories.

CHAPTER III

Cultivation

Sweet Peas—Hardy Annuals—Half-Hardy Annuals—Damping-off—
In the Greenhouse—Window-boxes—Hanging Baskets.

WITH FEW exceptions, Annuals do not require a great deal in the way of specially cultivated or artificially enriched soil. In fact, the majority of them do best in soil which is not too rich, as any excess of plant food in the ground will often encourage a leafy growth, attended by a reluctance to produce flowers. Provided the soil is neither too sandy nor of too heavy clay, and is well dug and in good order, the cultivation of Annuals presents little difficulty.

Ground intended to be used for Annuals should be well dug in the autumn to allow the top surface to become broken down by the weather until it is easily worked and in a fit state for sowing the many small-seeded Hardy Annuals during the following spring.

Poor soils may be improved by the addition of well-rotted stable manure, and heavy soils may be lightened by working in mortar rubble, sifted ashes, decayed leaf soil, peat or rough stable manure containing plenty of straw. Certain Annuals require more food from the soil than others, for instance the Sweet Pea, which needs generous treatment if the best results are to be obtained.

The ground upon which it is desired to grow Sweet Peas should be well prepared.

Old, rich, well-rotted farmyard manure, if it can be obtained, is the ideal fertilizer for the production of really good Sweet Peas. The soil should be moved to a depth of two spits—double dug that is—and the manure should be worked into the lower spit as the digging proceeds. The surface soil should be kept free from manure as the tender roots of the Sweet Peas do not flourish in direct contact with the manure and in any case it is desirable to encourage the roots to go down in search of their nourishment. When farmyard manure is not available, and that is usually more often than not in these days, the best that can be procured should be used—well-decayed compost and processed hop manure are excellent substitutes. To produce fine blooms with long stems it is necessary to see that the plants do not suffer from lack of moisture during dry spells and also to apply frequent weak doses of liquid manure, or a suitable proprietary fertilizer. Exhibition blooms are grown by training the plants cordon fashion on single stakes, but for ordinary garden use and for cutting for the house this is not necessary. Dead flowers should be removed regularly to encourage a long period of flowering.

Hardy Annuals

As to the best time for sowing seeds, it is only possible to give some general directions, since so much depends upon the kind of plant, the locality, and the situation in the garden in which the seeds are to be sown. In general, it is usually possible, except in very rough or frosty seasons, to choose a suitable day for sowing seeds of most of the Hardy Annuals in the open ground during the latter half of March in southern gardens; during the first half of April in the Midlands, and towards the end of April in Scotland and the North. As already pointed out, these are only general directions, and the amateur who has not yet won his experience of the correct times to sow the many different kinds of Annuals is referred to the notes on cultivation included in the description of each genus on pages 45–235.

The depth at which seeds should be sown is another point

which often worries the beginner, and he should be guided
by the size of the seed, just covering the smaller seeds with a
very thin sprinkling of soil, and burying the larger kinds,
such as those of Sweet Peas and Nasturtiums, to a depth of
about 1½ ins. For sowing rows of Annuals for edgings, or in
order to raise batches of plants to provide cut flowers, a
shallow drill may be taken out with a hoe, the seeds deposited
therein, and the soil raked over them. A more popular and
pleasing effect for garden decoration is obtained by sowing
the seeds very thinly in fairly large irregular-shaped patches
and then either raking them in or sprinkling a covering
of finely sifted soil over them.

And here it is necessary to repeat the advice which is given
countless times every year—sow very thinly. Its importance
cannot be too greatly emphasized, as every year thousands of
Annuals are robbed of their chance of reaching perfection
solely through overcrowding in their early stages. The germination of seeds of Annuals, if purchased from reliable
seedsmen, is usually of such a high standard that thin sowings can confidently be made. There can be no more de-
pressing sight than Annuals grown lank and spindly, starved
of air and sunshine, and resulting in a travesty of the sturdy,
handsome plants they would have made had they been given
room to develop. So let our slogan be, "Buy the Best Seeds
and Sow Thinly."

After sowing, the next attention which the seedlings will
require is weeding and thinning out. These two processes
may be carried out simultaneously, and as some varieties
take longer to develop than others, no definite time after
sowing can be given for this operation. A first thinning, however, may be made as soon as the plants are sufficiently
rooted, so that they will be reasonably undisturbed by the
uprooting of their neighbours, and it is well at this first thinning to leave about double the number of plants which the
bed will eventually contain, just in case of attacks by slugs or

other enemies. After about two weeks have elapsed it will usually be possible to see which plants are safely established and a final thinning may be carried out, this being done by simply removing about every other plant. If slugs are particularly troublesome, they may be trapped by placing a handful of bran mixed with a little powdered Metaldehyde according to the maker's instructions here and there, covered with a cabbage leaf.

When the plants begin to show signs of flower it is a good plan with the taller growing, as well as with the more straggly of the dwarfer kinds, to give them a little support by a few twigs placed among them, and after that is done the only attention they should need is the regular removal of all dead flowers. This will help to prolong the flowering period of the great majority of Annuals and, moreover, will give a much tidier appearance to the plants.

Half-Hardy Annuals

The Half-Hardy Annuals, being unable to withstand frost, are unsuitable for sowing direct into the open ground, but require to be raised and sheltered in a greenhouse or cold frame until such time as the weather has become warm enough to plant them out of doors.

Although Annuals classified as Half-Hardy are usually treated in this manner, it is quite possible with many of them to secure good results from late open-air sowings during May, but usually the resulting plants are considerably later and not of the same quality as those raised under glass. Many Hardy Annuals also are frequently sown under glass and transplanted to the open ground with a view to obtaining strong plants which will flower earlier than those sown at the normal time in their flowering positions.

As with the Hardy Annuals, it is not possible to lay down hard-and-fast rules for the times of sowing. The successful raising of Annuals under glass, although not difficult, calls

for a certain amount of care and knowledge of the requirements of very small seedlings in the matter of water and air,
and this knowledge comes only from the actual handling of
such seedlings.

Although not all amateur gardeners are fortunate enough
to possess a greenhouse, it is a great advantage in the raising
of most of the Half-Hardy Annuals, especially such kinds as
Salvias, Ageratums and Lobelias, which require to be sown
early in the year if the best results are to be obtained.
During February and March a temperature of $55°-60°$
should be maintained in the greenhouse, but after the end of
March slightly lower temperatures will prove adequate.

The seeds are best sown in pans, pots or shallow boxes of
a convenient size to handle, and if wooden boxes are used
they should be sufficiently strong to withstand frequent
handling. Good drainage is essential in all seed-sowing re-
ceptacles; if pots or pans are used they should be thoroughly
cleaned and then a large piece of broken pot placed over the
hole in the bottom and a few smaller pieces placed on top of
it. They are then ready to be filled with soil, and the question
of the best compost for raising seedlings requires a little consideration. Recent experiments have shown that greatly
superior results are obtained from seed-sowing soils which
have been partially sterilized by steam, and fertilized by the
addition of small quantities of superphosphate and chalk or
lime. For most amateurs the cost and labour of sterilizing the
soil will be too great, but the addition of fertilizers is a
simple and inexpensive matter, and will be found to have
most beneficial effects upon seedling growth. The best compost for seed sowing and pricking out is the following: 10
parts (by bulk) medium loam, 8 parts moss peat (or well-
rotted leaf soil), 6 parts coarse sand, and to every bushel of
this compost are added $1\frac{1}{2}$ ozs. superphosphate (16 per cent.
P_2O_5) and 1 oz. of chalk or lime. The prepared pots are filled
with this compost, which should be pressed firmly down,

and they are then ready for sowing. If boxes are employed, a small strip of wood should be placed over the space between the bottom boards and they should then be half-filled with rough fibrous soil, and the potting compost added to within half an inch of the top.

With regard to the actual operation of sowing the seeds little need be said except to repeat the familiar warning, "sow thinly," as seedlings which are overcrowded cannot possibly develop properly and are more prone to disease than those which can obtain all the air and light necessary to their growth.

The smaller seeds and those most subject to the "damping-off" disease should be covered with finely sifted silver sand, while for other seeds the ordinary compost passed through a fine sieve will suffice.

After sowing, water the pots or boxes with a fine-rosed can and shade them with paper. When the seedlings are large enough to handle, usually by the time they have produced the first pair of rough leaves (after the smooth cotyledons or seed leaves) they must be pricked off into boxes and gradually hardened off until they are ready to transplant into the open ground. It is during the hardening-off process that the possession of a cold frame as an adjunct to a greenhouse is of the greatest value.

A useful tool may be made for the operation of pricking off the seedlings. A piece of flat board, just a little smaller than the seed boxes to be used, is fitted with the same number of evenly spaced, short, pointed wooden pegs as the number of plants the box will hold. After the soil in the boxes has been made fairly firm it is possible by means of this tool to make all the holes for the seedlings at one operation, with the advantage that they are all evenly spaced in the box. After being pricked off, the seedlings should be shaded for a day or so until they have recovered from the shift.

The disease known as "damping-off" is caused by a fungus (Pythium) which, under conditions favourable to it, attacks the stems of the young seedlings, causing them to wither and die. The best safeguards against it are briefly, to sow thinly, pay great attention to the watering of the seedlings and keep the atmosphere in the house from becoming damp or stuffy. Certain plants, Kochia, Zinnia, Amaranthus and several others, are very susceptible to this disease, and should be watered by immersing the pot up to the brim in water for a minute or two, and not watered overhead. This method of watering should be adopted in all cases where damping-off is experienced.

Another important point which should not be overlooked concerns the covering of the shelves or stages upon which the pots are to be stood. The most suitable covering is undoubtedly pea gravel, although excellent results are obtained by placing the pots on finely sifted ashes, while many gardeners prefer to stand them on a surface of dampened peat. The presence of some covering matter upon the stages is important, as the bottoms of the pots are thereby kept moist but at the same time are not standing in a pool of water as they might be if they were placed on a solid surface.

In the Cool Greenhouse

The cultivation of Annuals as pot plants in the greenhouse is a matter upon which much has been written. Treatment varies considerably with various kinds of Annuals, and space does not permit of this subject being dealt with in detail. However, mention may be made of the best soil compost for use when growing Annuals in pots, which is similar in some respects to that recommended above for seed sowing. As the plants become established and ready for potting they are able to absorb more food from the soil than they can in their seedling stage, and the following compost has been found to give excellent results with all kinds of plants grown in pots:

10 parts (by weight) loam, 7 parts moss peat (or rotted leaf soil), 2 parts ballast (graded to $\frac{1}{8}$–$\frac{3}{8}$ in.); and to every bushel of this are added $1\frac{1}{2}$ ozs. hoof and horn (12·75 per cent. N), $1\frac{1}{2}$ ozs. superphosphate, $\frac{3}{4}$ oz. potash (48·5 per cent. K_2O) and 1 oz. chalk or lime.

Window-boxes

Many Annuals are splendid subjects for cultivation in window-boxes. The bottom of the boxes should be covered to a depth of about three inches with broken pots or rough cinders, to ensure good drainage. Then they should be filled with the compost recommended above for growing Annuals as pot plants. It should be remembered that window-boxes, especially those in hot sunny places, require a considerable amount of water, and care must be taken not to allow them to dry out.

Hanging Baskets

A number of trailing Annuals are very effective grown in hanging baskets. Wire baskets for this purpose may be obtained from all sundriesmen. They should be lined inside with damp moss and then filled with the same compost as that advised above for pot plants. Watering must be very carefully carried out, and is best done by plunging the baskets in water for about twenty minutes.

CHAPTER IV

The Uses of Annuals

In an Annual Border—As Climbing Plants—For Carpeting—Edging—
Bedding and Massing—Cutting—In the Rock Garden—For their
Scent—As Everlasting Flowers—As Foliage Plants—For Window-
boxes and as Pot Plants—In the Cool Greenhouse.

THE WIDE range of types, the great differences in height,
habit and time of flowering, as well as the endless variety of
their brilliant colourings, give Annuals the right to be considered the gardener's special friends.

In order to assist readers in the choice of varieties suitable
for the many purposes to which they may be put, lists are
given on pages 35–44, and although they are by no means
exhaustive, used in conjunction with the descriptions given
in Part II they should prove helpful and informative.

Annuals are perhaps never seen to better advantage than
when grown in great variety in a long border; irregular
patches, carefully chosen with due regard to colour, height
and flowering period, make a gay show during the best of the
summer months. When planning such a border it is well to
make the patches of each variety fairly large, not less than
two or three feet in length, and to avoid any formal arrangement. If the border is backed by a wall or fence which is not
screened by Roses or other climbing plants, an effective
background can be made with some of the rapid-climbing
Annuals, such as Sweet Peas, Convolvulus, Ipomoea, or
some of the Ornamental Gourds which have lately returned
to favour. Some form of support is, of course, necessary for
these climbers, either in the form of strings, wires or pea
sticks. A border which is flanked by lawn or paths may be

treated in a similar manner, and small clumps of climbing Annuals trained on pea sticks or rustic-poles; or any of the varieties of Sunflower, or the variegated Maize, *Zea japonica* var. *variegata*, will answer admirably as a background for the rest of the border.

In choosing the Annuals for the middle and front parts of the border, attention must be paid to the height and flowering time, no less than the colour, of each variety, as with a little care and forethought the display may be prolonged until the coming of the autumn frosts. A border may be planned with little difficulty so that it can be kept attractive over as long a period as possible, an aim which can be materially assisted by sedulously picking off the flowers as they wither. I have already referred to this point in an earlier chapter, but its effect on nearly all Annuals is so valuable that it can bear repetition.

As the elaborate designs of the carpet bedding so beloved by the gardeners of the past century have gradually given way in our parks and public gardens, no less than in our private gardens, to more natural and less stiffly formal types of bedding, Annuals have found a full measure of popularity. As bedding plants they vie successfully with the Geranium and the Chrysanthemum; and no matter what effect we are anxious to obtain nor what scheme of colours we wish to work out, we can nearly always find a variety of one of the members of this serviceable class of plants which will solve the problem.

It is often difficult to find suitable subjects for carpeting beds of tall plants which lack foliage near the ground; although some people prefer to see beds of such plants as Roses left clear of ground cover, the practice of using Violas and other low-growing plants for carpeting appeals to many gardeners, and in some cases, such as for carpeting plantings of Lilies, a dual purpose is served—shade being provided for the shallow-rooting Lily bulbs and a pleasing colour contrast being obtained for the brightly coloured flowers above.

The Tom Thumb varieties of Antirrhinum or the new colourful mixture known as Magic Carpet, which forms a low creeping mat about four to six inches in height, are very suitable for all kinds of carpeting work, while the soft blues of the dwarfer varieties of Ageratum are perhaps more useful when the colours of the main feature of the bed are in themselves very bright and dominating, as with Lilies or Gladioli.

For use as edging plants we have a wide choice of Annuals. Lobelia, Alyssum, the dwarf varieties of *Lychnis Coeli-rosa*, as well as several neat shapely little Annuals whose foliage is bright and attractive, such as the dwarf forms of *Chrysanthemum Parthenium*, are deservedly popular for edgings to borders and beds, but among the recent introductions we find numerous plants readily adaptable for use in this connection. The new *Nierembergia caerulea*, which will be found mentioned often in these pages, is one of these plants, and owing to its compact shapely habit, abundance of flowers and soft pleasing colour can be used in a variety of ways—not least effectively as an edging plant. A word of special mention is also due to the brilliant *Mesembryanthemum pyropeum*. Grown in a fairly sunny border nothing could be more attractive than a patch of this cheerful South African Annual. In addition to the mixture of many shades, separate varieties are now obtainable which breed fairly true from seeds and will undoubtedly in the course of time find their way into many gardens.

Although individual tastes differ about the degree of formality an edging plant should present, some gardeners preferring to keep it rigidly in its front-rank position, I prefer an irregular, informal planting along the front of a border or bed, with the edging plant allowed to run back among the taller plants here and there, giving the most natural effect.

Many Annuals rank among our most popular flowers for

cutting—Sweet Peas, Stocks, Asters, Centaureas—to mention but a few. It is a good plan to plant a patch or two of these in an odd corner of the vegetable garden to provide a supply of bloom for the house, without spoiling the beauty of beds or borders. A selection of some of the best Annuals for cutting is given on page 38.

Useful, too, in the rock garden are the colourful Mesembryanthemums, while Gilias, Dwarf Ursinias such as *U. pygmaea* and *U. pulchra*, *Dimorphotheca* Tom Thumb Golden Gem, the lilac Annual *Alyssum* Lilac Queen, *Antirrhinum* Rock Hybrid and Magic Carpet, dwarf-growing Verbenas such as *V.* Fireball and *V.* Carmine Ball, are but a few examples of splendid plants which can be judiciously employed to replace bona-fide rock plants which have died, so maintaining a show of colour until the time comes in the autumn for planting more lasting plants.

I have met gardeners who dislike the idea of mixing Annuals and alpine plants in a rock garden, but after the spring and early summer flowering the rock garden often tends to be rather drab and uninteresting, so if the reader is not an alpine devotee but merely a gardener whose aim is to make his plot of land attractive and pleasant to look upon for as long a period of the year as possible, I think that it is pardonable to associate Annuals with rock plants in this way.

The complaint is often made that so many of our most attractive Annuals have little or no scent, and while this is true of perhaps the majority of the Annual flowers commonly grown in gardens to-day, there are nevertheless enough sweetly scented subjects to plant a border near a French window or round a summerhouse which can be a positive joy, both during the hot, lazy afternoons of summer and in the cool of the evening, when the majority of the sweetly scented Annuals give off their best fragrance. Easily raised from seeds sown early in the year, Heliotrope, although not really an Annual, may well be permitted to form a basis of a scented border; Annual Scabious, Stocks, *Oenothera trichocalyx*, a particularly lovely white Evening Primrose, which possesses the advantage over many members of its family of remaining open during the daytime; Nicotianas, the incomparable Mignonette—and many more we can find, whose delightful sweetness follows us borne upon the evening breeze sometimes far from the plants themselves. The modern Sweet Pea, although of a size and texture much in advance of that of the older varieties, has undoubtedly lost some of its delicious scent in the process of improvement, but if its critics would go into a plantation of Sweet Peas early in the morning or about sunset, they would discover for themselves that the Sweet Pea of to-day still has a scent, at once powerful and fragrant, of a subtle sweetness, matching the exquisite lightness of its fragile flowers.

Another use to which certain kinds of Annuals may be put is for drying for winter decoration, when fresh flowers are scarce and consequently costly. These Everlasting Annuals possess undeniable decorative qualities whether growing in the garden or used as cut flowers in the home. During the past twenty years plant selectors have brought about many improvements in the size and colour of the flowers, and as the demand for better and new types has increased, they have redoubled their efforts to produce them. They are without exception easy to grow, and the only special care necessary is at the time of cutting and drying the flowers. The blooms should be cut when they are fully open in the case of the Composite, or Daisy-flowered Everlastings, such as Helichrysum and Helipterum, and all Everlasting flowers should be cut on dry sunny days, so that no moisture may be present on the flowers to hinder the drying process. Next they should be tied into small bunches and hung up in a dry, warm place with a sheet of muslin or even newspaper tied loosely round them to prevent them from becoming dusty.

During recent years small baskets of these Everlasting flowers, neatly arranged, the colours tastefully chosen, have proved exceedingly popular as Christmas gifts, and many find pleasure in making up their own designs and effects.

In addition to those Annuals whose actual flowers can be used in this way, there are quite a number which form decorative seed pods. The large-flowered Poppies, *Nigella* Miss Jekyll—Love-in-a-Mist—whose curious seed pods are extremely ornamental, and the hairy seed heads of the Annual Scabious may all be turned to account. Some prefer to colour them artificially by spraying them with suitable paints—gold or aluminium—but whether treated in this fashion or left in their natural state they are of undoubted value during the dark winter months. This practice of colouring seed pods has been extended on a large scale during the past few years to many of the Ornamental Grasses, some of them Annual varieties, and if the reader is inclined to experiment with this form of decoration the lists on pages 39 and 42 may prove helpful in choosing suitable varieties.

Certain Annuals are grown solely for their foliage, while others combine the attractions of striking variegated or colourful foliage with showy flowers. Of the latter type the "Queen" or variegated class of both Tall and Dwarf Tropaeolums and certain individual varieties, e.g. *T.* Tom Thumb, Golden Morn, a scarlet-flowered golden-leaved kind, and Empress of India, the well-tried favourite with leaves so dark as to be almost black, are worth growing; among the Antirrhinums, too, are several dark-leaved sorts, notably *A. nanum* var. Black Prince and the tall variety, Crimson King, but of the Annuals whose sole virtue lies in their handsome foliage the choice is not embarrassing. Perhaps the best known of these is the "Burning Bush," *Kochia trichophylla*, a beautiful dome of feathery, pale-green foliage always cool and fresh-looking on the hottest summer day, turning gradually to a burnished crimson as the golden days of autumn warn us of the approaching end of the garden's glories. Rather more sombre in colour, the varieties of Perilla have their uses as plants for contrast; the dark metallic leaves—so dark that they remind one more of a raven's plumage than anything else—serve to intensify, by their stark coldness, the delicate beauties and glowing colours of other plants around them.

Unusual and cheerful in their rather exotic colourings are the species of Amaranthus—*A. salicifolius*, the Fountain Plant, which bears long, willowy leaves shading gradually from bronze to orange-red, and *A. gangeticus* var. *tricolor splendens*, sometimes known as "Joseph's Coat." Its broad leaves are a rich red in colour and curiously marked with yellow and green, giving a most decorative effect dotted here and there among other plants. The Castor Oil plant, Ricinus, may be satisfactorily treated as an Annual and is usually sold in a mixture of several shades of colour. *Ricinus communis* var. *Gibsonii* is a useful kind, rather dwarfer than the other members of the genus, bearing large reddish-coloured leaves.

For window-boxes and hanging baskets a wide selection of Annual subjects may be employed. *Nierembergia caerulea* flourishes in any kind of window-box, wooden tub or stone sink, while the many varieties of Petunia are ideal for this purpose. In fact, as a glance at the list given on page 41 will show, the possible combinations of colours one can obtain in a window-box with Annuals, whether used by themselves or with other plants, are limitless.

Although Annuals are essentially plants for the open, most of them being sun-loving plants, many are nevertheless splendid subjects for the cool greenhouse or conservatory. The Celosias, Salpiglossis, many of the brilliant South African Composites (such as the Ursinias and Venidiums), Petunias, Browallias, and the deliciously scented *Nicotiana suaveolens*, are but a few examples of the type of Annual that revel in the moderate temperature of the cool greenhouse. A list of Annuals suitable for this purpose will be found on page 37; with its help a show of blooms may be obtained during many months, and by delaying or advancing the sowing times it is often possible, with some of the plants mentioned, to have supplies of bloom available for cutting at times when outside flowers are unobtainable. This, however, is a matter for the professional rather than the amateur gardener, and requires a good deal of practical experience before successful results can be relied upon.

Of those Annuals only suitable, owing to their delicacy, for cultivation in very warm or stove houses only a fleeting mention is made, as their appeal is not sufficient to justify space being devoted to their description.

The following classified lists of Annuals are not intended to be exhaustive, but if used in conjunction with the descriptions of Annuals in Part II should prove helpful to readers in selecting plants for various purposes.

DWARF BORDER ANNUALS

Ageratum
Alonsoa
Alyssum
Amaranthus
Anagallis
Antirrhinum (dwarf varieties)
Asperula
Begonia
Bellis
Brachycome
Calandrinia
Calceolaria (bedding varieties)
Calendula

Celosia
Cheiranthus
Cineraria
Clarkia
Collinsia
Coreopsis
Cuphea
Dahlia (Coltness varieties)
Delphinium
Dianthus
Diascia
Dimorphotheca
Echium
Emilia
Emmenanthe

Dwarf Border Annuals—*continued*

Erysimum
Eschscholzia
Gaillardia
Gilia
Godetia (dwarf)
Gomphrena
Heliophila
Helipterum
Iberis
Impatiens
Layia
Linaria
Lobelia
Lychnis
Matricaria
Mesembryanthemum

Myosotis
Nasturtium (Tom Thumb)
Nemesia
Nemophila
Nierembergia
Omphalodes
Petunia
Phacelia
Phlox (Drummondii)
Platystemon
Reseda
Tagetes
Ursinia
Verbena (dwarf)
Viola
Zinnia (dwarf)

Blue-flowered Annuals

Ageratum
Anagallis
Anchusa
Aster (see Callistephus)
Brachycome
Browallia
Campanula
Centaurea
Cineraria
Collinsia
Convolvulus
Delphinium
Felicia
Gilia
Heliophila
Ipomoea

Jasione
Linum
Lobelia
Lupinus
Nemesia
Nemophila
Nigella
Nolana
Omphalodes
Phacelia
Salvia
Statice
Verbena
Viola
Viscaria (see Lychnis)

ANNUALS FOR THE COOL GREENHOUSE

Acroclinium (see Helipterum)   Heliophila
Alonsoa   Heliotropium
Anagallis   Helipterum
Anchusa   Hunnemannia
Antirrhinum   Impatiens
Arctotis   Linaria
Begonia   Lobelia
Brachycome   Matthiola
Browallia   Mesembryanthemum
Calceolaria   Mimulus
Calendula   Nemesia
Campanula   Nemophila
Celosia   Nicotiana
Celsia   Petunia
Centaurea   Phlox (Drummondii)
Clarkia   Primula
Datura   Reseda
Delphinium   Rudbeckia
Dianthus   Salpiglossis
Diascia   Schizanthus
Didiscus   Senecio
Dimorphotheca   Statice
Echium   Trachelium
Eschscholzia   Tropaeolum
Exacum   Ursinia
Gaura   Venidium
Gilia   Verbascum
Godetia   Verbena
Gypsophila   Zinnia

ANNUALS FOR CARPETING

Ageratum   Antirrhinum (dwarf sorts)
Alyssum   Felicia
Anagallis   Gilia

Annuals for Carpeting—*continued*

Iberis   Mesembryanthemum
Ionopsidium   Mimulus
Linaria   Nemophila
Lobelia   Phacelia
Malcomia   Verbena

CLIMBING ANNUALS

Adlumia   Ipomoea
Cobaea   Lathyrus
Convolvulus   Maurandia
Eccremocarpus   Vicia
Humulus

ANNUALS SUITABLE FOR CUTTING FOR INTERIOR
DECORATION

Acroclinium (see Helip-   Helipterum
    terum)   Lathyrus
Antirrhinum   Leptosyne
Aster (see Callistephus)   Linaria
Calendula   Lupinus
Calliopsis   Lychnis
Centaurea   Matricaria
Cheiranthus   Matthiola
Chrysanthemum   Nierembergia
Clarkia   Nigella
Cosmos   Penstemon
Cyanus   Reseda
Dahlia   Rhodanthe (see Helipterum)
Delphinium   Rudbeckia
Dianthus   Salpiglossis
Eschscholzia   Scabiosa
Gaillardia   Statice
Godetia   Tropaeolum
Gypsophila   Verbena
Helichrysum   Zinnia

ANNUALS FOR EDGINGS

Abronia
Ageratum
Alyssum
Asperula
Bellis
Bellium
Calandrinia
Chrysanthemum
Crepis
Downingia
Felicia
Gilia
Godetia (dwarf)
Grammanthes
Iberis

Lobelia
Malcomia
Matthiola
Mesembryanthemum
Nemesia
Nemophila
Phacelia
Pyrethrum (see Chrysanthemum Parthenium)
Saponaria
Tagetes
Tropaeolum (dwarf)
Ursinia
Verbena
Viola

ANNUAL EVERLASTING FLOWERS FOR WINTER BOUQUETS

Acroclinium (see Helipterum)
Ammobium
Catananche coerulea
Gomphrena
Helichrysum

Helipterum
Rhodanthe (see Helipterum)
Statice
Xeranthemum
Waitzia

ANNUAL PLANTS HAVING ATTRACTIVE FOLIAGE

Amaranthus
Atriplex
Centaurea
Coleus
Euphorbia
Humulus

Kochia
Malva
Perilla
Pyrethrum (see Chrysanthemum Parthenium)
Ricinus

Bedding Annuals for Partly Shaded Places

Anchusa	Linaria
Antirrhinum	Matricaria
Begonia	Mimulus
Bellis	Nemophila
Campanula	Oenothera
Cineraria	Oxalis
Claytonia	Papaver
Delphinium	Salvia
Impatiens	Viola

Annuals from Seed for the Rock Garden

Abronia	Felicia
Adonis	Gilia
Alyssum	Grammanthes
Anagallis	Iberis
Antirrhinum (Rock Hybrids)	Ionopsidium
	Linaria
Bellis	Lobelia
Bellium	Malcomia
Brachycome	Mesembryanthemum
Calandrinia	Mimulus
Centranthus	Nemesia
Claytonia	Nemophila
Diascia	Nierembergia
Dimorphotheca (dwarf varieties)	Omphalodes
	Papaver
Downingia	Phacelia
Erysimum	Platystemon
Eschscholzia	Ursinia
Euphorbia	Verbena

ANNUALS WHICH MAY BE SOWN WHERE THEY ARE TO FLOWER

Adonis
Alyssum
Anchusa
Borago
Calendula
Calliopsis
Campanula
Centaurea
Chrysanthemum
Clarkia
Claytonia
Collinsia
Collomia
Convolvulus
Cynoglossum
Delphinium
Dimorphotheca
Downingia
Echium
Emilia
Erysimum
Eschscholzia
Euphorbia
Gilia

Glaucium
Godetia
Gypsophila
Helianthus
Iberis
Lathyrus
Lavatera
Leptosyne
Limnanthes
Linaria
Linum
Lupinus
Malcomia
Malope
Matthiola
Nemophila
Nigella
Papaver
Phacelia
Reseda
Rudbeckia
Viscaria
Tropaeolum

ANNUALS FOR WINDOW-BOXES

Abronia
Ageratum
Antirrhinum (dwarf)
Aster (dwarf)
Begonia
Celosia

Coleus
Eschscholzia
Grammanthes
Ipomoea
Linaria
Lobelia

Annuals for Window-boxes—*continued*

Matthiola	Reseda
Mesembryanthemum	Salvia
Nemesia	Statice (dwarf)
Nierembergia	Tropaeolum (dwarf)
Petunia	Ursinia
Phlox (Drummondii)	Verbena

TALL-GROWING ANNUALS FOR SCREENING AND BACKGROUNDS

Adlumia	Humulus
Althaea	Ipomoea
Atriplex	Lathyrus
Cleome	Lavatera
Convolvulus	Lupinus
Dahlia	Nicotiana
Delphinium	Polygonum
Eccremocarpus	Ricinus
Gourds (see Cucurbita and	Tropaeolum
Lagenaria, pages 43–44)	Vicia
Helianthus	

ANNUAL ORNAMENTAL GRASSES

In the following list of Grasses the names used are those generally adopted in most trade catalogues.

Agrostis laxiflora
Agrostis nebulosa
Agrostis pulchella
Anthoxanthum gracile
Avena sterilis (Animated Oats)
Briza gracilis (Little Quaking Grass)

Annual Ornamental Grasses—*continued*

Briza maxima (Larger Totter Grass)
Bromus aureus
Bromus brizaeformis
Chloris gracilis
Coix Lachryma-Jobi (Job's Tears)
Coix variegata
Eragrostis abyssinica
Eragrostis elegans (Love Grass)
Hordeum jubatum (Squirrel-tail Grass)
Lagurus ovatus (Hare's-tail Grass)
Lamarckia aurea (Golden-top Grass)
Tricholaena rosea (Half-Hardy)
Zea japonica var. gigantea quadricolor (Half-Hardy)
Zea japonica var. gracillima variegata (Half-Hardy)
Zea japonica var. quadricolor perfecta (Half-Hardy)
Zea japonica var. variegata (Variegated Maize, Half-Hardy)

ORNAMENTAL GOURDS

In the following list of Gourds used for ornamental purposes the names given are those generally adopted in most trade catalogues.

Apple-shaped	
Bi-coloured	
Egg-shaped	
Miniature	
Onion-shaped	Varieties of
Orange	*Cucurbita Pepo*
Pear-shaped	
Striped	
Turk's Cap or Turban	
Warted	

Ornamental Gourds—*continued*

Anaconda
Bottle, large
Bottle, small
Hercules' Club   Varieties of
Powder Horn   *Lagenaria vulgaris*
Serpent or Snake
Siphon
Spoon
Gooseberry (*Cucumis Anguria*)
Ostrich Egg (*Cucumis dipsaceus*)

Part II

Abronia (Gr. *habros* = elegant, graceful, delicate). Sand Verbena. *Nyctaginaceae.* 50 species; North America.

Although actually perennial, these trailing plants, when treated as Annuals, are useful for hanging baskets, tubs, window-boxes, rock work or the open border, and bear clusters of showy, sweetly scented flowers, closely resembling those of Verbena. Seeds may be sown in the open ground in April or under glass in February or March.

A. UMBELLATA. The most popular species; flowers bright rose with white centre, about ½ in. diameter. California, 1823. There is a garden variety, *grandiflora*, having slightly larger flowers and leaves.

Although not commonly cultivated nor readily obtainable, the following species are said to be serviceable plants: *A. fragrans, A. latifolia, A. mellifera* and *A. villosa.*

ACROCLINIUM see HELIPTERUM ROSEUM.

Adlumia (in honour of Major John Adlum, 1759–1836, an American horticulturist). Fumitory or Allegheny Vine. *Fumariaceae.* 1 species; Eastern North America, 1788.

A. CIRRHOSA (*A. fungosa*). A rapid-growing Biennial, not quite hardy, but a very suitable subject for planting against a wall, fence or trellis and most effective when allowed to ramble over shrubs and small trees. It bears pale, rose-coloured flowers about ½ in. long from June to September. Seeds may be sown out of doors in April.

Adonis (named after Adonis, the beloved of Aphrodite). *Ranunculaceae.* 10 species; Temperate Europe and Asia.

The annual species of this genus, with their varieties, are highly ornamental in mixed borders, on rock gardens and on the margins of shrubberies. The flowers are similar in shape to those of a Buttercup, and the finely cut foliage greatly enhances the appearance of the plant. Seeds may be sown in the open ground towards the end of March or during April.

A. AESTIVALIS. Pheasant's Eye, Flos Adonis, Summer Adonis. Erect stems about 1½ ft. in height bear deep-crimson flowers during June and July. 1629. A little-grown garden variety, *citrina*, has pale golden-yellow flowers.

A. ALEPPICA. A brilliant blood-red species 1½ ft. in height. Somewhat difficult to grow and not often obtainable, but strikingly beautiful.

A. AUTUMNALIS. Corn Adonis, Pheasant's Eye, Red Camomile, Red Morocco. Stems erect, 1–1½ ft. in height, and flowers crimson with deeper centre, produced from June to September. Although it is doubtful if this plant is native to Great Britain, it is found established in certain parts of the country.

Aethionema (Gr. *aitho* = to scorch, *nema* = filament, in allusion to the burnt appearance of the stamens). *Cruciferae*. 55 species; Mediterranean regions.

A. CAPPADOCICUM (*A. Buxbaumii*.) An uncommon little plant, 6 ins. in height, happiest on dry sunny banks and thriving in light sandy loam. The flowers, which appear in June, are pale rose in colour. It is best treated as a Half-Hardy Annual, although it may be sown in the open during May.

AFRICAN MARIGOLD see TAGETES ERECTA.

AGATHAEA COELESTIS see FELICIA AMELLOIDES.

Ageratum (Gr. *a* = not, *geras* = age, in reference to the long-lasting nature of the flowers). Floss Flower. *Compositae*. 45 species; Tropical America. *A. conyzoides* is a common weed of the Tropics.

A. CONYZOIDES (*A. mexicanum*). Best known under the name of *A. mexicanum*, this is the only species commonly grown in gardens. The many varieties introduced in recent years, the best of which are enumerated below, rank among the most popular of Half-Hardy Annuals. Ideal for all kinds of bedding work, the dwarfer and more compact varieties are eminently suitable for edging and carpeting purposes. The taller varieties, which grow to about $1\frac{1}{2}$ ft. in height, are sometimes cultivated as cut flowers for the market. Easy to grow, they have a long flowering period and will give a good show until the coming of the autumn frosts.

Seeds should be sown in a greenhouse in February or March, while if the season is favourable, quite good results can often be obtained by sowing in the open ground in May, although this practice is not always attended by a great measure of success, and the resulting plants flower rather late in the season. *A. conyzoides* grows about 1 ft. in height and bears large loose heads of lavender flowers. It is rather a straggly plant and for garden purposes the more compact varieties are better suited. Among the best of the numerous sorts now on sale are the following:

Blue Ball, a handsome dwarf type, the deep blue flowers are large and carried in ball-shaped clusters—one of the finest varieties for all purposes; Blue Cap, small-flowered but very free, a neat compact variety, splendid for edging; Imperial Dwarf Blue and Imperial Dwarf White, two old varieties still widely grown and very satisfactory; Little Dorrit White, a decorative, dwarf variety; Purple Perfection, although of not so deep a colour as its name suggests, this is nevertheless the deepest blue Ageratum on sale, and its habit is dwarf, compact and very showy.

A. MEXICANUM see A. CONYZOIDES.

AGROSTEMMA see LYCHNIS.

ALLEGHENY VINE see ADLUMIA.

Alonsoa (in honour of Z. Alonso, at one time Spanish Secretary for Santa Fé de Bogota). *Scrophulariaceae*. 6 species; Tropical America.

As bedding or border plants the Alonsoas are of great value, since by keeping dead flowers removed or even by cutting down the stems after flowering, a succession of bloom may be obtained, while as pot plants they can be successfully grown with little trouble. Treated as Half-Hardy Annuals and planted out in May, their culture presents little difficulty.

A. ACUTIFOLIA (*A. myrtifolia*). A cinnabar-scarlet-flowered species, growing to a height of about 2–2½ ft. A white variety, *candida* (*A. albiflora*), may be used satisfactorily for pot culture in the conservatory, to provide a display during the winter months.

A. ALBIFLORA see A. ACUTIFOLIA var. CANDIDA.

A. CAULIALATA. A scarlet-flowered species about 1 ft. in height. Peru, 1823.

There is a garden variety of this species sold under the name of *A. Mutisii*, chamois rose, which makes a bushy plant producing a profusion of delicately coloured flowers.

A. INCISIFOLIA. Mask Flower. About 2 ft. in height, bearing deeply cut leaves, and bright scarlet flowers. Chili, 1795.

A. MUTISII see A. CAULIALATA.

A. MYRTIFOLIA see A. ACUTIFOLIA.

A. WARSCEWICZII. Although better known than most of the species enumerated above, this plant should be much more widely grown, as its brilliant rosy-scarlet flowers are a constant pleasure in the garden during the summer months. Growing to a height of about 1½ ft., it is admirably suited for bedding or planting in patches in a mixed border. A slightly dwarfer variety is available under the name *compacta*. Central America, 1858.

Althaea (Gr. *althein* = to heal, in reference to certain medicinal qualities of some of the species). Hollyhock. *Malvaceae*. 15 species; Temperate regions.

The Hollyhock is usually grown as a Biennial or Perennial, but there is a variety of *Althaea rosea* sold under the

I. ANCHUSA CAPENSIS VAR. BLUE BIRD

2. ANTIRRHINUM MAJUS

Left: Majestic   *Right:* Old Variety

name of Annual Hollyhock, which can be easily flowered as an Annual. Double and single forms are obtainable and are usually grown in many-shaded mixtures.

Alyssum (Gr. *a* = not, *lyssa* = rage, in reference to its supposed property of curing canine madness). *Cruciferae.* 120 species; Mediterranean Europe.

A. MARITIMUM. Sweet Alyssum (*Königa maritima*). This species has given rise to numerous varieties, many of which are deservedly popular for all kinds of bedding and carpeting work. It is low growing, and its white flowers are deliciously scented and very attractive to bees. Seeds may be sown in the open ground during April. Some of the best varieties are: *Benthami compactum*, a dwarf compact type 4–6 ins. in height, with white flowers; *procumbens*, a white variety of low-spreading habit, ideal for carpeting and filling odd spaces on the rock garden: Little Dorrit, a white garden variety most suitable for edging purposes, which makes a dwarf bushy little plant only about 4 ins. in height, and bears large heads of pure white flowers; Lilac Queen, of similar habit, but a splendid contrast in colour, being of a rich deep lilac; Purple King, an even deeper and richer variety than the last.

Amaranthus (Gr. *amarantos* = unfading, in reference to the long-lasting nature of the flowers). *Amaranthaceae.* 60 species; Tropical and Temperate Regions.

This unusual genus includes many highly ornamental and widely differing types, and contains species and varieties of great merit as foliage plants, as well as a number whose curiously shaped inflorescences are in themselves bright and showy. Of the latter the long, trunk-shaped, crimson ropes of flowers of Love-Lies-Bleeding, *Amaranthus caudatus*, is an example. Among those kinds grown solely for their foliage are numerous brilliant species which display unusual combinations of colours and markings. There are, however, many dark and sombre species, whose effect is funereal and to many gardeners unattractive. The more cheerful forms are attractive when grown in pots and are an asset to the cool greenhouse or conservatory. Unless otherwise stated, seeds should be sown under glass in April and attention paid to watering, as several members of the genus are susceptible to damping-off. Fairly dry sunny positions suit them best, and it is unwise to manure the ground too heavily, as this encourages the plants to become coarse and often unsightly.

A. BICOLOR see A. GANGETICUS var. MELANCHOLICUS RUBER.

A. CAUDATUS. Love-Lies-Bleeding. Grows to a height of 2–3 ft.; the leaves are a pale green, and the flowers hang in long drooping cord-like formations, their ends often reaching to the ground. The colour of these strange flowers is a rich blood-red, contrasting markedly with the foliage. The plant is hardy and seeds may be sown in the open ground in April.

A. GANGETICUS. This species has given rise to many popular varieties which are widely used as foliage plants for bedding purposes. They are mostly about 1–1½ ft. and of a Half-Hardy nature, extremely varied in colour. The following varieties are noteworthy: *melancholicus ruber* (*A. bicolor*), a crimson-leaved, compact-growing variety, flowers unimportant, Japan; *tricolor* (*A. tricolor*), Joseph's Coat, a well-known ornamental variety with oddly coloured leaves. The base of the leaf is crimson-scarlet, merging to bright yellow and green at the tip; most effective when well grown. Other forms are Aurora, leaves red, yellow and dark green, and *marmoratus*, leaves green and yellow, mottled with rose. Tropics.

A. HENDERI. This is an attractive foliage plant with rosy-carmine leaves mottled and marked with various colours from golden-yellow to pale green. It is generally considered to be a hybrid of *A. salicifolius*.

A. HYPOCHONDRIACUS. Prince's Feather. The leaves are a greenish-purple and the dense erect flower spikes are of a dark blood-red. The plant usually attains a height of about 2–3 ft. Tropical America. Two varieties worthy of mention are: *sanguineus*, growing to a height of about 3 ft.; the flowers and leaves are a rich blood-red; and *viridis*, Love-Lies-Bleeding, White, about 2–3 ft. in height; the leaves and stems are a bright green and the long ropes of flowers white.

A. PANICULATUS (*A. speciosus*). A tall-growing handsome species often attaining a height of 3–4 ft. The colour of the leaves varies from dark purplish-green to dark crimson and the flowers are a dark crimson-purple. Tropical regions.

The variety *flavescens* (*A. speciosus* var. *aureus*), Golden Prince's Feather, is of similar height, but the flowers are a greenish-yellow; a useful border plant.

A. SALICIFOLIUS. Fountain Plant. A handsome species often growing to a height of 2–3 ft., it bears long drooping willow-like leaves changing from bronze-green to orange-red. A valuable foliage plant for bedding purposes. Philippine Islands, 1871.

A. SPECIOSUS see A. PANICULATUS.

A. TRICOLOR see A. GANGETICUS var. TRICOLOR.

AMBERBOA see CENTAUREA MOSCHATA.

Ammobium (Gr. *ammos* = sand, *bio* = to live, in reference to the sandy soil in which it thrives). Winged-Stalked Everlasting Flower. *Compositae.* 2 species; New South Wales.

A somewhat unattractive member of the group of Everlasting Flowers. It is principally grown on account of the long-lasting characteristic of its flowers, which can be cut and dried and used for winter decoration. Seeds may be sown in the open ground towards the end of March or during April.

A. ALATUM. The only species commonly cultivated. A

gaunt-looking plant about 2–2½ ft. in height bearing pure
white flowers with a golden-yellow centre. A larger-flowered
garden variety is obtainable under the name *grandiflorum*.

Anagallis (Gr. *anagelao* = to laugh; allusion doubtful).
Pimpernel. *Primulaceae*. 25 species; Europe, Asia, Africa
and South America.

A showy and attractive family of low-growing annual and
perennial plants. Only one species, *A. arvensis*, is a true
Annual but the other species and their varieties may be
successfully flowered as Annuals. They do best in warm
sunny positions and are splendid for rock-work or in the front
row of a mixed border. Seeds may be sown in the open
ground during April in the case of *A. arvensis* and its varieties; the other kinds are best treated as Half-Hardy.

A. ARVENSIS (*A. indica*). A charming, trailing Annual bearing small flowers varying in colour from scarlet to white.

A. GRANDIFLORA see A. LINIFOLIA.

A. INDICA see A. ARVENSIS.

A. LINIFOLIA (*A. Monellii, A. grandiflora*). A charming
little plant, growing to a height of about 4–6 ins. The flowers
are a brilliant blue in colour and about ½ in. in diameter.
This species has given rise to many varieties of which some
of the best are described below. Although they are all
varieties of *A. linifolia*, they are generally listed in catalogues
under the name *A. grandiflora: carnea*, pale flesh-pink;
coccinea (*A. sanguinea*), flowers large, deep scarlet in colour;
caerulea, large bright blue flowers, a valuable plant for the
cool greenhouse; *Phillipsii*, a dwarf blue large-flowered form,
ideal for rock-work, usually sold under the name *A. Monellii*
var. *Phillipsii*.

A. MONELLII see A. LINIFOLIA.

A. SANGUINEA see A. LINIFOLIA var. COCCINEA.

During the early part of the last century many varieties
and hybrids, such as *A. Breweri, A. Wellsiana, A. Will-*

moreana, made their appearance, but are seldom seen in present-day gardens.

Anchusa (Gr. *anchousa* = alkanet, from *ancho* = I constrict, referring to certain healing properties for the skin possessed by some species). *Boraginaceae*. 45 species; Europe, North Africa, Western Asia.

A. CAPENSIS. A biennial species which may be very successfully grown as an Annual. The plant is free-flowering and grows to a height of about 1–1½ ft. The colour of the flowers is a brilliant blue, of a shade not too plentiful among annual plants. There is a strikingly beautiful garden form, Blue Bird, dwarfer and more compact than the type; it makes a small bush, about 1 ft. in height, literally covered with large brilliant blue flowers. A noteworthy plant of exceptional value for all kinds of bedding work.

ANGELONIA SALICARIAEFOLIA see p. 17.

ANTICHARIS see p. 19.

Antirrhinum (Gr. *rhis* = nose, in reference to the shape of the flowers). Snapdragon, Dragon's Mouth. *Scrophulariaceae*. 36 species; Northern Hemisphere.

Although not strictly annual plants the Antirrhinums grown extensively in gardens are usually treated as such, unless it is desired to obtain an early show of bloom by sowing in the autumn and wintering the plants in a greenhouse or cold frame. Seeds should be sown under glass during January, February or March and the young plants moved into their flowering positions during April. Seeds may be sown in the open ground during April but the plants will flower late in the year and seldom make such fine specimens as those raised under glass.

A. MAJUS. The Common Snapdragon, which has become naturalized in Great Britain. It grows to a height of about 2 ft. and the flowers, which vary considerably in colour, are about 1½–2 ins. long. Europe.

The garden varieties of *A. majus* are legion, and surprising results have been obtained by breeders who have specialized in their improvement during the past twenty years. Numerous new varieties are introduced every year, and while some of the older sorts gradually disappear from cultivation many out-of-date kinds which could well be dispensed with are still on sale, although they have been superseded by better and more handsome varieties. A selection of some of the best varieties of Antirrhinum is given below, under the classification usually adopted in most seedsmen's catalogues.

A. MAJUS or Tall. 2½–3 ft. Vermilion Brilliant; also Striped varieties, a mixture of many differently coloured striped kinds.

A. MAJUS var. GRANDIFLORUM. Apricot Beauty; Cerise King; Crimson King; Feltham Beauty, a delightful shade of rose-pink; Goliath, salmon-rose, shaded apricot-orange; Harmony, rich pink, yellow centre; Orange Glory; Primrose Queen; Queen Victoria, pure white; Rose King; Torchlight, orange-scarlet, yellow centre; and Yellow King.

A. NANUM. Intermediate or Semi-dwarf. 1–1½ ft. Black Prince, crimson, dark foliage; Flame, brilliant orange-scarlet; Ladybird, cherry-pink and white.

A. NANUM var. COMPACTUM or Bedding. 9 ins. Bright Rose; Canary Yellow; Dark Crimson; Orange-Scarlet; Pale Pink; White.

A. NANUM var. GRANDIFLORUM. Advance, orange-scarlet, white throat; Beacon, salmon-rose, gold centre; Charm, rose-pink; Cherry Ripe, terra-cotta red; Cottage Maid, pale pink, white throat; Dazzler, bright scarlet; Empress, crimson; Gloria, deep rose; Golden Monarch; Madonna Improved, pure white; Malmaison, silvery pink; Orange Glow; Primrose Monarch; Radiance, salmon-red; Victory, terra-cotta orange; Silver Queen, silvery lilac; Welcome, rich crimson.

A. NANUM var. GRANDIFLORUM Majestic. 1½ ft. A handsome

type with enormous flowers. Avalanche, pure white; Dawn
o' Day, pale rose-pink, fading apricot; Eldorado, golden-
yellow; Evensong, chamois-pink, shaded apricot; Fair Lady,
clear·rose-pink; Fire-dragon, scarlet-cerise; Golden Dawn,
golden-buff, shaded salmon; Orange King, terra-cotta
orange, yellow tip; Primrose; Purple King; Rosamond, rich
rose; Rose Marie, rose, golden centre; Rose Princess, rose-
cerise, gold centre; Royal Gold, golden-orange, flushed
salmon; Splendour, rich rose-pink, orange centre; Startler,
rich, glowing cerise; Sunset, terra-cotta, shaded salmon;
Twilight, pale apricot, shaded salmon.

A. ROCK HYBRID or TRAILING. Resulting from crosses between *A. majus*, *A. glutinosum* and *A. molle*, several varieties
have been obtained which, although comparatively small-
flowered, are splendid for carpeting or rock-work. They are
of a very low-growing trailing nature and are extremely
floriferous. Rock Hybrid Pink Gem and Rock Hybrid White
Gem are notable varieties, while the many-coloured mixture
on sale is exceedingly effective. Baby Rose is a very compact
deep pink variety; Magic Carpet, a race of compact very low-
growing, semi-trailing Snapdragons, consists of a mixture of
many colours, and is unrivalled for all types of planting
where a close-growing subject is required.

A. TOM THUMB. 6 ins. Canary Yellow; Brilliant Crimson;
Dainty Gem, delicate rose; Henry IV, bronze and gold;
Pinkie, bright rose-pink; Rosie, salmon-rose; Snowflake,
pure white.

APPLE OF PERU see NICANDRA PHYSALOIDES.

ARCTOMECON see p. 18.

Arctotis Gr. *arktos* = a bear, *ous* = an ear, in reference
to the shaggy seeds). *Compositae.* 65 species; Tropical and
South Africa, Australia.

A genus of striking beauty, all its members are sun-loving
plants. The brilliant colourings of many of the species con-

trast pleasingly with the large, often woolly, leaves, and few
Annuals can compare with these dazzling Daisy-flowered
plants. While some are Perennial, those mentioned below
may be treated as Half-Hardy Annuals. A strain known as
Sutton's Hybrids is reputed to have been derived by crossing
A. grandis with a Venidium; the colours range through
white, cream and buff to rich orange and are enhanced by
a bright blue disc as in *A. grandis*. Their cultivation is simple,
and if a fairly dry, sunny position is given them in a light
sandy soil, they will provide a gay display for several months.

A. BREVISCAPA see A. LEPTORHIZA var. BREVISCAPA.

A. GRANDIS. An elegant species 1½ ft. in height; the flowers
are borne on long stems and are a glistening white, the
reverse of the petals is shaded a delicate lavender, and the
centre of the flower is a rich blue. Singularly beautiful as a
border plant or used as a cut flower. S.W. Africa. 1710.

A. HYBRIDA. Forms deriving from various species are
beginning to appear in trade lists and a mixture known as
Sutton's Special Hybrids is said to have been the result of
inter-crossing *A. leptorhiza* var. *breviscapa*, *A. scapigera* and
other species. A fine range of colours from white to cream,
yellow, orange, red and crimson is the result.

A. LEPTORHIZA var. BREVISCAPA. Commonly sold under the
name of *A. breviscapa*, this is one of the most vividly striking
members of the family. The plant is dwarf and shapely,
about 1 ft. in height, and the large bright orange flowers are
carried on short stalks 4–6 ins. long. There is a larger-
flowered, deeper-coloured variety, *aurantiaca*, which is
considerably more showy.

A. SCAPIGERA see A. SPECIOSA var. HAYANA.

A. SPECIOSA var. HAYANA (*A. scapigera*). The handsome
plant until recently known as *A. scapigera* is now referred to
this sub-species. The leaves are dark green, white-felted on
the reverse, and when young are covered with a silvery cob-
webby film. The plant reaches a height of about 1½ ft. and

the flowers borne on long stems vary in colour from white, pink and yellow-orange to blood-red.

A. SPECIOSA var. JACQUINII. Commonly found in seed catalogues under the name of *A. speciosa*, this attractive plant is about 1½ ft. in height, and the orange-coloured flowers are rendered more attractive by a reddish shading on the reverse of the petals.

There are several desirable species not at present in cultivation, two of the most noteworthy being *A. Fosteri* and *A. Gumbletonii*.

Argemone (Gr. *argema* = cataract of the eye, in allusion to properties of this plant supposed to cure this disease). Devil's Fig, Prickly Poppy, Mexican Poppy, Yellow Thistle. *Papaveraceae*. 12 species; Tropical America, one naturalized throughout the Tropics.

A valuable genus of biennial plants (one perennial), successfully grown as Annuals. Their large white, yellow or purplish Poppy-like flowers are singularly handsome in mixed borders and are produced with great prodigality during the summer months. The foliage is stiff, prickly and usually white-spotted and resembles that of certain kinds of Thistle; the plants are sturdy and upright, often 2–3 ft. in height. They thrive in a light soil and a sunny position; seeds should be sown during March in the open ground where the plants are to flower. They may be flowered earlier if sown under glass during February, but Argemones dislike being transplanted, and if this method of treatment is adopted care must be taken when moving the young plants to disturb the roots as little as possible.

A. ALBIFLORA see A. MEXICANA.

A. GRANDIFLORA see A. MEXICANA.

A. HISPIDA. White-flowered, 2 ft. in height. A serviceable plant. California, 1879.

A. MEXICANA. Pale lemon-yellow flowers; the plant is 2 ft.

in height and is moderately prickly. It is said to possess
certain medicinal properties and is a troublesome weed in
parts of Tropical America and Mexico, whence it was introduced in 1592. The following varieties are noteworthy:
albiflora (*A. albiflora*) white-flowered, with glaucous spiny
leaves; 2–3 ft. in height; Southern States of America, 1820;
grandiflora, large white-flowers; widely grown and exceedingly handsome; usually found in catalogues as *A. grandiflora*; the foliage is spiny and somewhat glaucous. Mexico,
1827.

A. OCHROLEUCA. Flowers yellowish-white. Stems and
leaves very prickly. Mexico, 1827.

A. PLATYCERAS. Large glistening white flowers sometimes
varying to purple, 2 ins. in diameter. A handsome species.
North and South America.

Arnebia (from Arabic vernacular name *arneb*). Prophet's
Flower. *Boraginaceae*. 12 species; Mediterranean, Tropical
Africa, Himalayas.

Easily grown, decorative little Half-Hardy Annuals, the
Arnebias are not very widely cultivated, but are nevertheless
interesting subjects for a mixed sunny border. Seeds should
be sown under glass in February or March and the plants
moved to their flowering positions in May.

A. CORNUTA. A bushy plant, 2 ft. in height; the flowers
resemble those of a Marigold and are yellow, black-spotted,
changing to a pure yellow as they develop. Orient, 1888.

A. GRIFFITHII. About 9 ins. in height, this dwarf species
is not often seen in cultivation. The flowers are a bright
orange and marked with black spots. North-West India.

Asperula (L. *asper* = rough, in allusion to the leaves).
Woodruff. *Rubiaceae*. 80 species; Europe, Asia, Australia.

Excellent little plants for edging, or planting in patches in
mixed borders. Seeds of the annual species, sown in the open
in April, will flower in June–July.

A. ORIENTALIS. Better known in the trade as *A. azurea* var. *setosa*, this charming little sky-blue-flowered plant grows to a height of about 1–1½ ft. and covers itself with a wealth of sweetly scented flower-heads. 1867.

A. TRICHODES. A white-flowered species rarely seen and probably not now in cultivation. 1838.

ASTER, CHINA, see CALLISTEPHUS HORTENSIS.

ASTER TENELLUS see FELICIA FRAGILIS.

ATHANASIA ANNUA see LONAS INODORA.

Atriplex (Gr. *a* = not, *traphein* = to nourish). *Chenopodiaceae.* 180 species; Temperate and Sub-tropical regions.

A. HORTENSIS var. ATRO-SANGUINEA (*A. h.* var. *cupreata*). A crimson-leaved variety of the common Orach, sometimes used as a vegetable, the leaves being eaten like Spinach. Growing to a height of about 4 ft., it may be treated as a Hardy Annual, and is quite effective as a foliage plant in the back row of a border.

BABY'S BREATH see GYPSOPHILA.

BALSAM see IMPATIENS.

BARTONIA see MENTZELIA LINDLEYI.

BEARD TONGUE see PENSTEMON.

BEEFSTEAK-PLANT see PERILLA.

Begonia (in honour of Michel Begon, 1638–1710, a French botanist). *Begoniaceae.* 750 species; Tropical and Sub-tropical regions.

Both the tuberous- and fibrous-rooted kinds of Begonia may be successfully treated as Annuals as they will flower quite well during their first year from seed. The varieties and hybrid forms now available are so numerous that it is only possible to mention here a few of those which have been found most popular for general garden purposes. Seeds should be sown in a temperature of 70° during January or

February, and the seedlings potted on. They should be ready
for planting out towards the end of June. Great care must be
observed in sowing the seeds as they are very minute.

Begonias are usually grouped in seedsmen's catalogues
into two classes, Tuberous-rooted and Fibrous-rooted. The
former group contains many splendid large single- and
double-flowered hybrid forms, as well as varieties whose
flowers are fringed or crested. It is of the utmost importance
to obtain only the very best strains available. In the Fibrous-
rooted group there are numerous, compact varieties, producing a profusion of small showy flowers, which are
strikingly handsome when massed in beds or borders. Some
of the most popular of these are described below.

B. GRACILIS. The type, which has produced several fine
varieties and many hybrids, is about 6 ins. in height, with
dark green, smooth, shining foliage and rose-pink flowers.
Many hybrids are now available under the name *heterosis*;
the seed of these hybrids is obtained by cross-fertilizing two
different kinds, and it is only the first generation of seedlings
obtained in this way which can be relied upon to breed true
to description.

Some of the best varieties and hybrids are: Fireball,
brilliant crimson; *heterosis* Dresden, 1936, carmine-scarlet;
heterosis Pink Profusion, clear rose; *luminosa*, dark scarlet
flowers with deep reddish-brown foliage; White Pearl, snow-
white.

B. SEMPERFLORENS. The originator of many beautiful
varieties, this species is about 1 ft. in height and bears an
abundance of rose-coloured flowers, sometimes varying to
white. The varieties may be divided into two classes, tall and
dwarf. Some of the best of the tall varieties, which reach a
height of about 12–15 ins., are: Albert Martin, brilliant carmine; Bedding Queen, rose-pink; Vernon, blood-red;
Salmon Queen, salmon-red; and White Queen, pure white.

Among the dwarf types, about 6 ins. in height, are:

heterosis Gruga, carmine-pink; Lightning, deep scarlet; Triumph, white-tinged pale pink.

BELLE DE NUIT see MIRABILIS.

Bellis (L. *bellus* = pretty, beautiful, in reference to the flowers). Daisy. *Compositae.* 15 species; Europe and Mediterranean regions.

The Daisies, those indispensable flowers for spring bedding, can be easily flowered in their first year from seeds, if sown under glass early in the year, during February or early March, and although to many people they are essentially April flowers, they have their uses later in the season. They are all perennial, and usually treated as Biennials. As edging plants they are ideal, while certain species and varieties serve a useful purpose in the rock garden.

B. PERENNIS, the Common Daisy, native of Great Britain. Numerous double varieties are obtainable, notably: *helichrysoides*, a pink form having curiously incurved petals; Longfellow, a rich deep rose-coloured variety; Quilled Etna, bright red; Snowball, pure white; *monstrosa alba*, very large double white flowers; *monstrosa rosea*, similar in type to the above with bright rose-pink flowers; *monstrosa grandiflora alba*, the largest flowered white form of all.

B. ROTUNDIFOLIA var. CAERULESCENS see BELLIUM MINUTUM var. CAERULESCENS.

Bellium (L. *bellis* = a Daisy, in reference to the resemblance the flowers bear to those of the Daisy). False Daisy. *Compositae.* 6 species; Mediterranean regions.

Small Daisy-like plants easily grown as Annuals, their creeping habit renders them valuable as rock or edging plants. They are very free-flowering and may be sown under glass in February or March to flower the same year, although they are generally treated as Biennials and sown in the open ground in June to flower the following year.

B. BELLIDIOIDES. A creeping plant 3 ins. only in height,

bearing a profusion of white flowers resembling a miniature Daisy. 1796.

B. CRASSIFOLIUM. Although not readily obtainable, this downy-leaved, creamy-white-flowered species is worth cultivating for the rock garden. It is about 6 ins. high. 1831.

B. MINUTUM. A tiny pale lilac-flowered species, small flowered, about 3 ins. only in height. 1772. There is a variety, *caerulescens* (*Bellis rotundifolia* var. *caerulescens*), Blue Daisy, in which the flowers, about 1 in. in diameter, are pale blue and are produced very freely. A dainty little plant for the rock garden, it grows 6–9 ins. high. 1873.

BELMONTIA see p. 19.

BIDENS PROCERA see p. 18.

BINDWEED see CONVOLVULUS.

BLACK-EYED SUSAN see HIBISCUS TRIONUM, RUDBECKIA and THUNBERGIA.

BLACKSTONIA see p. 19.

BLADDER KETMIA see HIBISCUS TRIONUM.

BLANKET-FLOWER see GAILLARDIA.

BLUE BOTTLE see CENTAUREA CYANUS.

BLUE DAISY see BELLIUM.

BLUE LACE FLOWER see TRACHYMENE CAERULEA.

BLUMENBACHIA LATERITIA see LOASA LATERITIA.

BLUET see CENTAUREA CYANUS.

Borago (derivation uncertain, possibly from low L. *burra* = a shaggy cloak). Borage. *Boraginaceae*. 3 species; Europe, Mediterranean regions, Asia.

B. OFFICINALIS. Sometimes grown for decorative effect, the common Borage is beloved by bees. It is generally found in the herb garden, and is used for flavouring various dishes, also claret cup and fruit drinks. Seeds sown during March or April in the flower garden will give quite a pleasing display later in the year. The deep-blue flowers contrast well with the silvery appearance which a covering of woolly hairs gives to the foliage and stems. The plant reaches a height of about 2 ft.

Brachycome (Gr. *brachus* = short, *kome* = hair). Swan River Daisy. *Compositae.* 50 species; Australia, New Zealand, Africa, North America.

One of the daintiest Half-Hardy Annuals, it gives of its best when planted in a dry sunny position. A first-rate plant for a mixed border, flowering continuously for a long period. Although seed may be sown in the open ground during May, better results are achieved by sowing under glass in March or April and transplanting the seedlings towards the end of May.

B. IBERIDIFOLIA. About 1 ft. in height, the flowers are often 1–1½ ins. in diameter and are produced very freely. There are numerous varieties, some of the most attractive of which are: *alba*, a pure white form of the above; and the following which are slightly more compact: Blue Gem, a clear lavender-blue variety with a white zone at the base of the petals; Mauve Beauty, deep mauve, with a dark disc or centre; White Star, a useful white variety; Purple King, rich purple, one of the best varieties; Summer Beauty, a charming soft mauve with a contrasting dark disc.

A pleasing effect may be obtained by planting these varieties in mixture.

BRAZILIAN MORNING GLORY see IPOMOEA SETOSA.

BROOM CYPRESS see KOCHIA.

Browallia (in honour of J. Browall, 1707–1755, Bishop of Abo in Finland). *Solanaceae*, 6 species; Tropical America.

Blue-flowered Annuals are always desirable both in the garden and in the cool greenhouse or conservatory, and while the Browallias, given favourable weather conditions, will often flower well in a sheltered border, they are splendid pot plants,

and as such deserve greater popularity. Plants raised from
seeds sown under glass during March will flower from July
onwards, and sowings may be made about the end of July or
early August to produce winter-blooming plants for the
conservatory. These late plants should be stopped several
times to encourage bushy growth, except in the case of
B. viscosa var. Sapphire, which is itself a dwarf compact
type.

B. DEMISSA. Usually sold and cultivated under the name
of *B. elata*. About 1–1½ ft. in height; the flowers are of an
attractive shade of pale violet-blue and are carried singly on
short stems. 1735.

The variety *alba* (*B. elata* var. *alba*), is similar to the
above, but bears pure white flowers.

B. GRANDIFLORA. About 1½ ft. in height, this little-grown
species varies in colour from white to pale lilac. 1829.

B. SPECIOSA. A fine pot plant producing large flowers varying from white to pale lilac; 1½–2 ft. in height. There is a
variety, *major*, with very large violet-blue flowers often 2 ins.
in diameter. It is extremely showy when grown in pots and
banked in a conservatory. Height 1½–2 ft.

B. VISCOSA. 1–1½ ft. in height. A very free-flowering
species. The flowers are small, but of a bright violet-blue,
enhanced by a white eye. A garden variety, Sapphire, is
dwarfer and more compact and attains a height of only 9–10
ins. Its flowers are a deeper blue than the type, and the
contrast between the blue and the white eye is more sharply
defined. A noteworthy plant.

BUTTERCUP PRIMROSE see PRIMULA FLORIBUNDA.

BUTTERFLY-FLOWER see SCHIZANTHUS.

CACALIA see EMILIA.

CAJOPHORA LATERITIA see LOASA LATERITIA.

CALAMPELIS see ECCREMOCARPUS.

3. CALANDRINIA UMBELLATA

4. CALENDULA OFFICINALIS
Showing Different Forms of Flower

Calandrinia (in honour of J. L. Calandrini, a Genoese botanist). Rock Purslane. *Portulacaceae*. 80 species; North and South America, Australia.

Several members of this genus are extremely effective for rock-work, as edging plants and in mixed borders, and it is to be regretted that they are not seen more often in gardens. Some of the species are annual, while the perennial kinds respond well when treated as Annuals. Seeds may be sown in the open ground during April, or if plants are required to flower early in the summer, sowings may be made under glass in March, and the seedlings transplanted to a warm sunny position towards the end of May.

C. GRANDIFLORA. Grows to a height of about 1 ft.; the flowers are about 2 ins. in diameter, of a rosy-purple colour and resemble those of the Poppy. The foliage is of a fleshy nature and is an attractive shade of pale green. Chile, 1826.

C. MENZIESII (*C. speciosa*). A pretty plant, 6 ins. in height, bearing rosy-purple flowers ½–1 in. in diameter. 1831. A white variety of the foregoing is the variety known as *alba* (*C. speciosa* var. *alba*).

C. SPECIOSA see C. MENZIESII.

C. UMBELLATA. A very showy and effective plant for the rock garden and other garden purposes. It is a dwarf trailing species about 4–6 ins. in height, bearing brilliant violet-crimson flowers in clusters on short stiff stems. In favoured localities it is sometimes perennial. The best conditions for satisfactory flowering are a sunny position and a light sandy soil. The flowers close up at evening or in dull cloudy weather. A splendid plant, deserving a greater popularity than it enjoys at present. Chile, 1826.

Although not frequently seen, nor easily obtainable, the following species are said to be desirable plants: *C. Buridgii*, *C. caulescens*, *C. chromantha*, *C. compressa*, *C. discolor* (*C. elegans*), *C. spectabilis*.

Calceolaria (L. *calceolus* = a slipper, in reference to the shape of the flowers). Slipperwort. *Scrophulariaceae.* 200 species; South America, Mexico.

The genus *Calceolaria* contains several annual species and a great many perennial species, some of which may be treated successfully as Annuals. It is divided into two sections, shrubby kinds and herbaceous kinds, and it is from certain species of the latter group that most of the hybrid varieties commonly grown as Annuals for pot culture and bedding purposes have been derived. Seeds of the annual species should be sown under glass during February or March, the seedlings being transplanted towards the end of May or during June.

The hybrid kinds, usually grown for greenhouse or conservatory decoration, should be sown during July to obtain large plants which will flower early the following spring. Seeds of the hybrid varieties sown as late as August or early September will produce later supplies of plants, which may be bedded out after the weather has become warmer during the early summer of the following year.

C. CHELIDONIOIDES. A neat annual species 1–1½ ft. in height, bearing small lemon-yellow flowers.

C. CLIBRANII see C. PROFUSA.

C. HERBEOHYBRIDA see C. HYBRIDA.

C. HETEROPHYLLA see C. SCABIOSAEFOLIA.

C. HYBRIDA (sometimes now referred to as *C. herbeohybrida*). The numerous hybrids and garden varieties now in cultivation have been derived from the herbaceous species, and there is a wide choice of different types and colourings suitable for both pot culture and bedding purposes. The following are some of the best obtainable: Albert Kent Improved, a splendid variety with large golden-yellow, crimson-blotched flowers carried in immense trusses and extremely showy; Albert Kent Hybrids, a mixture of many shades of colour, varying from creamy-yellow to rose, carmine and crimson; the habit of the plants is similar to the last type; Covent Garden Strain, a selection of many brilliant shades of colour; the flowers are very large and curiously marked and mottled—a fine type for show purposes; Eclipse, a new race of hybrids having a more woody tendency than most. The colours of the flowers, which are carried in dense bunches, are very bright and varied, and the plants, about 2 ft. in height, are more hardy than the majority of Calceolaria hybrids. They may be safely wintered in a cold frame, and if planted out in a fairly sheltered spot in the garden about the beginning of June will flower profusely for many weeks—splendid additions to the many fine strains at present in commerce; Feltham Glory, resembling the Albert Kent type in the shape of its flowers and in general habit, the colours range from scarlet orange, golden-brown to pure yellow; Feltham Scarlet, a selection of the last strain, the flowers being a rich velvety scarlet; James' Strain, a selected mixture of many fine large-flowered, blotched, marked and also self-coloured varieties; *multiflora nana*, a new strain, in which the vividly coloured medium-sized flowers are borne in large clusters; the plants are dwarf and shapely, excellent for pot-work and largely grown for the market.

C. MEXICANA. A small-flowered pale yellow annual species growing to a height of about 1 ft. A useful and showy plant.

C. MULTIFLORA see C. HYBRIDA.

C. PROFUSA (*C. Clibranii*). Growing to a height of about 1½–2 ft., this is a delicate yellow-flowered species. The small flowers are longer in shape than those of the hybrid types.

C. SCABIOSAEFOLIA (*C. heterophylla*). An interesting species. The rather hairy foliage forms an admirable background for the small pale yellow flowers. The height of the plant is 1½–2 ft.

Calendula (L. *calendae* = the first day of the month, in allusion to its long flowering period). Pot Marigold. *Compositae*. 15 species; Mediterranean regions.

C. CHRYSANTHEMIFOLIA see DIMORPHOTHECA CHRYSANTHE-MIFOLIA.

C. GRAMINIFOLIA see p. 17.

C. OFFICINALIS. The Common Marigold, also known as Garden and Pot Marigold.

Always popular, the Calendulas have during the past few years received a fresh impetus by reason of the numerous varieties and new types which have been placed on the market. The extreme ease with which they may be grown in almost any soil or position, combined with their long-flowering characteristic and their adaptability for use as a cut flower, entitle them to a place in every garden, large or small. Perfectly hardy, they may be sown in the open ground at any time from early March until May. Autumn sowing will produce plants flowering early in the following summer. *C. officinalis*, the type from which all the garden varieties have been derived, is, by comparison with the modern refined sorts, a rather coarse and to many people unattractive plant. It grows to a height of about 2 ft. and bears single orange-coloured flowers. 1573.

The following is a selection of some of the best varieties: Apricot Queen, 2 ft. in height, deep apricot in colour, the flowers are double and freely produced; Art Shades, a mixture of many pleasing shades; The Ball, the deep rich orange flowers are globular in shape and very useful for cutting, height 2 ft.; Golden King, the largest-flowered double golden variety yet introduced, a dwarf type very suitable for culture in pots, height 1 ft.; Lemon Queen (Sulphur), an old lemon-yellow variety still very popular, height 2 ft.; Meteor, an interesting striped double variety, height 2 ft.; Orange King, a splendid companion to Golden King, resembling it closely in height and form, while the flowers are a rich deep glowing orange; Radio, a distinct break in Calendulas, the flowers are a rich orange and the florets are curiously quilled and pointed, useful and decorative as a cut flower; Radio Golden Beam, the yellow counterpart of the last; Sunshine, a splendid variety, one of the very best for cutting—the stems are long and to a large extent free from side growths and the flowers are a pure golden-yellow, the florets being long and rather loose, resembling the effect of a double Chrysanthemum; Orange Sunshine, the orange form of the last.

C. PLUVIALIS see DIMORPHOTHECA PLUVIALIS.

CALIFORNIAN POPPY see ESCHSCHOLZIA, also PLATYSTEMON.

CALIFORNIAN WHISPERING BELLS see EMMENANTHE.

CALLIGLOSSA DOUGLASII see LAYIA CALLIGLOSSA.

CALLIOPSIS see COREOPSIS.

Callirhoë (Gr. *kallirroe,* daughter of the classic river-god Acheloos). Poppy Mallow. *Malvaceae.* 8 species; North America.

It is to be regretted that this charming genus, of very simple cultivation, is not seen more often in gardens. Certain species are readily obtainable, and all those mentioned here are worthy of consideration. There are both annual and perennial species, the latter generally being treated as Annuals. Seeds may be sown under glass in March, the seedlings being transplanted in April, or sowings may be made in the open ground during April. Light sandy soil and an exposed, sunny position suit them best.

C. DIGITATA. An elegant species growing to a height of about 2½ ft. The flowers are a bright magenta in colour and resemble those of the Poppy.

C. INVOLUCRATA. A trailing species bearing large crimson flowers about 1½ ins. in diameter. There is a variety, *lineariloba* (*C. lineariloba*), similar to the last but with smaller leaves and lilac-pink flowers.

C. PAPAVER. Height 2–3 ft. The flowers are large and of a brilliant violet-red colour with a contrasting white centre.

C. PEDATA. Height 1 ft. The stems are of a somewhat

trailing nature, and the flowers are a rich crimson with a white centre.

Callistephus (CALLISTEMMA) (Gr. *kallistos* = most beautiful, *stephanos* = a crown). China Aster. *Compositae.* 1 species; China, Japan.

C. HORTENSIS (*C. chinensis, C. sinensis, Callistemma hortensis*). This indispensable race of garden plants, commonly but erroneously referred to as China Asters, have all been derived from the monotypic genus *Callistephus*. The type plant, *C. hortensis*, is in itself a beautiful subject for garden decoration and cutting alike. A woodland plantation of this plant at Kew Gardens excites great admiration every year. The flowers are a pale shade of violet-mauve, about 3 ins. in diameter, and are carried on stems 1–1½ ft. in length. Cultivation is simple, but care must be taken not to allow the plants to become drawn and spindly. Seeds should be sown in a greenhouse during March, or in a cold frame in April, and the seedlings transplanted as soon as they are large enough, after all danger of frost is past—usually towards the end of May or early June.

A selection of some of the best types has been made from the multitude of varieties now obtainable. Different types vary considerably in time of flowering, and a note is made of the relative earliness or lateness of each particular section, but as the actual flowering time depends to a great extent on the sowing date, it is not possible to give more than comparative information.

A disease known as " Black Leg " or " Wilt " is sometimes troublesome in certain districts. This is caused by a fungus *Fusarium conglutinans* var. *callistephi*, whose spores can exist in the soil for a considerable time. It is advisable, when this disease is detected, not to plant Asters for several seasons, but in cases where this is not possible, use may be made of the specially selected " Wilt Resistant " strains which have been produced in America, and which are said to be in a large measure resistant.

Anemone Flowered or Sunshine. Obtainable in many shades of colour, this unique type produces flowers with a ring of long flat florets surrounding a curiously quilled centre, giving the effect of a double Anemone. They are very handsome Asters for indoor decoration. Mid-season; height 2 ft.

Chrysanthemum Flowered, Dwarf. A splendid bedding type; the flowers are full double and freely produced. Ideal for pot culture. Mid-season; height 9 ins. Similar in type but slightly taller, the variety Beacon is the brightest scarlet-flowered Aster yet introduced and well worth growing.

Chrysanthemum Flowered, Tall. Similar to the dwarf type described above, but growing to a height of about 1½ ft. Mid-season.

Comet, Dwarf. Similar in height and time of flowering to the Dwarf Chrysanthemum-flowered type, but differing in the shape of the flowers, which are not so tight and compact, and in some respects more attractive.

Comet, Giant. A taller-growing form of the last, deservedly popular for bedding and cutting. Height 1½ ft.

Early Dawn. A very early flowering type recently introduced and becoming increasingly popular. Height 1–1½ ft.

Early Hohenzollern. Similar to the Ostrich Plume class mentioned below but very early flowering. Height 1 ft.

Eclipse or Ray. A very beautiful quilled type, elegant and graceful, one of the most beautiful for indoor decoration. Mid-season; height 1½ ft.

Giants of California. A very large double-flowered type about 2 ft. in height and latest of all to flower.

Hercules. The largest type of all. Mid-season; height 1–1½ ft.

Late Branching. Following on the Ostrich Plume type in time of flowering, this long-stemmed double class has many uses. Height 2 ft.

Leviathan. The longest-stemmed and most striking type of all. The flowers are very large and fully double. Mid-season; height 2½ ft.

Lilliput. A small-flowered but very floriferous strain, ideal for bedding, cutting or pot culture. Not as often seen in gardens as its many qualities warrant. Mid-season; height 1½ ft.

Ostrich Plume. The well-known long-stemmed type in great demand for cutting and bedding. Obtainable in many beautiful shades of colour. Mid-season; 1½–2 ft. in height.

Paeony Flowered. An unusual and very beautiful class. The petals are incurved and the flowers bear a striking resemblance to a Japanese Incurved Chrysanthemum. Mid-season; height 1½ ft.

Single or Sinensis. Preferred by many to the double forms for indoor decoration, this pretty type is about 1½ ft. in height. Mid-season.

Single Large Flowered. Similar to the last-mentioned in time of flowering but slightly taller, larger flowered and more free from side growths, thus providing longer stems for cutting.

C. SINENSIS see C. HORTENSIS.

CALOTIS CUNEIFOLIA see p. 17.

Campanula (L. *campana* = a little bell). Bell Flower. *Campanulaceae*. 300 species; Northern Temperate regions extending to Tropical Mountain regions.

The genus consists principally of perennial and biennial species, but those mentioned below are Annuals of considerable worth. They may be sown in the open ground in April, but in the case of *C. media*, annual form, better results are obtained by sowing under glass in March and transplanting the seedlings towards the middle of May.

C. ATTICA see C. DRABAEFOLIA.

C. CECILII. Height about 1½ ft. A beautiful species suitable for cultivation in the cool greenhouse. The flowers are large, lavender-blue in colour and delicately veined with a deeper shade.

C. DRABAEFOLIA (*C. attica*). Height 4 ins. Suitable for edging, carpeting or rock-work; a dwarf compact plant bearing large violet-blue flowers.

C. LOREYI see C. RAMOSISSIMA.

C. MEDIA. Canterbury Bell. The ever-popular Canterbury Bell is a Biennial, but an annual form has been introduced of recent years which has gained a certain degree of popularity. At present this form is available in mixture, and also in two separate colours, rose and blue. They grow to a height of about 1½ ft. and are best treated as Half-Hardy Annuals.

C. RAMOSISSIMA (*C. Loreyi*). Height 1 ft. A useful border plant; the dainty bells are a deep shade of violet-blue. There is a white form *alba* (*C. Loreyi* var. *alba*).

C. SULPHUREA. Height 9 ins. This pretty species, which has greyish foliage and pale-yellow flowers, has recently reappeared in cultivation. It is best sown under glass in March and transplanted during May, or it may be successfully grown as a pot plant for the cool greenhouse. Syria.

CANARY CREEPER see TROPAEOLUM PEREGRINUM.

CANDYTUFT see IBERIS.

Canna (derivation uncertain). Indian Shot. *Cannaceae*. 60 species; Tropical and Sub-tropical regions.

A genus of greenhouse Perennials which may be easily and quickly raised from seeds. They may be successfully treated as Annuals, and if seed is sown in a greenhouse during February or March the seedlings will grow rapidly and be ready for planting out about the end of May, after all danger of frost is past. They will produce their brilliantly coloured flowers during the late summer and early autumn. Difficulty is sometimes experienced with the germination of the seeds, which is materially assisted by chipping or cutting a small piece off the side of the seeds, and by giving strong bottom heat until germination takes place.

Cannas do best in fairly rich soil and prefer a sunny sheltered position. The hybrid forms are most suitable for cultivation as Annuals, as they come to maturity more quickly than the majority of the species. The following is a selection of the best varieties: Crozy's, a fine mixture of many brilliant colours, gorgeous bedding subjects; Dark Leaved, dark foliage contrasting pleasingly with the vivid colourings of the flowers; Madame Crozy, flowers rich scarlet edged with gold, and very showy; Vilmorin's Giant Red, a recent introduction, large-flowered and of a striking colour; Vilmorin's Giant Rose, a companion type to the last.

Cannabis (L. *cannabis* = hemp). Hemp. *Cannabinaceae*. 1 species; Central Asia.

C. GIGANTEA see C. SATIVA var. GIGANTEA.

C. SATIVA. The common Hemp is cultivated in many tropical and temperate countries for its fibre and also for the narcotic drug which is extracted from it. Its graceful and decorative foliage renders it a useful plant for wild parts of the garden or for planting in clumps at the back of a border or in a shrubbery. The variety *gigantea* is a more robust garden form.

CANTERBURY BELL, ANNUAL, see CAMPANULA MEDIA.

CAPE PRIMROSE see STREPTOCARPUS.

CARNATION see DIANTHUS CARYOPHYLLUS.

CARPET PLANT see IONOPSIDIUM ACAULE.

CASTOR OIL PLANT see RICINUS.

Catananche (Gr. *katanangke* = a strong incentive, in reference to the custom among Greek women of using it in love potions). *Compositae*. 5 species; Mediterranean regions.

These pretty Perennials may be easily treated as Annuals

and are useful plants in a mixed border. Seeds should be sown in March under glass and transplanted during May.

C. CAERULEA. Height 1½ ft. The pale violet flowers, embellished with a dark-blue centre, are borne on long stems. and are useful as cut flowers, being of the "everlasting" type; *bicolor*, a garden variety having blue-centred white flowers.

CATCHFLY see SILENE.

Celosia (Gr. *kelos* = burnt, in reference to the dry burnt appearance of some of the species). Cockscomb. *Amaranthaceae*. 60 species; Tropical and Temperate regions of Africa and America.

Although these beautiful and highly decorative plants are more at home in a cool greenhouse than in the open flower bed, they are nevertheless used largely for bedding purposes during the late summer. Ideal pot plants, both the Feathered and Crested forms are used with effect in the conservatory, and possess the advantage of remaining in bloom for a considerable length of time. Seeds should be sown during March in a greenhouse at a temperature of 75° and the seedlings potted on as soon as they are large enough. They should not be allowed to become starved but should be moved into larger pots as this becomes necessary, to encourage bold sturdy growth. They may be planted out at any time after the middle of June.

C. ARGENTEA var. CRISTATA (*C. cristata*). The Crested Cockscomb. The curiously shaped inflorescence of the wild plant has been developed by plant selectors until the large, full heads of the modern varieties have been produced. These are usually found in seed catalogues under the name of *C. Thompsonii* var. *magnifica*, a trade name of apparently no botanical standing. Another form of *C. argentea* which bears handsome feathery plumes is commonly referred to as *C. pyramidalis* or *C. plumosa*. There are several varieties of this graceful feathered type which are preferred by many gardeners to the stiff, curious Cockscombs.

The following are among the most popular garden varieties: *C. argentea* var. *cristata plumosa* Pride of Castle Gould, a mixture of many shades of colour. The spikes are longer but not quite so full as the following variety. Prize Strain, best for both pot-work and bedding; obtainable in mixture and in two separate colours, red and yellow.

C. CRISTATA see C. ARGENTEA var. CRISTATA.

C. PLUMOSA see C. ARGENTEA var. CRISTATA.

C. PYRAMIDALIS see C. ARGENTEA var. CRISTATA.

C. THOMSONII see C. ARGENTEA var. CRISTATA.

Celsia (in honour of Professor Celsius of Upsala, 1670–1756). *Scrophulariaceae*. 40 species; Asia, Africa and Mediterranean regions.

A genus of pretty biennial or perennial plants, suitable for cultivation as border Annuals. In the case of *C. Arcturus* pot culture is recommended. They resemble the Verbascums or Mulleins, to which they are very closely related botanically. They are easily raised from seeds sown in a greenhouse during March, the seedlings being potted on and transplanted to their flowering positions during May.

C. ARCTURUS. A beautiful yellow-flowered species, often cultivated in pots for the cool greenhouse or conservatory. Planted out in the open, the spikes of bloom will rise to a height of about 2–3 ft. and present a most handsome appearance during mid-summer.

C. CRETICA. The golden-yellow flowers are larger than those of the foregoing and are quaintly marked with two large brown spots. The height of the plant is about 1½ ft.

Centaurea (*L. Kentaurion*, name given by Dioscorides to the plant which was said to have cured an arrow wound in the foot of the Centaur Chiron). *Compositae*. 600 species; cosmopolitan.

The genus includes both annual and perennial species, most of which make splendid cut flowers. Unless otherwise stated, seeds should be sown in the open ground in September or April; early blooming and finer plants result from autumn sowings.

C. AMBERBOII see C. MOSCHATA.

C. AMERICANA. A strong-growing species about 2-3 ft. in height, bearing large lilac-purple flowers. Best treated as a Half-Hardy Annual. N. America, 1824. There is a white form, *alba*.

C. CINERARIA (*C. candidissima*). Commonly, and commercially, known as *C. candidissima*, this is one of the most useful plants for edging. It is a Perennial, but when sown under glass in February or early March the young plants with their effective large silvery leaves will grow to a suitable size in their first year for all edging purposes. Very effective when used in conjunction with such plants as Begonias. Mediterranean regions, 1710.

C. CLEMENTEI. A Spanish species of fairly robust growth often reaching a height of 3 ft. The plant presents a woolly white appearance and the flowers are pale yellow. A useful foliage plant.

C. CYANUS. Blue Bottle, Bluet, Cornflower. Often simply catalogued as *Cyanus minor*; the profusion of beautiful colours now available among the Cornflowers entitles them to a place in every garden. The blue varieties especially are of a shade all too scarce among garden plants and no mixed border of Annuals is complete without them. If supplies are required for cutting, autumn sowing is preferable, as the plants produce many more flowers than those from spring sowings, and the stems are considerably longer. Some of the best varieties are: Emperor William, a semi-double deep-blue variety; Double Blue, of which fine strains selected for depth of colour and doubleness are now obtainable; Double Carmine Rose, a recently introduced shade, very effective;

Double Rose, a pleasing soft shade of delicate rose-pink; Double White, a pure white variety contrasting well with the coloured forms; Double Dwarf Jubilee Gem, a recent introduction which has proved very popular; the plants are bushy, about 1 ft. in height, and the large flowers are a deep blue in colour. This is a useful bedding variety and very effective when grown in pots; seeds sown under glass in September will make a good show in the conservatory about the middle of May.

C. DEPRESSA. An annual species not very widely grown but useful for borders and bedding, also as a cut flower. It grows to a height of about 1–1½ ft. and the flowers are a deep blue with a reddish-brown centre. Persia and Caucasus, 1818.

C. IMPERIALIS see C. MOSCHATA.

C. MARGARITAE. A white variety of *C. moschata*.

C. MOSCHATA (*C. Amberboii, C. odorata, C. suaveolens, Amberboa moschata*). Sweet Sultan.

From this species and its varieties numerous valuable garden forms have been produced. Some of the best are mentioned below. The type *C. moschata* varies in colour, and the purple, white and yellow forms are widely grown for their delightful scent and their decorative effect both in the garden and as a cut flower. Height 2 ft. Orient, 1629. The giant Sweet Sultan or *C. imperialis* of gardens is generally supposed to be the offspring of *C. moschata* and its variety *C. Margaritae*; this splendid race is specially suitable for cutting. The large sweetly scented flowers are carried on long stems and last well in water. Among the best varieties are *imperialis alba*; Bright Rose; Delicate Lilac, a very popular colour; Purple; and Rose with white centre.

C. ODORATA see C. MOSCHATA.

C. SUAVEOLENS, a yellow form of *C. moschata*.

CENTAURY see ERYTHRAEA.

Centranthus (Gr. *kentron* = a spur, *anthos* = a flower). Valerian. *Valerianaceae*. 12 species; Europe and Mediterranean regions.

This genus includes both annual and perennial species, the latter being easily treated as Annuals. They are excellent for borders or large rockeries and will do well on dry walls. Seeds may be sown in the open ground during March or April or under glass early in March, the seedlings being transplanted when they are large enough, usually during May.

C. CALCITRAPA. Height 6 ins. to 1 ft. A little-grown species producing rose-purple flowers. Southern Europe, 1623.

C. MACROSIPHON. Growing to a height of about 1½ ft., this is an easily cultivated Hardy Annual species of compact habit and is a plant of considerable merit. The bright rose flowers are abundantly produced and are very effective in masses. Spain. There is also a white variety, and a mixture of several shades of colour is obtainable.

C. RUBER. Red Valerian, Pretty Betsy. These perennial Valerians may be treated as Annuals and are free-flowering. This species grows to about 2–3 ft. in height, and bears rosy-red flowers. Europe and Syria. There is a white variety, *albus*, also a form *atrococcineus* similar to the type but with dark-red flowers. The two red sorts are effective when grown in association with each other.

CERATOTHECA see p. 19.

Cerinthe (Gr. *keros* = wax, *anthos* = a flower, in reference to the wax that bees were supposed to obtain from the flowers). Honeywort. *Boraginaceae*. 7 species; Europe and Mediterranean regions.

Although not widely grown, some of the members of this genus deserve to be more generally cultivated. Seeds should be sown under glass during March and transplanted to a sunny position towards the end of May. Sowings may also be made out of doors in April.

C. MAJOR. Growing to a height of about $2\frac{1}{2}$ ft. the plant produces brown and yellow flowers. Grown mostly for bees. 1596.

C. MINOR. A less attractive species, growing to a height of about 2 ft. The yellow-brown spotted flowers hang downwards and their effect is to a large extent lost. 1570.

C. RETORTA. A showy species, about 2 ft. in height, which freely produces yellow purple-tipped flowers. Greece, 1825.

CHALK PLANT see GYPSOPHILA.

Charieis (Gr. *charieis* = elegant, in reference to the beauty of the flowers). *Compositae.* 1 species; South Africa.

C. HETEROPHYLLA (*Kaulfussia amelloides*). A dwarf, compact, free-flowering Daisy-like Hardy Annual, about 6 ins. in height, bearing deep-blue flowers. Seeds may be sown in the open ground during April, or if it is desired to have plants in flower early in the summer, sowings may be made under glass during March and the seedlings transplanted as soon as they are large enough. The varieties include : *atroviolacea*, dark violet, and *kermesina*, a violet-red form.

Cheiranthus (Gr. *cheir* = a hand, *anthos* = a flower, the allusion being that the flower makes a good nosegay). Wallflower. *Cruciferae.* 20 species; Mediterranean and Northern Temperate regions.

The genus consists, strictly speaking, of perennial or sometimes biennial species such as *C. Cheiri*, the progenitor of the race of present-day Wallflowers. Mention is here made only of those which can be treated as Annuals.

C. ALLIONII. Probably a hybrid; growing to a height of about 12 ins., the plant is one of the most brilliant of all orange flowers. It is rarely seen at its best when sown in the spring and the best time for sowing is June or July.

C. ALPINUS see ERYSIMUM OCHROLEUCUM.

C. CHEIRI. Height $1-1\frac{1}{2}$ ft. Annual forms of the common

5. DELPHINIUM CONSOLIDA
Giant Imperial Varieties

6. DIASCIA BARBERAE

Wallflower will bloom for several months during the summer if sown under glass during February or March. The following are among the best varieties: Annual Belvoir Castle, Golden Yellow, Blood Red, Early Paris Market, a pleasing shade of light brown; Golden Gem, Primrose Gem and White Gem.

C. KEWENSIS. Height 1 ft.; a valuable winter-flowering plant for the conservatory or cool greenhouse. It is the result of crosses made at Kew in 1897 between *C. mutabilis* and various coloured forms of *C. Cheiri*. The colour of the flowers changes from brown when in bud to primrose-yellow, fading to a pale purple as the flowers wither. Seeds sown in July will provide a show of colour for many months during the winter.

CHERRY PIE see HELIOTROPIUM.

CHICKLING VETCH see LATHYRUS SATIVUS var. AZUREUS.

CHILIAN BELLFLOWER see NOLANA.

CHINA ASTER see CALLISTEPHUS.

CHINA CREEPER see IPOMOEA QUAMOCLIT.

CHINESE PINK see DIANTHUS CHINENSIS.

CHINESE PRIMROSE see PRIMULA SINENSIS.

Chrysanthemum (Gr. *chrusos* = gold, *anthemon* = a flower). *Compositae*. 180 species; Europe, Asia, Africa and America.

Deservedly popular, the annual species and their numerous brilliantly coloured varieties possess the advantages of being extremely easy to grow, exceedingly showy as garden plants and light and decorative as cut flowers. Indeed, there are few Annuals which will give such a splendid show in return for so little trouble. Seeds may be sown in the open ground during April, or if early supplies of blooms are required sowings may be made under glass in March.

C. ANNULATUM see C. CARINATUM var. CHAMELEON.

C. CARINATUM (*C. tricolor*). This species, which has given rise to so many fine garden forms, grows to a height of about 2 ft., and bears white rays, enhanced by a yellow ring at the base. The disc of the flower is dark purple, completing the three-coloured effect alluded to in the now obsolete name of *C. tricolor*. Among the best varieties are: *atrococcineum* The Sultan, bright crimson; *Burridgeanum*, a strain introduced in 1858 by Mr. F. K. Burridge; the flowers are similar to those of the type but have a crimson ring in addition to the yellow ring at the base of the rays; *Burridgeanum* Golden Feather, similar to the last but with golden leaves; Chameleon (*C. annulatum*), flowers a pale coppery shade, the base of the rays being shaded with rosy-purple which changes gradually to yellow as the flowers age; Double Fringed, a showy mixture of rich bronze, red and yellow shades; Dunnetti Golden, a double golden-yellow form. There is also a white variety of similar type; John Bright, a showy bright golden-yellow variety; Northern Star, a large-flowered strain, the flowers are white, with yellow ring and dark-purple disc; White Queen, a white variety in which the yellow zone is very pale and almost invisible.

For garden decoration many people prefer to sow the varieties of *C. carinatum* in mixture, when they are particularly effective.

C. CORONARIUM. A pale-yellow semi-double-flowered species attaining a height of about 3 ft.; numerous garden varieties have been derived from it, all of them useful and attractive plants. Golden, sulphur and white varieties, similar in height and habit to the type but bearing fully double flowers, are obtainable which are eminently suitable for cutting. Some of the best varieties include: *nanum compactum* Golden Queen, a dwarf compact golden-yellow double-flowered type useful for bedding; *nanum compactum* Primrose Queen, a pale sulphur-yellow-flowered form of the foregoing; *namum compactum* White Pearl, a white variety

similar in type to the above; Tom Thumb Golden Gem, a
very dwarf type, 1–1½ ft. only in height, often used for pot
culture; Tom Thumb Primrose Gem, a paler form of the
last; Single Golden Glory, a very large-flowered deep
golden-yellow form, attaining a height of 3–4 ft. and producing its flowers on long stems, admirable for cutting.

C. FRUTESCENS. Marguerite or Paris Daisy. A greenhouse
Annual, the familiar White Marguerite is much in demand
as a pot plant. Seed should be sown in February and the
plants may be potted on for indoor work or planted out for
summer bedding. There is a pale lemon-yellow variety; also
Comtesse de Chambord, a very fine large-flowered variety
and *grandiflorum*, the garden form commonly cultivated at
the present time, the flowers of which are considerably
larger than in the type.

C. INODORUM see MATRICARIA INODORA.

C. MULTICAULE. Not frequently seen in cultivation but a
useful plant for massing in a border. The flowers are golden-
yellow and are large and showy.

C. NIVELLEI. Of recent introduction, this is a free-flowering golden-yellow species, showy and of great garden value.
Morocco.

C. PARTHENIUM (*Pyrethrum Parthenium*). The useful
varieties of this plant, usually known in the trade under the
old name *Pyrethrum*, are in great demand for bedding and
for use as edging plants. Although perennial it is commonly
treated as an Annual, and seeds are sown in September and
the seedlings wintered in boxes in a cold frame, to be
planted out early the following summer. If preferred, sowings may be made during February or March and the seedlings planted out towards the end of April. The varieties
commonly grown are *aureum* or Golden Feather, the familiar
yellow-leaved form; Excelsior, a dwarf compact selection of
the former, and of a brighter golden colour; Golden Moss, a
dwarf crisped and curled form; *laciniatum* Perfection, a

dwarf variety with finely cut leaves; *selaginoides*, dwarf and compact with golden serrated leaves. The foregoing are cultivated chiefly for their golden foliage, the small white flowers being of slight decorative value.

C. segetum. Gowan, Corn Marigold. This is the wild species native to Britain and often found in cornfields. The type is about $1\frac{1}{2}$ ft. in height and bears small single yellow flowers. It has given rise to many useful garden forms, all of which are splendid for cutting. Some of the best are: *grandiflorum*, large bright yellow flowers; Eastern Star, a pale-yellow variety with a dark disc; Eldorado, a deep-yellow variety with a dark reddish-black disc; Evening Star, bright golden-yellow, very large-flowered; Morning Star, primrose-coloured; White Star, creamy-white with a yellow disc; Yellow Stone, a new double golden-yellow variety which promises to become very popular for cutting.

C. tricolor see C. carinatum.

Cigar Plant see Cuphea ignea.

Cineraria (L. *cinereus* = ash-coloured, in allusion to the grey down on the leaves). *Compositae.* 35 species; Africa and Madagascar.

The decorative Cinerarias are essentially greenhouse Perennials but are usually treated as Annuals and occasionally used for outdoor bedding. Seeds sown under glass during April and May will flower in the autumn of the same year, while sowings made during July and August produce plants which will bloom the following spring.

C. cruenta. It is from this species, either directly or by hybridization with certain other species, that the race of garden Cinerarias has been obtained. The type grows to a height of about 2 ft., and the flowers are reddish-purple in colour. There are several different forms among the modern garden varieties, some of which are described below under the names commonly used in seed catalogues.

C. CRUENTA var. HYBRIDA GRANDIFLORA. Height 1 ft. A very large-flowered form obtainable in several separate colours, such as blue, red, white, purple, also bicoloured forms having a white zone at the base of the petals. The named variety Matador is a unique and striking shade of cinnabar-scarlet.

C. CRUENTA HYBRIDA Double Flowered. To many gardeners the double forms lack the appeal of the single kinds, but for those who prefer the double type the mixtures obtainable reproduce fairly well from seeds.

C. CRUENTA HYBRIDA MULTIFLORA NANA. A dwarf compact, small-flowered strain, very showy and containing a wide variety of shades of colour. Some of the colours may be obtained separately.

C. CRUENTA var. STELLATA. About 2 ft. in height; the narrow-petalled star-shaped flowers are particularly dainty, and many shades of colour are to be found in the mixtures now on sale, while several shades may be obtained separately.

Clarkia (named in honour of Capt. W. Clark, companion of Lewis the explorer of the Rocky Mountain regions). *Onagraceae.* 8 species; Western North America.

The garden varieties of Clarkia are among our most useful Annuals. Of easy cultivation, their wide range of beautiful colours entitles them to a place in every annual border. Seeds may be sown in the open gound during March and April or, to obtain earlier-flowering plants, under glass early in March.

C. ELEGANS. Height 2–2½ ft. Splendid for massing or as a cut flower. There are many fine double garden varieties, among the best of which are the following: Albatross, a compact erect-growing white variety; Chieftain, a delicate mauve; Crimson Queen, a rich crimson-red; Dorothy, brilliant rose; Enchantress, salmon-pink; Glorious, crimson-scarlet; Orange King; Purple King; Rosy Morn, one of the best, a beautiful shade of rose-pink; Salmon Bouquet, of erect habit, salmon-pink, a fine variety; Salmon Perfection; Vesuvius, bright orange-scarlet.

C. PULCHELLA. About 1½ ft. in height. Differing from *C. elegans* mainly in the shape of the flowers, the varieties of *C. pulchella* have slightly broader petals, but the general effect is not so showy. *C. pulchella* is a lilac-flowered species varying to white. Several interesting forms are available, including: *integripetala*, in which the flowers are rosy-lilac single, and with broad petals; there is also a double form and a white form; Mrs. Langtry, flowers white with a crimson centre, a showy bright variety; Tom Thumb, a dwarf compact strain, obtainable both in separate colours and as a mixture. Useful for the front row of a border.

CLARY see SALVIA HORMINUM.

Claytonia (named in honour of John Clayton of Virginia, an early American botanist). Spring Beauty, Purslane, *Portulacaceae*. 24 species; North Temperate and Arctic regions.

An interesting genus of low-growing, mostly trailing species which often become naturalized in favourable places. They are useful for the rock garden. Seeds should be sown in the open ground in April.

C. PERFOLIATA. Winter Purslane. Height 3–6 ins. A small white-flowered annual species, naturalized in parts of Great Britain and in places a troublesome weed. 1794.

C. SIBIRICA. Siberian Purslane. A dwarf plant 6 ins. in height, bearing pale rose-pink flowers. Thrives in a damp peaty soil; a useful plant for the lower parts of a rock garden in semi-shade. Naturalized in many parts of Britain. Siberia, 1768.

Cleome (name adopted by Linnaeus, derivation uncertain). Spider Flower. *Capparidaceae*. 70 species; Tropical and Sub-tropical regions.

These curious and decorative plants have gained the name Spider Flower from the long purple stamens and rose-coloured petals of the most popular species. They are successfully grown as Annuals for bedding purposes. Seeds should be sown in a greenhouse in February or March and the seedlings potted on and planted out towards the end of May or early in June. They are frequently used as bedding plants in the London parks.

C. GIGANTEA. Height about 6–8 ft. The flowers are whitish-green with pink stamens. A handsome plant. There are variously coloured forms sold under the name of *C. gigantea hybrida* which are probably varieties of *C. spinosa*.

C. PUNGENS see C. SPINOSA.

C. ROSEA see p. 17.

C. SPINOSA (*C. pungens*). Height about 3–4 ft. The stems and leaves are armed with short spines and the plant has a strong, disagreeable smell. The flowers are rosy-purple and the stamens, often 3–4 ins. in length, are deep purple in colour.

C. VISCOSA. Height about 3 ft. The flowers are a pale flesh colour.

CLINTONIA see DOWNINGIA.

CLOUD PLANT see GYPSOPHILA.

Cobaea (in honour of Father B. Cobo, a Spanish Jesuit and naturalist). Cup and Saucers. *Polemoniaceae*. 9 species; Tropical America.

C. SCANDENS. The only species generally cultivated, it is a rapid-growing perennial climber which, treated as an Annual, is very suitable for planting against walls, fences, trellises, rustic arches and the like, as it will form ornamental cover in a short time. The flowers are single, about 1–1½ ins. in diameter, somewhat resembling those of a Canterbury Bell, and are light violet in colour. Seeds should be sown under glass during late February or March and the seedlings transplanted to a warm sunny position in June. Cobaeas may be cultivated in large pots, but they thrive best planted out in a light fairly rich soil. There is a white variety of the foregoing, *alba*, which breeds fairly true from seed.

COCHLEARIA ACAULIS see IONOPSIDIUM ACAULE.

COCKSCOMB see CELOSIA.

Coleus (Gr. *koleos* = a sheath, in allusion to the way in which the filaments of the stamens are fused at the base). *Labiatae*. 150 species; Tropics of the Old World.

A large genus of annual and perennial stove plants chiefly grown in pots for indoor decoration, also in window-boxes, but not now popular as bedding plants. The genus is interesting in several ways; certain species produce tubers strongly aromatic and rich in essential oils that are cooked and eaten, while those species and varieties commonly grown for their foliage possess unique and often brilliant colourings. They may be easily raised from seeds sown in February or March in a greenhouse, the seedlings being potted on as soon as they are large enough.

C. BLUMEI. It is from this species that most of the garden varieties grown to-day have originated. Many mixtures are obtainable which include a wide range of colours and types, one of the most popular being a form with narrow, laciniated leaves. The variety *Verschaffelti* is a crimson-leaved form, very striking and useful for contrasting effect in carpet bedding.

C. FREDERICII. A splendid deep blue-flowered species of recent introduction, which is destined to become very popular for greenhouse work. It grows to a height of about 3 ft. and carries its flowers in long racemes; winter-flowering.

C. THYRSOIDEUS. A beautiful species bearing long racemes of bright blue flowers, very useful for conservatory work as it blooms during the winter.

Collinsia (in honour of Zaccheus Collins, 1764–1831, at one time Vice-President of the Academy of Natural Sciences of Philadelphia). *Scrophulariaceae*. 25 species; North America.

Showy little plants suitable for massing in a mixed border of Annuals. Seeds may be sown outdoors in a sheltered position during September to flower early the following summer, or in the open ground in March or April to flower the same year.

C. BARTSIAEFOLIA. Height 1 ft. A little-grown species bearing purple flowers. A white variety is also known. California.

C. BICOLOR. Attaining a height of about 1 ft., this species and its varieties are the most widely grown. The flowers are produced freely and are lilac and white in colour. California, 1833.

There are several varieties, including: *alba* (*candidissima*), pure white; *multicolor*, a showy form bearing variegated, white, lilac, rose or violet flowers; Salmon Beauty, a recent introduction of a delicate salmon-rose shade.

C. GRANDIFLORA. Height 1 ft. A large blue-and-white-flowered species, very showy. There is a beautiful form *carminea*, which bears large carmine-purple flowers.

C. VERNA. Height 9 ins. A less popular species; the flowers are purple and bright blue. Best sown in the autumn.

Collomia (Gr. *kolla* = glue, in reference to a mucilaginous substance surrounding the seeds). *Polemoniaceae*. 10 species; Western America.

A genus of annual, biennial and perennial plants of which some are cultivated in gardens. The annual species are dwarf and shapely, and being brilliantly showy, are attractive to bees. Seeds may be sown in the open ground in September to flower early the following summer, or during March or April for flowering the same year.

C. COCCINEA (*C. lateritia*). A bright scarlet-flowered plant, about 1½ ft. in height. Chili, 1832.

C. GRANDIFLORA. Not so frequently seen in gardens as the above, but a desirable plant, growing to a height of about 2 ft. and bearing clusters of salmon-buff flowers, each about 1 in. long.

C. LATERITIA see C. COCCINEA.

Convolvulus (L. *convolvo* = I entwine). Bindweed. *Convolvulaceae*. 180 species; Temperate or Tropical regions.

C. MAJOR see IPOMOEA PURPUREA.

C. MINOR see C. TRICOLOR.

C. PURPUREUS see IPOMOEA PURPUREA.

C. TRICOLOR (*C. minor*). This species with its several varieties are the only annual forms commonly grown in gardens.

Seeds sown in September in the open ground will flower early the following year, while sowings made under glass in February or March will flower later in the year. Sowings may also be made in the open ground in April or early in May. It grows to a height of about 1½ ft. and bears large deep blue white-throated flowers curiously marked with yellow stripes. Among the numerous varieties, the following are noteworthy: *albus*, white-flowered; *compactus*, a dwarf form sometimes used for pot work; *monstrosus*, a large, deep blue-flowered variety, the centre of the flowers being pure white; *roseus superbus*, a curious form bearing yellow-striped, rose-coloured flowers, deepening towards the centre to a violet-purple, finally merging to pure white.

Coreopsis (Gr. *koris* = a bug, *opsis* = resemblance, in reference to the seed's similarity to a bug). Tickseed. *Compositae*. 80 species; America, Tropical Africa, Sandwich Islands.

It will be found that many catalogues list the annual kinds under the name *Calliopsis*, and the perennial species and varieties as *Coreopsis*. This invaluable genus has given rise to a number of varieties which, by reason of the profusion of their brilliantly coloured flowers and the ease with which they may be cultivated under all normal garden conditions, rank among our finest garden plants. The annual kinds are splendid subjects for massing in beds or planting in groups in a mixed border, the taller varieties being eminently suitable for cutting. Seeds may be sown under glass during March, the seedlings being transplanted towards the end of May, or in the open ground during April.

C. ATROSANGUINEA see C. TINCTORIA var. NIGRA SPECIOSA.

C. BICOLOR see C. TINCTORIA.

C. CALLIOPSIDEA see LEPTOSYNE CALLIOPSIDEA.

C. CORONATA. About 1–1½ ft. in height, this species bears showy, large orange-yellow flowers, the rays lightly marked at the base with brown spots.

C. DRUMMONDII. A handsome species about 1–1½ ft. in height; the flowers are deep orange-yellow marked with a brown zone at the base of the rays. Sometimes strains are sold producing pure orange flowers.

C. ELEGANS see C. TINCTORIA.

C. GIGANTEA see LEPTOSYNE GIGANTEA.

C. MARITIMA see LEPTOSYNE MARITIMA.

C. MARMORATA see C. TINCTORIA.

C. TINCTORIA (*C. bicolor*, *C. elegans*, *C. marmorata*, *C. nigra*). Height about 2 ft.; the large yellow flowers are enhanced by a broad crimson-brown zone at the base of the rays. There are numerous varieties of this species, the best of which are described below and classified as *nana* and *nana compacta* in most seedsmen's lists.

Semi-dwarf, or *nana* varieties, about 1½ ft. in height: Evening Star, the flowers are deep yellow with a deep scarlet zone; Fire King, bright scarlet, attractive flowers; The Garnet, a very free-flowering variety, the flowers are rich crimson-scarlet.

Tom Thumb or *nana compacta* varieties, height about 8 ins.: Beauty, a compact bushy plant, covered with golden-yellow flowers with a dark crimson zone; Crimson King, a dwarf compact crimson variety; Dazzler, a very large-flowered golden-yellow variety with a broad crimson zone, very fine compact habit; *purpurea stellata*, a curious purple-brown coloured variety; The Sultan, one of the finest dwarf crimson varieties—a good companion to C. Dazzler; Tiger Star, dwarf and compact, the flowers are a rich brown mottled with yellow.

There is also a tall-growing dark crimson form 1–2 ft. in height, *nigra speciosa (C. atrosanguinea).*

CORN ADONIS see ADONIS AUTUMNALIS.

CORNFLOWER see CENTAUREA CYANUS.

CORN MARIGOLD see CHRYSANTHEMUM SEGETUM.

CORONARIA COELI-ROSA see LYCHNIS COELI-ROSA.

Cosmos (COSMEA) (Gr. *kosmos* = ornament). *Compositae.* 20 species; America and West Indies.

The beauty of their delicately cut foliage and the large single or double flowers entitle these decorative Annuals to a place in every garden. They are never seen to better advantage than when allowed to form a background to a border of mixed Annuals, where they will provide a show of bloom for many weeks during the summer and early autumn. Seeds should be sown in March or April under glass and the seedlings transplanted at the end of May or early in June.

C. BIPINNATUS. It is from this species that most of the garden varieties have been derived. The plant grows to a height of about 4–5 ft. and the large single flowers are a pale lilac-purple colour. Mexico, 1799.

There are numerous types and varieties differing in time of flowering, and care should be taken to obtain those that will come into bloom early in the summer. The following are among the best: Early Mammoth Flowering, obtainable in several separate colours, such as crimson, lilac, pink and white; Fairy Queen, a bright rose-pink compact variety, about 2½ ft. in height; Giant Blush Queen, a large-flowered rosy-lilac variety, 3–4 ft. in height; Sensation varieties with flowers 4–5 ins. across, include Crimson, Pinkie, rose-pink and Purity, white; Double Early Flowering, obtainable in several separate colours.

C. SULPHUREUS. About 2½ ft. in height, this species differs from *C. bipinnatus* in its smaller flowers and less finely cut, glossy leaves. The flowers are golden-yellow but appear rather late in the season in this country. It is from this species that the modern yellow forms have been obtained, the best of these being Klondyke Orange Flare, a deep rich orange, flowering early in the season and producing splendid blooms for cutting.

CREAM CUPS see PLATYSTEMON.

Crepis (Gr. *krepis* = a sandal; reference obscure). Hawks-beard. *Compositae.* 240 species; Northern Hemisphere, South Africa and South America.

C. RUBRA. Height about 6 ins. An attractive little border Annual useful for edgings. The flowers, which resemble the common Hawkweed, are deep rosy-pink. A white form is also known. Seeds may be sown in the open ground during April.

CUCUMIS see p. 44.

CUCURBITA see list of varieties on p. 43.

CUP AND SAUCERS see COBAEA.

Cuphea (Gr. *kyphos* = bending, in reference to the form of the capsule). *Lythraceae.* 200 species; America.

Brilliantly showy for bedding purposes, certain of the Cupheas may be successfully treated as Half-Hardy Annuals. Seeds should be sown under glass during March and the seedlings transplanted to a warm sunny spot during June.

C. IGNEA (*C. platycentra*). Cigar Plant. An exceedingly bright plant, about 1 ft. in height. It bears long rich scarlet flowers with black tips and white mouth. Very useful for bedding. Mexico, 1845. The white variety, *alba*, is not often found in gardens.

C. MINIATA. A bushy plant, 1 ft. high. The flowers are bright cinnabar-red in colour, and are very showy. The white variety, *alba*, and a variety bearing crimson and purple flowers, *compacta*, are not easily obtainable and seldom seen in gardens.

C. PLATYCENTRA see C. IGNEA.

CYANUS see CENTAUREA.

Cynoglossum (Gr. *kyon* = a dog and *glossa* = a tongue, in reference to the form of the leaves of some of the species). Hound's Tongue. *Boraginaceae*. 50 species; Temperate and Sub-tropical regions, 2 in Britain.

This interesting genus of perennial and biennial plants includes certain species suitable for cultivation as Annuals. Seeds may be sown under glass during March and the seedlings transplanted during May, or sowings may be made in the open ground towards the end of April.

C. AMABILE. Height about 2 ft. An attractive plant, producing freely small blue sweet-scented flowers over a long period, it is effective when massed in mixed borders. Several varieties are available, notably: *album*, pure white; Fairy Blue, a distinct shade of Cambridge blue; and Pink, a deep rosy-pink.

C. LINIFOLIUM see OMPHALODES LINIFOLIA.

CYPRESS VINE see IPOMOEA QUAMOCLIT.

Dahlia (in honour of Dr. Dahl, a Swedish botanist) *Compositae*. 10 species; Central America.

In recent years the practice of raising Dahlias from seeds each year as Annuals has become increasingly widespread, and, especially with the very dwarf bedding types, has proved highly successful. Although plants from spring sowings flower later in the season and are never so large as those cultivated by cuttings or division of old tubers, the great advantage lies in not having to care for the tubers and cut-ings during the winter and early spring. The wealth of beautiful colours and the comparatively true-breeding qualities of most of the selected strains of Dahlias now avail-able reduce risk of disappointment to a minimum. Modern varieties of Dahlia have all been derived from four or five species, notably *D. coccinea*, *D. Juarezii*, *D. Merckii* and *D. rosea* (*D. variabilis*), of which *D. rosea* and *D. Juarezii* have played a large part. Seeds may be sown during March in a greenhouse and the seedlings transplanted to their flowering positions at the end of May, or they may be potted on and transplanted later in the summer.

The following are some of the best mixtures and varieties obtainable:

Double Decorative. Large-flowered forms, growing to a height of about 4 ft. Variations in the type of flower must be expected when raised from seed, the majority having very large broad petals. The range of brilliant colours is surprising.

Paeony Flowered. Similar in height to the foregoing and bearing large, full, double flowers in great variety of colour.

Miniature Paeony Flowered or Charm. About $3\frac{1}{2}$–4 ft. in height, this excellent strain produces large numbers of small double flowers in many beautiful shades of colour. The light, graceful form of the flowers, and the long stems, make them ideal subjects for cutting.

Unwin's Dwarf Hybrids. Somewhat resembling the last in type of flower, this strain grows to a height of only 2–3 ft., and contains many beautiful shades of colour. A good bed-ding strain. A mixture producing flowers whose petals are attractively quilled or twisted has appeared recently under the name of Unwin's Ideal Bedder. The variety of colours has been materially increased in this strain.

Pompon. The old-fashioned, very double small-flowered type which grows to about 4 ft. in height and reproduces remarkably well from seeds.

Apoldro. A distinct variety about 2–3 ft. in height, with dark bronze foliage and bright scarlet flowers. The golden-yellow anthers give a curious effect to the flowers.

Dark Leaved. A mixture of dark-leaved sorts, bearing small double or semi-double flowers, including many shades of colour. Height 3 ft.

Single Colossal. Growing to a height of about 4 ft., this strain carries very large single flowers in a great variety of colour.

Single Coltness Gem Hybrids Improved. Height 1½ ft. One of the finest subjects for bedding purposes. A great range of colour and a dwarf free-flowering habit combine to make this a strain of outstanding garden merit. In addition to the splendid mixture of many colours, several self-coloured varieties are now available which reproduce very well from seeds. The Coltness Yellow is notable, and, slightly taller and larger-flowered, the scarlet Mignon Fire-brand is also to be recommended.

Daisy see Bellis.

Datura (from its Arabic name *tatorah*). Thorn Apple. *Solanaceae.* 15 species; Tropical and warm Temperate regions.

Grown as Half-Hardy Annuals, certain of the Daturas are of value in mixed borders for their generous foliage and large trumpet-shaped flowers. Seeds may be sown in a green-house during March or early April, the seedlings being transplanted to their flowering positions after the end of May.

D. chlorantha. A perennial species easily cultivated as an Annual. It grows to a height of about 3 ft. and bears long pendulous golden-yellow flowers. 1845. The variety Golden Queen has bright yellow double flowers.

D. Cornucopia see D. fastuosa.

D. fastuosa (*D. Cornucopia*). An annual species, about

7. ESCHSCHOLZIA CALIFORNICA VAR. ORANGE KING

MASS CLUMPS OF SHASTA DAISY

4 ft. in height from which several interesting varieties have originated. The flowers are 6–7 ins. long and purple outside, white within. Among the varieties, there is a rather dingy white form, *alba*; also *Cornucopia*, Horn of Plenty, a curious plant bearing large triplicate white flowers, the outside of the inner trumpets being dark violet in colour; *Huberiana*, a garden variety with large double flowers varying in colour from yellow, blue, to reddish-purple. It is supposed to be a hybrid with *D. chlorantha*.

D. METELOIDES (*D. Wrightii*). A handsome species, about 3 ft. in height, bearing large fragrant white flowers suffused with violet-purple.

D. WRIGHTII see D. METELOIDES.

Delphinium (Gr. *delphin* = a dolphin, on account of the similarity of the shape of the spur to a dolphin). Larkspur. *Ranunculaceae*. 150 species; Northern Temperate regions, and mountains of Tropical East Africa.

Few Annuals can compare with the Larkspurs for beauty and elegance as well as for the delicate shadings of colour which are available among the newest varieties. Tall and stately, unrivalled as cut flowers, they are indispensable plants in any collection of Annuals. The most handsome plants are obtained from sowings made during late September in the open ground, plants raised in this way often reaching a height of over 6 ft. Seeds sown in March or April in the open ground will produce plants 3–4 ft. in height which will flower later than the autumn-sown ones, usually during July.

D. AJACIS. Rocket Larkspur. This species has given rise to the garden forms described below. The type is about 1½ ft. high, bearing spikes of showy flowers varying in colour from rose and white to purple. Tall and dwarf forms are available in mixture. There is a handsome double-flowered type known as Hyacinth-Flowered of which tall and dwarf forms may be had in separate colours, rose, white, brick-red, etc.

D. Consolida. It is from this species that the majority of the finest modern varieties have been obtained. A tall, branching, rather angular plant, it bears short spikes of flowers in various shades of purple, blue and white. The garden varieties are generally classified in seed lists as below.

D. Consolida fl. pl. Stock Flowered Larkspur. Very floriferous, loosely branching and fully double, this type has gained great popularity. The range of beautiful colours includes rosy-scarlet, dark blue, azure blue and white, and a soft salmon-rose variety, Rosamond.

The Spire, or Giant Imperial type, an upright-growing form of later introduction, less angular and definitely more suitable for garden decoration, is rapidly becoming popular. The varieties Blue Spire, Lilac Spire, White Spire, Miss California (brilliant rose), Daintiness (lilac and white) and Exquisite Pink, a delicate shade of soft pink, are among the finest Larkspurs yet introduced.

D. Consolida var. imperiale fl. pl. (*D. imperiale*). Emperor Larkspur. Height 2 ft. A very dwarf shapely type producing short closely packed spikes of double flowers in various shades of colour. Noteworthy varieties are Cameo Pink, Azure Blue and Brilliant Rose.

D. grandiflorum (*D. sinense*). A number of dwarf showy varieties of this species, usually found in catalogues under the name of *D. sinense*, are very easily raised as Annuals. Seeds may be sown in the open ground in March or April or under glass in March for early flowering. The type is about 2 ft. in height and the large single flowers are of varying shades of blue. Among the best varieties are: Azure Fairy, a beautiful free-flowering form bearing large Cambridge-blue flowers, height $1\frac{1}{2}$ ft.; Blue Butterfly, an excellent plant for the front of a border, about $1\frac{1}{2}$ ft. in height, with brilliant blue flowers marked with a small brown spot on each petal; Blue Gem, a dwarf variety 1 ft. only in height, with flowers of an intense shade of deep blue, ideal for all bedding purposes; *paniculatum*, an interesting form, 1 ft. in height, bearing small rosy-purple flowers, usually sold as *D. paniculatum*.

D. IMPERIALE see D. CONSOLIDA var. IMPERIALE FL. PL.

D. PANICULATUM see D. GRANDIFLORUM var. PANICULATUM.

D. SINENSE see D. GRANDIFLORUM.

DEPTFORD PINK see DIANTHUS ARMERIA.

DEVIL'S FIG see ARGEMONE.

Dianthus (Gr. *dios* =divine, *anthos* = a flower). Pink, also Carnation. *Caryophyllaceae*. 250 species; Europe, Asia, Africa.

There can be few garden lovers who have not come under the spell of the "divine flower." Its delicious scent and exquisite form have endeared it to countless gardeners, and with the passing of the years still more lovely varieties come to strengthen its indefinable appeal. The species and varieties described below, although in some cases more often grown as Perennials, are easily grown as Annuals with excellent results. Their cultivation in this way presents no difficulty and indication as to the proper time for sowing is given separately for each species described.

D. ARMERIA. Deptford Pink. Height 1–1½ ft. A useful annual species for the rock garden; the clusters of small fringed flowers are deep pink and speckled with white. It is a native of Great Britain but not common. Seeds should be sown under glass during March and the seedlings transplanted to the open ground in late April.

D. CARYOPHYLLUS. Carnation. The progenitor of all modern large-flowered Carnations, this species is believed by many to have played some part in the production of the annual or Marguerite type. It is not possible to state the parents of this type with any degree of certainty, but it is generally conceded that *D. chinensis*, *D. Armeria* or *D. Caryophyllus* was used in its development. Marguerite or

Margaret Carnations and the Chabaud varieties are splendid when used as Annuals in borders or for cutting, and if sown in February under glass and planted out in early April, will flower profusely for many weeks during the summer and early autumn. Although the form of their flowers cannot be compared with that of the large Perpetual Flowering or Border kinds, they are very double, sweetly scented, and obtainable in a wide range of beautiful colours.

The following varieties will be found to give very satisfactory results, grown as Annuals: Giant Chabaud, a sturdy strain, of which the separate colours Fire Queen, Purple King, Rose Queen, Ruby Queen and Marie Chabaud, pale golden-yellow, are all thoroughly reliable—height 1½ ft.; Grenadin, a very double scarlet variety; White Grenadin is of dazzling purity, a worthy counterpart; Margaret, obtainable in several fine shades of colour, dark red, rose-scarlet, white and yellow—it is never more effective than when grown in mixture; and the New Large Flowered Malmaison strain containing a great range of colours. Height 1½–2 ft.

D. CHINENSIS (*D. sinensis*). Chinese Pink, Indian Pink, Japanese Pink. A host of beautiful varieties, both single and double, have originated from this species and they rank among our most decorative and free-blooming Annuals. Seeds may be sown under glass during February or March and the seedlings transplanted to their flowering positions during April or early May. The type grows to a height of about 9–12 ins. and the flowers vary in colour from pink to rosy-lilac. China and Japan, 1713. The following varieties, grouped under the classification usually adopted in most seedsmen's catalogues, are among the best:

Heddewigii. Japanese Pink, height 9 ins. The large single flowers vary in colour from pink and crimson to white. The deep crimson form, Crimson Belle, and the striped rosy-pink, Eastern Queen, are well worth growing as separate colours.

Heddewigii fl. pl. A mixture of colours similar to the last but having double flowers. The variety *D. diadematus* is a large-flowered selection in many beautiful shades of colour, while Fireball, double brilliant scarlet; Pink Beauty, and Purity, a fine white variety, are the best of the self-coloured double types.

Giant or *superbissimus*. Height 6 ins. A very beautiful strain of single Indian Pinks; the flowers are very large, slightly fringed, and the petals are delicately crimped or crested in a most pleasing manner. The variety of colours to be found in this strain is surprising and includes all shades of crimson, scarlet, rose, flesh-pink and white. The variety Queen Alexandra is similar in type and has large glistening white flowers.

Fringed or *laciniatus*. Height 6 ins. A large single-flowered strain with delicately fringed petals, very showy in mixture. In addition to several self-coloured single varieties, the best of which is the brilliant orange-scarlet Vesuvius, there are several fine double forms such as Salmon Queen and the pure white Snowdrift, which should not be overlooked.

D. DIADEMATUS see D. HEDDEWIGII FL. PL. var. DIADEMATUS.

D. HYBRIDUS Delight. A hybrid between *D.* Sweet Wivelsfield and *D. Roysii*; the habit and general appearance of the plant are in many respects similar to *D.* Sweet Wivelsfield. The strain contains many beautiful shades of colour, including red and crimson. It can be successfully treated as an Annual in the manner indicated for *D.* Sweet Wivelsfield.

D. HYBRIDUS Sweet Wivelsfield. This valuable garden plant was obtained by crossing Sweet William (*D. barbatus*) with *D. Allwoodii*; the plant grows to a height of about $1\frac{1}{2}$ ft. and is very floriferous, resembling in habit the Sweet William, one of its parents. The individual flowers are large, both self-coloured and beautifully marked forms being found in brilliant mixture. Treated as an Annual, and sown under glass during March or April, it is an ideal subject for bedding, also for culture in pots. There is a double variety which breeds fairly true from seeds.

D. SINENSIS see D. CHINENSIS.

Diascia (Gr. *diaskeo* = I adorn, in reference to the showy flowers). *Scrophulariaceae*. 30 species; South Africa.

D. BARBERAE. Not so widely grown as it might be. The dainty coral-pink Nemesia-like flowers of this lovely little Annual are most attractive, either in a mixed border or when used as a pot plant for conservatory work. Seeds should be sown under glass in March or early April and the seedlings transplanted to their flowering positions during May. Height 1 ft.

D. BARBERAE var. Salmon Queen. A beautiful clear salmon-pink variety.

DIDISCUS CAERULEUS see TRACHYMENE CAERULEA.

Dimorphotheca (Gr. *dimorphos* = two forms, *theke* = a receptacle or box, the florets of the disc being of two forms). *Compositae*. 20 species; South and Tropical Africa.

These South African sun-loving, Daisy-flowered plants have become increasingly popular during recent years as their free-flowering nature and brilliant colourings render them extremely suitable for bedding or grouping in mixed borders. The flowers remain open most of the day but close up at evening or during cloudy weather. They are best treated as Half-Hardy and seeds should be sown in a greenhouse during March, the seedlings being transplanted towards the end of May.

D. AURANTIACA. Namaqualand Daisy. Height about 1–1½ ft. A very showy and floriferous plant, producing great numbers of beautiful glossy rich golden salmon-orange flowers over a long period during the summer months. Namaqualand, 1907.

D. AURANTIACA HYBRIDA. A mixture of variously coloured

forms which have probably been obtained by crossing *D. aurantiaca* with *D. pluvialis*. It is impressive when massed and includes shades ranging from yellow, salmon and orange to white. 1912.

Certain named varieties which breed fairly true from seeds, such as Golden West, Salmon Beauty and White Beauty, are also serviceable plants.

D. CALENDULACEA. Similar in height and habit to *D. aurantiaca*, the flowers are large and vary in colour from salmon, buff and yellow to white. Notable varieties include: Lemon Queen, a large-flowered, deep chrome-yellow variety, more compact than the type and very suitable for bedding, height 1 ft.; and Tom Thumb Yellow Gem, a very dwarf showy little plant useful for bedding, edging or rock-work; the large flowers are pure golden-yellow in colour.

D. CHRYSANTHEMIFOLIA (*Calendula chrysanthemifolia*). Height about 2 ft. As its name implies, it resembles a Chrysanthemum, and bears large single golden-yellow flowers on long thin wiry stems. Usually grown as a pot plant, it is a splendid subject for cutting.

D. EKLONIS. Height 1½–2 ft. A shrubby, upright plant, producing pure white star-shaped flowers, with deep blue disc, borne on long stems, useful as a summer bedding plant.

D. PLUVIALIS (*Calendula pluvialis*). The Great Cape Marigold. Height 1–2 ft. A free-flowering species producing great numbers of large single pure white flowers with a golden disc, the reverse of the rays being delicately shaded with blue.

There is an interesting variety, *ringens*, in which the pure white flowers are embellished by a wide deep blue zone at the base of the rays, rendering it much more effective; it is dazzlingly beautiful when massed. 1699; also a double form, *ringens fl. pl.*, which remains open all day but which is considered by most gardeners to be more unusual than beautiful.

D. SINUATA. Height 9 ins. to 1 ft. A very rich orange-coloured species; the flowers are often as large as 2½ ins. in diameter. It has recently become quite popular in gardens and is a valuable plant for the mixed border. A variety Orange Glory is of a deeper shade of orange.

Dolichos (Gr. *dolichos* = long, in reference to the long twining shoots). Hyacinth Bean, Soudanese Bean. *Leguminosae*. 60 species; Sub-tropical regions.

D. LABLAB. Although not suitable for cultivation in very cold localities, it may be successfully grown if planted in a warm sunny border with a south aspect. The pea-shaped flowers are rosy-purple in colour and the crimson seed pods are also highly decorative. Seeds should be sown in a greenhouse during February or early March and the seedlings planted out during June. There is a white form, *alba*.

Downingia (CLINTONIA) (in honour of Andrew J. Downing, an American pomologist and landscape gardener). *Campanulaceae*. 3 species; Pacific America.

Dwarf, elegant little Annuals usually grown under the name *Clintonia*, they may be used for rock-work, hanging baskets, or edgings and are most effective when sown where they are to flower in a mixed border. Seeds should be sown during April in the open ground or under glass during February or March, the seedlings being transplanted during May.

D. ELEGANS (*Clintonia elegans*). Height 6 ins. The flowers are blue with a white lip and are freely produced.

D. PULCHELLA. Similar in height and habit to the last, this showy species bears beautiful blue-and-white flowers marked with violet and yellow in the throat, the lip being yellow and white.

DRAGON'S MOUTH see ANTIRRHINUM.

Dracocephalum (Gr. *drakon* = a dragon, *kephale* = a head, in reference to the shape of the flower). *Labiatae*. 40 species; Northern Temperate regions.

D. MOLDAVICA. Height 1–1½ ft. Mostly cultivated for bees, the plant is dwarf and bushy, and bears long spikes of violet-blue flowers. Seeds may be sown in the open ground during early April or under glass during March.

Eccremocarpus (Gr. *ekkremes* = hanging, *karpos* = fruit, in reference to the pendent seed pods). *Bignoniaceae*. 3 species; Peru.

E. SCABER (*Calampelis scaber*). The only species commonly grown, it is a beautiful, somewhat tender, climbing Perennial which is successfully treated as an Annual. The tubular flowers are brilliant orange-scarlet in colour, about 1 in. in length and carried in loose racemes. Given a fairly sheltered sunny position against a wall or fence it will grow rapidly, often attaining a height of 10–14 ft. Seeds should be sown in a greenhouse during March, the young plants being transplanted during June. There is a pure golden-yellow-flowered form of the above, *aurea*.

Echium (from Gr. *echion*, the old name of the plant). Viper's Bugloss. *Boraginaceae*. 30 species; Europe, Mediterranean.

Splendid plants for bees, certain of the Echiums are also highly ornamental grown as Annuals for beds and borders. Seeds may be sown during April in the open ground but better results and earlier flowering are obtained by sowing under glass during early March.

E. CRETICUM. A branching plant 1½ ft. in height, bearing bright red flowers.

E. PLANTAGINEUM. A beautiful lilac-blue species, bushy and fairly compact and very free-flowering. About 1½ ft. in height. There is a variety Blue Bedder, a more compact form, in which the flowers are a slightly brighter shade of blue; it is a useful border plant and also a fine subject for growing in pots. A mixture of colour forms which include pale blue, light pink, rosy-mauve and white, is sold under the trade name of *E. plantagineum hybrids*.

EGG PLANT see SOLANUM MELONGENA.

ELEPHANT'S TRUNK PLANT see MARTYNIA.

Emilia (derivation doubtful). Tassel Flower. 25 species; chiefly Tropics of the Old World, but two species cosmopolitan.

E. SAGITTATA (*E. flammea, Cacalia coccinea*). Often referred to as *Cacalia coccinea*, this is the showy Scarlet Tassel Flower. The plant grows to a height of about 1½ ft. and the clusters of flowers are carried at the ends of the long slender stems.

Seeds may be sown in the open ground where they are to flower, during April. There is a golden-yellow garden form, *aurea* (*E. flammea* var. *aurea, Cacalia aurea*).

Emmenanthe (Gr. *emmenos* = enduring, *anthos* = a flower, in reference to the long-lasting flowers). Californian Whispering Bells. 6 species; North-West North America.

E. PENDULIFLORA. Height 1 ft. An interesting and desirable plant which should be more often seen in gardens. It forms a small bush bearing numerous sprays of golden-yellow bell-shaped flowers of the "everlasting" type. At times it almost disappears in its native habitat but is found in thousands after a forest fire, and seeds will be found to germinate easily if sown under glass during March or April in soil made almost untouchably hot. 1892.

Erigeron (Gr. *ear* = spring, *geron* = an old man, in reference to the leaves being hoary with white down when young). *Compositae*. 180 species; cosmopolitan.

Although most of the members of this genus are Perennial, many may be easily treated as Annuals and, if sown under a glass during February or March and planted out during May, will give a good show of bloom during the late summer and autumn. They are most effective when planted in large masses in borders or in the wild garden.

E. COULTERI. A handsome plant about 1 ft. in height; the

flowers are pure white, about 2 ins. in diameter, and are very suitable for cutting.

E. DIVERGENS. Height 1½ ft. An annual species very free-flowering and easy to grow. The flowers are small, but produced in great numbers over a long period, and are pale lavender-mauve.

Erysimum (Gr. *eryo* = I draw, in allusion to its supposed property of drawing blisters). *Cruciferae*. 80 species; Mediterranean regions, Europe, Asia.

These brightly coloured Wallflower-like plants, although mostly biennial or perennial, include three species which are often grown most successfully as Annuals. They are suitable for beds and borders, also for the rock garden. Seeds may be sown in the open ground during March or April to flower the same year.

E. ASPERUM. Height 1–1½ ft. A gay plant; the flowers vary in colour from light yellow to rich orange. *E. asperum* var. *arkansanum* is a pale yellow large-flowered form.

E. OCHROLEUCUM. Alpine Wallflower. A bushy dwarf compact plant about 9 ins. in height, bearing pale golden-yellow flowers. Sometimes known as *Cheiranthus alpinus*.

E. PEROWSKIANUM. Height 1½ ft. An annual species, free-flowering and very effective when planted in groups in a mixed border. The flowers are a rich deep orange colour and are sweetly scented. 1838.

Erythraea (Gr. *erythros* = red, in reference to the flowers of certain species). Centaury. *Gentianaceae*. 30 species; Temperate regions.

A genus of considerable garden merit not so frequently seen as its qualities warrant; there are several elegant annual species both easy to cultivate and distinctly showy. Seeds may be sown in the open ground in April or under glass during March.

E. CENTAURIUM. Height about 6 ins. An annual species bearing Gentian-like flowers, of a delicate shade of rose; it is charming when used in the rock garden. A native of Britain.

E. VENUSTA. Height about 9 ins. The star-like flowers, often 1 in. in diameter, are clear rose-pink with a contrasting white throat. A valuable plant for the rock garden. California, 1878.

Eschscholzia (in honour of Dr. J. F. von Eschscholz, 1793–1831, a German naturalist, companion of Kotzebue on his expedition round the world). Californian Poppy. *Papaveraceae.* 150 species; Pacific North America.

For brilliance and general garden decoration, this genus and its host of gorgeous varieties have become an indispensable feature of our gardens. New shades, double forms and types with crinkled petals, continue to make their appearance, all of them undeniably beautiful and easy to grow. Commonly treated as Annuals, they often prove perennial, and two- or three-year-old plants that have become well established flower very freely and are extremely showy. Seeds may be sown in the open ground in September to flower early the following summer, or in March to flower the same year.

E. CAESPITOSA. Referred by some authors to E. *californica*, but generally obtainable under the name of *E. caespitosa*. It is a dwarf species, about 4–6 ins. in height with small yellow flowers, and is a useful rock-garden subject.

E. CALIFORNICA. Height about 1 ft. This is the original species from which the great majority of the garden forms have been derived. It has been adopted as the State flower of California. The flowers are rich deep yellow, and very freely produced. 1790.

The varieties in commerce are usually arranged in three sections, viz.: Tall Single, Dwarf Single and Double, and some of the best are classified in this way below. They are never seen to better advantage than when grown in mixture and many fine strains are now on sale.

Tall Varieties. Height about 1 *ft.*

Alba, creamy-white; *canaliculata* Flambeau, a semi-double variety, rich orange-red in colour and having curiously crimped or wrinkled petals; *canaliculata* Ramona, a golden-bronze variety similarly frilled to the last, the exterior of the petals being of a soft shade of coppery-rose; *carminea grandiflora rosea*, a beautiful shade of rosy-carmine; Chrome Queen, an unusual shade of soft chrome-yellow; *crocea*, warm orange yellow; Mandarin, rich deep orange, shaded crimson on the exterior of the petals; Orange King, one of the largest-flowered of all, and a glistening deep orange in colour.

Dwarf or erecta compacta Varieties. Height 6–9 *ins.*

Carmine King, a very brilliant shade; Dainty Queen, delicate pale rose; Dazzler, a large-flowered, flame-coloured variety; Fireflame, orange-scarlet; Gloaming, coral-rose, apricot within; Golden Rod, bright golden-orange; *intus rosea*, an old carmine variety still popular; Mikado, an old favourite, but by comparison with modern varieties somewhat small-flowered, yet still outstanding by reason of the unique deep orange-crimson colour of its flowers; Moonlight, a popular, compact, pale chrome-yellow variety; Rose Queen, pale carmine-rose.

Double-flowered Varieties. Height about 9 *ins.*

Alba fl. pl., a large-flowered ivory-white form; Autumn Glory, a semi-double coppery-orange variety, very attractive; Carmine Queen, a great favourite, and well worth growing, it is a rich carmine-crimson in colour and the large shapely flowers are very double; Cherry Ripe, rich cerise, terra-cotta base; *crocea fl. pl.*, there can be few more striking garden plants than this fine rich orange variety; Enchantress, a particularly pleasing combination of soft carmine-rose suffused with cream, large-flowered and most attractive;

Golden Glory, golden-yellow with an orange centre; Robert Gardiner, fully double flowers, rich orange in colour, with petals fluted or crimped in a most pleasing way; Toreador, orange-crimson golden-bronze within.

Other varieties of less garden value than the foregoing, but not without a certain charm, are: *maritima*, a procumbent, silver-leaved plant bearing golden-yellow flowers, and *tenuifolia*, a small yellow-flowered form with very narrow leaves, considered by some authors to be a distinct species, but more often referred to as a variety of *E. californica*.

Eucharidium (Gr. *eucharis* = agreeable). *Onagraceae.* 3 species; California.

A small genus of showy little Annuals bearing a close resemblance to Clarkia and very effective if massed in borders. Their cultivation is simple and seeds may be sown in the open ground during late March or in April.

E. BREWERI. Height 1–1½ ft. Although not easily obtainable this species is a desirable plant; the flowers are deep crimson-purple in colour with a white base to the petals, and possess a delightful Honeysuckle-like scent.

E. CONCINNUM. Height 9–12 ins. The flowers are deeply cut and bright rose in colour. Not widely grown in gardens.

E. GRANDIFLORUM. The most common species and a plant of considerable merit. It grows to a height of about 1 ft. and bears deep rosy-purple flowers. A white variety *E. grandiflorum* var. *album*, and a pink form *E. grandiflorum* var. *roseum* are recorded, but not generally grown or easily obtainable.

EUCNIDE see MENTZELIA GRONOVIAEFOLIA.

Eupatorium (said by Pliny to be in honour of Mithridates Eupator, King of Pontus). *Compositae.* 450 species; America, Europe, Asia and Tropical Africa.

E. AGERATOIDES (*E. Fraseri*). White Snakeroot. A perennial species, about 2–3 ft. in height, sometimes cultivated as a

Hardy Annual. The flowers, which are useful for cutting, are pure white and carried in small clusters. Seeds may be sown under glass during March for early flowering, the seedlings being transplanted during late April or May.

E. FRASERI see E. AGERATOIDES.

Euphorbia (classical name, said by Pliny to be in honour of Euphorbus, a physician to Juba, King of Mauritania). Spurge. *Euphorbiaceae.* 750 species; chiefly Sub-tropical and warm Temperate regions.

E. HETEROPHYLLA. Mexican Fire Plant, Hypocrite Plant, Fire on the Mountain, Annual Poinsettia. An annual species about 2 ft. in height. It forms a bushy plant and the green and scarlet leaves are highly ornamental. The small flowers are orange-red in colour. Cultivation is simple and seeds may be sown in the open ground during April. It is also a suitable subject for cultivation in pots. There is a white variegated form similar in height and habit known as *variegata* (Snow on the Mountain).

EUTOCA see PHACELIA DIVARICATA.

EVENING PRIMROSE see OENOTHERA.

EVERLASTING FLOWERS see p. 39.

Exacum (name used by Pliny, allusion doubtful). *Gentianaceae.* 30 species; mainly in Tropics and warm Temperate regions of Asia, but also in Tropical East Africa.

The Exacums are often cultivated with effect as pot plants for the cool greenhouse. Seeds sown in March will produce plants which, if potted on into 5-in. pots, will flower during the summer of the same year. Sowings are often made during August to produce larger plants for flowering the following year.

E. AFFINE. Height about 6 ins. The most popular species, it is dwarf, bushy and carries numerous light blue fragrant flowers; widely grown as a pot plant for market work on the

Continent. There is a new dark lavender variety, *atro-caeruleum*, which promises to become popular.

Although not in general cultivation, *E. zeylanicum* and *E. Forbesii* are said to be desirable plants, the latter being described by some authors as the finest of the genus.

FAIRY PRIMROSE see PRIMULA MALACOIDES.

Felicia (L. *felix* = happy, in allusion to the cheerful appearance of the plant). False Daisy. *Compositae*. 60 species; South Africa.

Several members of this Daisy-flowered genus are splendid subjects treated as Annuals, for edgings, while some are useful for the rock garden. Seeds should be sown under glass during March and the seedlings transplanted towards the end of April or in May.

F. ADFINIS. A species recently introduced bearing large blue flowers on stems 8 or 9 ins. in length. It is also a decorative plant for the cool greenhouse.

F. AMELLOIDES (*Agathaea coelestis*). Usually grown as a greenhouse Perennial, this shrubby species can also be used as a Half-Hardy Annual. The large flowers are of an exquisite shade of blue. Height 1–2 ft.

F. BERGERIANA. Introduced several years ago, this low-growing free-flowering species is suitable for rock-work and for carpeting purposes. The flowers are about 1 in. in diameter, of a bright blue colour. Height 4–6 ins.

F. FRAGILIS (*F. tenella, Aster tenellus*). A bushy little species about 6 ins. in height, bearing clear blue flowers; a good edging plant.

F. ROTUNDIFOLIA. Height 9–12 ins. This dwarf, extremely floriferous species is excellent as an edging plant in a sunny position. As there seems to be some confusion regarding the nomenclature of the plant it is given here under the name generally used in trade catalogues.

F. TENELLA see F. FRAGILIS.

9. HELENIUM TENUIFOLIUM

10. IBERIS

Planted out of Pots in Early Summer

FENZLIA see GILIA DIANTHOIDES.

FIRE ON THE MOUNTAIN see EUPHORBIA HETEROPHYLLA.

FLAX see LINUM.

FLOS ADONIS see ADONIS AESTIVALIS.

FLOSS FLOWER see AGERATUM.

FLOWER OF AN HOUR see HIBISCUS TRIONUM.

FOUNTAIN PLANT see AMARANTHUS SALICIFOLIUS.

FOUR O'CLOCK see MIRABILIS.

FRENCH HONEYSUCKLE see HEDYSARUM CORONARIUM.

FRENCH MARIGOLD see TAGETES PATULA.

FULLER'S HERB see SAPONARIA.

FUMITORY see ADLUMIA.

Gaillardia (in honour of M. Gaillard, a French patron of botany). Blanket Flower. *Compositae.* 15 species; America.

Unsurpassed for brilliance and the duration of their flowering period, the annual Gaillardias rank among the most useful of our summer border plants. In addition to their merits as garden plants, they provide us with cut flowers which remain fresh for a long time in water. Seeds should be sown in a greenhouse during March and the seedlings transplanted as soon as they are large enough, usually early in May.

G. AMBLYODON. Height about 1–1½ ft. The flowers are rich blood-red but not so large as the following species. 1873.

G. PULCHELLA. Height 1½ ft. A large-flowered handsome plant bearing yellow-tipped crimson-purple flowers. It is principally from this species that the large number of garden varieties now available have been derived. The best of these include: *picta*, the form generally grown in gardens, the flowers are large, of a rich coppery-red colour, tipped with golden-yellow; *picta aurea*, a pure yellow form; *picta albo marginata*, a showy variety, the flowers are reddish-brown tipped with white; *picta* Chameleon, an interesting form bearing scarlet flowers margined with white and yellow; *picta* Indian Chief, introduced a few years ago, this variety gained immediate popularity, and makes a shapely plant bearing large bronze-red flowers with little or no margin of any kind; *picta Lorenziana*, in this curious and decorative form the ray florets are tubular in shape, and the flowers are double; it is sold in a mixture of many shades and markings, but the following separate colours may be obtained: *bicolor*, red and yellow; *rubra*, red, white-tipped; *sulphurea*, pale golden-yellow; The Bride, creamy-white.

Gamolepis (Gr. *gamos* = union, *lepis* = a scale, in reference to the involucre). *Compositae*. 12 species; South Africa.

G. TAGETES (*G. annua*). A showy dwarf Annual growing to a height of about 6–9 ins. Useful for edging or massing in borders, it bears golden-yellow Daisy-like flowers about 1 in. in diameter. Seeds may be sown under glass during March or in the open ground during April.

GARDEN BALSAM see IMPATIENS BALSAMINA.

Gaura (Gr. *gauros* = superb, in reference to the appearance of the flowers of certain species). *Onagraceae*. 25 species; North America.

G. LINDHEIMERI. This is the most ornamental species, and although a Perennial, is often cultivated as an Annual either in the garden or in pots for the cool greenhouse. The flowers, carried in long spikes, are white with rosy-tinted calyx tubes. Height about 3 ft.

Gazania (in honour of Theodore of Gaza, 1393–1478, who translated the botanical works of Theophrastus into Latin). *Compositae*. 24 species; Cape Colony.

Large-flowered Daisy-like plants, sun-loving and gorgeous in the brilliance of their colourings, the Gazanias, although perennial, may be flowered during their first year from seeds sown in a greenhouse.

G. HYBRIDA. Several species have entered into the showy hybrid forms now available, and in addition to the many-coloured mixture, usually sold under the name *G. splendens hybrida grandiflora*, the varieties Orange Glow, a deep attractive shade of orange, enhanced by a black-and-white zone, and Tangerine Red, a handsome shade, are obtainable.

G. LONGISCAPA. An interesting species with grey woolly foliage and showy golden-yellow flowers rendered more brilliant by a pronounced black-and-white zone.

G. PAVONIA. The flowers of this striking species are rich red in colour with an attractive zone of chocolate and white.

G. RIGENS. The well-known *G. splendens* of gardens is now referred by botanists to this species. It is a splendid plant, dwarf and free-flowering and the large flowers are often $2\frac{1}{2}$–3 ins. in diameter, and their bright orange rays are marked at the base with a black spot with a white dot in the centre of it. Hybrid forms are available, generally under the name *hybrida grandiflora*.

G. SPLENDENS see G. HYBRIDA and G. RIGENS.

Gilia (in honour of P. S. Gil, a Spanish botanist). *Polemoniaceae*. 120 species; Temperate and Sub-tropical America.

Consisting of annual, biennial and perennial species, this genus contains many splendid plants which, treated as Annuals, are very valuable for massing in groups in mixed borders. Most of them are dwarf and free-flowering and many are suitable for growing in rock gardens or as edging plants. Seeds of the hardy kinds may be sown in the open ground during September to flower the following year, or during March or April to flower the same year. Cultural directions are given for those species which require treatment differing from the above.

G. ABROTANIFOLIA. A light graceful plant about $1\frac{1}{2}$ ft. in height, bearing large heads of very pale blue flowers.

G. ACHILLAEFOLIA. Height 1 ft. A bushy small-leaved plant; the first of the large violet-blue flowers are carried in compact heads, but later, on the side growths, they are borne more widely separated. Garden forms are *G. achillaefolia* var. *major* and *G. achillaefolia* var. *alba*, a white variety. 1833.

G. AGGREGATA (*Ipomopsis elegans*). Height about 2½ ft. Similar in type to *G. coronopifolia*, but differing from that species by its dwarfer habit. The flowers vary in shade, brilliant scarlet, orange and almost white forms being known. It is a Biennial but may be cultivated as an Annual by sowing seeds in a greenhouse during March and transplanting the seedlings to the open ground during May.

G. ANDROSACEA (*Leptosiphon androsaceus*). An erect-growing plant 1–1½ ft. in height; the flowers, which vary in shade from lilac or pink to white, are carried in fairly close heads and are very ornamental.

G. CAPITATA. A tall-growing plant often 2 ft. in height. The foliage is very finely cut and the flowers, borne in dense heads, are a delightful shade of blue. A white form, *alba*, and a larger more robust variety, *major*, are also known. 1826.

G. CORONOPIFOLIA. Height 3–4 ft. One of the most lovely and strikingly handsome plants for beds or borders. The magnificent tall spikes of long brilliant scarlet flowers are very leafy, the delicately cut foliage adding greatly to the beauty of the plant, which is of outstanding merit. It is best to sow seeds under glass during September, wintering the plants in pots in a cold frame, and planting them out during May, but seeds sown in a greenhouse during February will flower well in the autumn of the same year. Variations in the colour of the flowers sometimes occur, pink, yellow and orange forms being known. Beds of this plant have been greatly admired during recent years in the London parks.

G. DIANTHOIDES (*Fenzlia dianthiflora*). Often grown as a pot plant for the cool greenhouse, this pretty species grows to a height of about 6 ins. and may be successfully treated as a Hardy Annual. The large flowers vary somewhat in shade, being generally lilac or rosy purple, usually with a white or yellow eye; white forms are also known (*Fenzlia alba*). It is a charming little plant, splendid for edgings or rock-work. 1855. There is a garden form, *speciosa*, bearing larger flowers.

G. LACINIATA. Height 6–12 ins. Similar in form to *G. capitata*, this species is rather more compact, and although not in general cultivation is said to be a desirable garden plant. 1831.

G. LINIFLORA. Height about 1 ft. Not often seen in gardens or trade lists, but a useful bushy Annual; its numerous white flowers, borne singly, are distinctly showy. 1833.

G. MICRANTHA (*Leptosiphon roseus*). Height 6–8 ins. A splendid bedding Annual, very effective if massed in a mixed border. The flowers vary considerably in colour, from purple to lilac, red, rose, yellow and white. Several garden varieties are available, usually described in seed catalogues as *Leptosiphon aureus*, *L. carmineus*, *L. hybridus*, a mixture of many shades, *L. luteus*, and *L. roseus*.

G. TRICOLOR (*G. nivalis*). Height 1 ft. A popular border annual for a sunny position; the flowers are white, edged with purple, deepening towards the centre, and rendered more striking by a yellow tube or eye. 1833.

There are many varieties, notably: *compacta*, a dwarfer bushy form; *nana*, a dwarf type; *nivalis*, white; *rosea splendens*, a large-flowered rose variety; *rubro-violacea*, a reddish violet form.

GILLIFLOWER see MATTHIOLA.

Glaucium (Gr. *glaukos* = greyish-green, in reference to the colour of the leaves). Horned Poppy, Sea Poppy. *Papaveraceae*. 25 species; Europe, Asia.

These handsome Poppy-like plants are brilliantly showy and could be more generally employed in large borders or in wild parts of the garden. While most of the species are

biennial or perennial a few are annual, and certain others
may be treated as such. Their cultivation is simple and they
will thrive in almost any soil or situation. Seeds are generally
sown during June or July in the open ground to flower the
following summer, but sowings made in March will produce
flowering plants during the same year.

G. CORNICULATUM. Height about 1 ft. The flowers are
orange-red, sometimes purplish, and each petal has a black
spot at the base. Two varieties are recognized: *phoeniceum*
with purplish-crimson flowers, each petal having a black
spot at its base; *rubrum*, similar but of a deeper colour.

G. FLAVUM (*G. luteum*). Yellow Horned Poppy. A splendid
plant for sandy soil, it bears large yellow flowers and is a
native of Great Britain. Height 2 ft. In the variety *tricolor*,
the flowers are large, often 3 ins. in diameter, and are bright
orange-scarlet in colour, each petal being marked with
yellow and black. Height 2–3 ft.

G. LEIOCARPUM. Not such a handsome plant as the last,
but the brilliant orange-red flowers are nevertheless quite
showy. Height 1½ ft.

G. LUTEUM see G. FLAVUM.

G. PHOENICEUM see G. CORNICULATUM var. PHOENICEUM.

G. RUBRUM see G. CORNICULATUM var. RUBRUM.

GLOBE AMARANTH see GOMPHRENA.

Gloxinia (in honour of P. B. Gloxin of Strasbourg, a
botanical writer of the eighteenth century). *Gesneriaceae*.
6 species; Tropical America.

Gloxinias are Perennial, but if seeds are sown during
February they will flower about August of the same year.
They are essentially stove plants and consequently are not
dealt with at any length in these pages. Many fine strains,
which include a wide range of lovely colours and exceedingly
handsomely marked flowars, are available, and a well-grown
group of modern Gloxinias is unsurpassed by any other

tuberous plant. Some of the best varieties are: *caerulea*, rich sky-blue with a white throat; Defiance, a striking rich scarlet; Queen Victoria, pure white; and *violacea*, deep velvety violet.

Godetia (in honour of C. H. Godet, a Swiss botanist). *Onagraceae.* 25 species; Western America.

The Godetias are among our most valuable garden Annuals, and the introduction of new types and shades of colour continues year by year. Their bright and abundant flowers are a constant source of delight for many weeks during the summer. Ideal for bedding, strikingly beautiful when sown in large patches in a mixed border, they may also be grown in pots for greenhouse or conservatory decoration, while certain varieties are much in demand as cut flowers. They are of simple cultivation, and seeds may be sown in the open ground during September to flower the following year, or during March or April to flower the same summer. Earlier flowering plants may be obtained by sowing in a greenhouse during February and transplanting the seedlings in May.

G. AMOENA. Height 1–2 ft. A slender lilac-crimson-flowered plant which has given rise to several varieties, notably: *Schaminii*, large double salmon-rose flowers; *Schaminii* Rosy Morn, double coral-pink; *Schaminii* Shell Pink, a delightful shade.

G. BOTTAE. Height about 1–1½ ft. A pale lavender-pink-flowered species resembling the last in habit.

G. DUDLEYANA. Height about 2 ft. A large rosy-mauve-flowered species of slender upright habit.

G. GRANDIFLORA (*G. Whitneyi, Oenothera Whitneyi*). Height about 1–2 ft. A most attractive species from which the majority of the popular garden varieties have been derived. The type bears large rosy-red flowers shaded deeper towards the centre. There are numerous varieties, some of the best of which are described under the classification usually adopted in seedsmen's catalogues.

Tall or Grandiflora Double Varieties

Cherry Red, a most attractive shade; Flesh Pink, a delicate shade; *kermesina*, bright crimson; *lilacina*, pale lilac; Rich Pink, one of the best of this class.

Whitneyi Varieties. Large-flowered Varieties growing to a height of about 1 ft.

Azalaeiflora, double, brilliant rose; Carmine Glow, large double rich carmine; Firelight, rich crimson; Flamingo, crimson-scarlet; Kelvedon Glory, a new shade of rich salmon-pink; Lavender Gem, a beautiful clear shade; Lavender Queen, light lavender; Pelargonium, pale pink with a large carmine blotch on each petal; Sweetheart, bright pink double flowers; Sybil Sherwood, bright salmon-pink; Sybil Sherwood Double, similar to the last but with double flowers; White Swan, the largest pure white-flowered variety.

Compact Varieties. Height about 9 ins.

Crimson Glow, brilliant crimson; Gorgeous, blood-red; New Blue, a deep rich shade; Sunset, rosy crimson; Wild Rose, a delicate shade of rose-pink.

G. WHITNEYI see G. GRANDIFLORA.

GOLDEN PRINCE'S FEATHER see AMARANTHUS PANICULATUS.

Gomphrena (derived from *Gromphraena*, a name given by Pliny to a kind of Amaranth). Globe Amaranth. *Amaranthaceae*. 100 species; Tropical and Sub-tropical regions.

G. GLOBOSA. This species and its varieties are cultivated for their attractive ball-shaped flowers which are of the "everlasting" type. They are much in demand for including in the attractive baskets and posies of everlasting flowers which have become so popular in recent years. The type grows to a height of about $1\frac{1}{2}$ ft. and the flowers are variable in colour. Seeds should be sown under glass during March and the seedlings transplanted towards the end of April or during May.

Some of the best of the many varieties are: *alba*, pure white; *aurea superba* (*G. Haageana*), a narrow-leaved, golden-flowered form; *rosea*, flesh pink, most attractive; *rubra*, deep purple, one of the most popular colours; *striata*, a variegated form; *nana compacta rubra*, a dwarf purple-flowered variety, 6 ins. in height.

G. HAAGEANA see G. GLOBOSA var. AUREA SUPERBA.

GOOD NIGHT AT NOON see HIBISCUS TRIONUM.

GOURDS, ORNAMENTAL, see p. 43.

GOWAN see CHRYSANTHEMUM SEGETUM.

Grammanthes (Gr. *gramma* = writing, *anthos* = a flower, in reference to the V-shaped markings at the base of each petal). *Crassulaceae*. 1 species; South Africa.

G. GENTIANOIDES. Although not often found in trade catalogues, this dwarf fleshy-leaved little Annual is very useful for edgings, hanging baskets or the rock garden. It is a Half-Hardy Annual, and seeds should be sown under glass during March. The flowers open a creamy-white, later deepening to rich orange-scarlet, and are produced in abundance. The plant forms a little bush about 3 ins. only in height and is most attractive during the summer months. There are several forms which differ slightly in the size of the leaves or the flowers; these are notably: *vera* and *chloraeflora*, the latter variety having slightly larger flowers than the type.

GRASSES, ORNAMENTAL, see p. 42.

Gypsophila (Gr. *gypsos* = lime, *philos* = loving, in reference to its preference for calcareous soils). Baby's Breath, Chalk Plant, Cloud Plant. *Caryophyllaceae*. 55 species; Europe, Asia.

The familiar Gypsophila has come to be regarded as an indispensable plant for cutting purposes. Few plants are better adapted for table decoration and the effective combinations which can be made with its light and graceful flowers are infinite. Seeds may be sown in the open ground during April.

G. ELEGANS. Height 1½ ft. The delicate and charming white flowers present a pleasingly soft contrast to other border Annuals, and their popularity as cut flowers is widespread. By selection, the form and size of the flower have been greatly improved and the variety *grandiflora* is a distinct advance on the type. There is also a variety *carminea*, which bears rosy-pink flowers.

G. MURALIS. A dwarf species sometimes used for rockwork, or allowed to hang down from stone walls. The height of the plant is about 6 ins. and the small flowers are a pale shade of rosy-pink.

HAWKSBEARD see CREPIS.

HEARTSEASE see VIOLA.

Hebenstretia (in honour of Prof. J. E. Hebenstreit, 1703–1757, Professor of Medicine at the University of Leipzig). *Scrophulariaceae.* 30 species; South and Tropical Africa.

H. COMOSA. Introduced in 1902, this pretty Annual does not now appear to be in general cultivation. It grows to a height of about 1½ ft. and bears long spikes of small, white, red-spotted, fragrant flowers, sometimes varying to yellow or pink. Seeds may be sown under glass during March or in the open ground towards the end of April or in May.

Hedysarum (from Gr. name *Hedysaron*, used by Dioscorides). *Leguminosae.* 100 species; Northern Temperate regions.

H. CORONARIUM. French Honeysuckle. A handsome border plant, not, as its popular name suggests, a climber. The scarlet flowers are carried in long spikes on plants 3–4 ft. in height. It is a Biennial, but seeds sown in the open ground during March will produce flowering plants the same year. There is also a white variety, but this is not widely cultivated.

Helenium (from *Helenion*, an old Greek name used by Hippocrates and probably derived from Helen of Troy). *Compositae*. 30 species; Western America.

H. TENUIFOLIUM. Height 1–1½ ft. A showy annual species which forms a small bush of very fine pale green foliage covered with pale golden flowers about 1½–2 ins. in diameter. Seeds should be sown under glass during March and the seedlings transplanted towards the end of April.

Helianthus (Gr. *helios* = the sun, *anthos* = a flower). Sunflower. *Compositae*. 60 species; America.

The Common Sunflowers, estimable though they may be when planted with discretion, are often misplaced, and especially in a small garden are apt to present a coarse, flamboyant appearance, devoid of grace and of small decorative value. The taller kinds may be rendered more in harmony with the other members of a mixed annual border by removing the centre shoot, causing the plant to branch more freely, and in recent years varieties have appeared dwarfer and more compact than the old yellow-flowered giant, which are among the best plants obtainable for the back row of a border. The larger forms, however, have their uses and often are quite ornamental planted in small groups in shrubberies or on the fringe of the wild part of the garden.

Certain varieties are cultivated in some countries for the oil which is obtained from their seeds, and the seeds of the large-seeded kinds are sold on the streets in Russia and eaten raw, being considered a delicacy. The cultivation of Sunflowers is simple, seeds being sown during April in the open ground where the plants are to flower.

H. ANNUS (*H. lenticularis*, *H. macrocarpus*, *H. ovatus*). Common Yellow Sunflower. Height 5–8 ft. A giant in every

way, its immense single yellow flowers are often more than
1 ft. in diameter. Useful for the wild garden, or in shrubberies. 1596. Among the numerous varieties the following
are noteworthy: *Bismarckianus*, a tall, very free, single,
large-flowered yellow variety, height 5–8 ft.; *californicus
fl. pl.*, a double yellow-flowered form, height 8–10 ft.; Chrysanthemum-flowered double, a large golden-yellow form
with twisted and laciniated petals, height 5–8 ft.; *citrinus*,
pale primrose-yellow, a pleasing change from the golden
varieties, height 5–8 ft.; *fl. pl.*, the double form of the common Sunflower, height 6–8 ft.; *globosus fistulosus fl. pl.*, a
very large-flowered double golden-yellow variety growing
to a height of about 6–8 ft.; Golden Nigger, golden-yellow
flowers, of medium size, with a black centre, height 4–6 ft.;
nanus fl. pl., a dwarf double yellow-flowered type, more
suitable for garden purposes than the foregoing varieties,
height 3–4 ft.; Sutton's Red, the large flowers are yellow
with a broad chestnut-red band round the centre, height 5–8
ft.; *variegatus*, a form not often grown, which has yellow
flowers and variegated leaves, height 5–8 ft.

H. ARGYROPHYLLUS. Silvery-leaved Sunflower. The large
golden-yellow flowers are similar to those of *H. annuus*, but
the whole plant is covered with a silvery-white down which
gives it a most effective appearance, height 5–7 ft.

H. DEBILIS (*H. cucumerifolius*). Miniature Sunflower. A
useful and decorative type of Sunflower, dwarfer and more
shapely than the larger kinds. The yellow flowers are small
but are very freely produced, and the plant grows to a height
of about 3–4 ft.

There are several varieties, the best of which include:
Diadem, a sulphur-yellow form: *nanus*, a curious dwarf type
bearing golden-yellow flowers, height 2–3 ft.; Dazzler, the
flowers rich chestnut-red, tipped with golden-yellow, height
3 ft.; Excelsior, said to be a hybrid form between this species
and *H. annuus*, the mixture contains many beautifully zoned

forms, including a wide range of chestnut-red and bronze shades; the flowers are in every case tipped with either pale or deep yellow, height 3–4 ft.; Golden Fleece, a rich golden-yellow variety with dark centre, the florets being twisted in an elegant and pleasing manner, height 3–4 ft.; Star-shaped Double, the double golden-yellow flowers have twisted florets similar to the last, height 4 ft.; Starlight, similar in height and form of flower to *H.* Golden Fleece but pale sulphur-yellow in colour; Stella, a tall-growing single, with large flowers, height 5 ft.; Sunlight, a dwarfer and more compact form of *H.* Golden Fleece, one of the best for garden purposes, height 2½–3 ft.

H. LENTICULARIS see H. ANNUUS.

H. MACROCARPUS see H. ANNUUS.

H. OVATUS see H. ANNUUS.

Helichrysum (Gr. *helios* = the sun, *chrysos* = gold, in reference to the colour of the flowers). Everlasting flower. *Compositae.* 350 species; Europe, Asia, Africa, Australia.

Several species and the varieties which have been derived from them are largely grown for their beautiful "everlasting" flowers which, in addition to their value for winter decoration when dried, are plants of great merit in a mixed border. Seeds should be sown under glass during March, and the seedlings transplanted early in May. Sowings may also be made in the open ground during April, but the resulting plants often bloom too late in the year to be of much service. They thrive best in a rich loamy soil.

H. BRACTEATUM. Height 1½–3 ft. The single flowers are rich golden-orange in colour. There are several varieties which include: *album* (*H. niveum*), pure white single flowers; *atrococcineum*, dark scarlet single-flowered variety; *atrosanguineum*, dark blood-red, single flowers; *bicolor*, flowers golden-yellow, tipped with red; *monstrosum*, the very large-flowered double form popularly grown for garden decoration and for cutting, height 2–3 ft. There are numerous fine varieties which include many beautiful shades of colour, notably crimson, rose, rosy carmine, terra-cotta, salmon-pink, silvery-pink, sulphur-yellow, violet and white; Fireball, a bright orange-red; Golden, deep rich yellow.

H. NIVEUM see H. BRACTEATUM var. ALBUM.

Heliophila (Gr. *helios* = the sun, *phileo* = I love). Cape Stock. *Cruciferae*. 70 species; South Africa.

Several elegant members of this charming genus have recently taken a prominent place in our gardens, and when thickly massed are an asset to any border of mixed Annuals, while as pot plants for the cool greenhouse they are at once graceful and showy. Seeds should be sown, four or five in a small pot, under glass during March, and the seedlings thinned out, leaving two or three plants in each pot. They may then be planted out during May without being separated. For pot culture in the greenhouse it is best to prick five or six seedlings into each 5-in. pot so as to obtain an effective display.

H. LEPTOPHYLLA. Height 9 ins. The bright blue flowers, enhanced by a pure white eye, are produced freely in long racemes. The plant is slightly more bushy and compact than the following species.

H. LINEARIFOLIA. Height 1 ft. Slightly taller and less bushy than the last, bearing beautiful clear blue flowers.

The following, although at one time grown in gardens, are seldom seen and not easily obtainable: *H. amplexicaulis*, *H. coronopifolia*, *H. pilosa*, *H. pilosa* var. *incisa* (*H. arabioides*).

Heliotropium (Gr. *helios* = the sun, *trope* = a turning, in reference to its supposed characteristic of turning towards the sun). Heliotrope. Cherry Pie. *Boraginaceae*. 220 species; Tropical and Temperate regions.

Although strictly speaking, a greenhouse Perennial, the Heliotrope may be successfully flowered during its first year from seeds and will attain a considerable size during a relatively short period. Its delightful scent and handsome appearance more than justify its inclusion in a mixed border of Annuals. Seeds should be sown under glass during February or early March and the seedlings moved into small pots as soon as they are large enough, being transplanted to their flowering positions in the open ground towards the end of May. Most of the fine cultivated forms are either varieties or hybrids of *H. corymbosum* and *H. peruvianum*; they breed fairly true from seeds, although some variation must be expected. Among the best varieties to raise from seeds are: Florine, dwarf, and free flowering, flowers light-violet in colour, height 1 ft.; Marguerite, large heads of deep violet-blue flowers, height 1½ ft.; Roi des Noirs, very dark blue, height 1½ ft.; Rose, a curious mixture of rose and pink shades, height 1½ ft.; White Lady, pure white, height 1½ ft.; Regale, a compact free-flowering mixture containing many shades of lilac and blue.

In addition to the above there are several choice mixtures of many shades of colour from which the white and paler forms have been eliminated.

Helipterum (Gr. *helios* = the sun, *pteron* = a feather, in reference to the plumed pappus). Australian Everlasting Flowers. *Compositae*. 50 species; Australia, South Africa.

Among the most graceful of the Everlasting Flowers, the Helipterums, which now include the genera commonly referred to as *Acroclinium* and *Rhodanthe*, are Annuals of easy cultivation and considerable garden merit. Groups of them in mixed borders are singularly effective, possessing the advantage of remaining in flower for a long time, while they may also be easily grown in pots for the cool greenhouse, and the flowers, when cut and dried, are useful for winter decoration. Seeds should be sown under glass during March, and the seedlings transplanted early in May.

H. CORYMBIFLORUM (*Roccardia corymbiflora*). A branching small white-flowered species of little garden value, height about 6 ins.

H. HUMBOLDTIANUM (*H. Sanfordii, Roccardia Humboldtiana*). The small golden-yellow flowers are carried in dense terminal corymbs or clusters and are sometimes cut and dried for winter use, but the golden colour fades when the flowers are cut, becoming a dull greenish-white. Height about 9 ins.

H. MANGLESII (*Rhodanthe Manglesii, Roccardia Manglesii*). Usually grown and catalogued under the name *Rhodanthe*, this species is a neat, erect-growing Annual 1–1½ ft. in height, bearing large single pale rose-pink flowers. The flowers retain their colour when dried. There are several varieties including: *album*, a white form of the type; *atrosanguineum*, a dark red form; *maculatum*, a more robust form bearing larger flowers, bright rose-pink in colour, with a deeper ring at the base of the papery petals; *maculatum album*, a white form of the last.

A mixture of the above varieties of *H. Manglesii* is sometimes found in trade catalogues under the name of *Rhodanthe varium*.

H. ROSEUM (*Acroclinium roseum*). Commonly described as *Acroclinium*, this species is a most attractive and showy member of the Everlasting group. It grows to a height of about 1–1½ ft., and the single rose-pink flowers are about 1½ ins. in diameter. They close up in dull weather, but the double varieties are less inclined to do so and are generally more decorative subjects for garden purposes. There is a white form, known in gardens as *H. album* (*Acroclinium album*), also a double rose-coloured form *roseum* (*H. roseum fl. pl., Acroclinium roseum fl. pl.*) which is less prone to close its flowers during dull weather than the single varieties; and the variety *album fl. pl.* (*H. album fl. pl., Acroclinium album fl. pl.*), the white counterpart of the foregoing.

11. MATTHIOLA CRIMSON BEAUTY

12. MESEMBRYANTHEMUM CRINIFLORUM

A new strain of double-flowered varieties in many pleasing shades, varying from deep carmine-rose to pink-white and creamy-yellow, has recently made its appearance under the name of *Acroclinium grandiflorum* mixed. This represents a distinct improvement on the existing varieties in size of flower and in the variety of colouring.

H. Sanfordii see H. Humboldtianum.

Hemp see Cannabis.

Hibiscus (an old Greek name used by Dioscorides for the Mallow). *Malvaceae.* 160 species; Tropical and Sub-tropical regions.

There are several species belonging to this strikingly beautiful genus which are annual and several which, although biennial or perennial, may be successfully flowered during their first year from seeds. As the treatment required differs for some of the species, cultural directions are given for each one.

H. africanus see H. Trionum.

H. diversifolius. An uncommon, decorative perennial species easily treated as an Annual. It grows to a height of about 2 ft. and is of a branching, rather untidy habit, but nevertheless is well worthy of cultivation. The flowers are about 2–3 ins, in diameter, creamy-white in colour with a deep purplish-brown centre. Seeds should be sown under glass during early March and the seedlings transplanted to the open border towards the end of May.

H. Manihot. Height 3–4 ft. A splendid greenhouse Perennial sometimes treated as a Half-Hardy Annual. The large sulphur-yellow flowers are often 3 ins. in diameter with a deep purple centre. White forms are also known. Seeds should be sown in a greenhouse during February, and the seedlings potted on. They may be planted out in the open ground at the end of May, but better specimens are obtained if they are grown in pots in a cool greenhouse.

H. Trionum (*H. africanus, H. vesicarius*). Flower of an Hour, Bladder Ketmia, Good Night at Noon, Venice Mallow. A showy Annual of a rather loose untidy habit, attaining a height of about 1½ ft. The flowers, which are freely produced, are very short-lived, and are sulphur-yellow in colour, embellished with a dark purple centre. Seeds of this species and the variety described below should be sown under glass in March and transplanted during May, or in the open ground during April.

The variety *major* (*H. africanus major*), Black Eyed Susan, is a larger flowered, primrose-yellow form, the flowers having a deep violet-purple centre, height 2 ft.

H. vesicarius see H. Trionum.

Hollyhock see Althaea.

Hologymne glabrata see Lasthenia glabrata.

Honeywort see Cerinthe.

Hop see Humulus.

Horn of Plenty see Datura fastuosa.

Horned Poppy see Glaucium.

Hound's Tongue see Cynoglossum.

Humulus (L. *humus* = the ground, in reference to the plant's habit of trailing on the ground unless supported). Hop. *Moraceae.* 2 species; Northern Temperate regions.

H. japonicus. Annual Hop. A very rapid-growing ornamental climber which in a short time will produce a delightful light-green covering of foliage upon trellis work, fences, pergolas, etc. Seeds are best sown under glass during April and the seedlings transplanted towards the end of May, but sowings may also be made in the open ground during May. There is an interesting variety, *variegatus*, in which the leaves are curiously streaked with white, which is preferred by many to the green-leaved type.

Hunnemannia (in honour of John Hunneman, an English botanist). Mexican Tulip Poppy. *Papaveraceae.* 1 species; Mexico.

H. FUMARIAEFOLIA. Height 1–1½ ft. An interesting and decorative Biennial or Perennial which is often treated as an Annual. In the annual border, in pots or in a cool greenhouse it can be most effective; the bushy habit of the plant, together with its feathery glaucous foliage combine with the attractive bright-yellow Poppy-like flowers to make it an elegant feature of the garden. The flowers are also useful for cutting. Seeds should be sown under glass during March and the seedlings transplanted in May, or in the open ground during May.

A variety, Sunlite, recently introduced, is slightly taller than the type and bears flowers a little deeper in shade and sometimes semi-double.

HYACINTH BEAN see DOLICHOS.

HYPOCRITE PLANT see EUPHORBIA HETEROPHYLLA.

Iberis (from *Iberia*, the ancient name of Spain, where many species are found). Candytuft. *Cruciferae.* 30 species; Europe, Asia.

The genus contains Biennial and Perennial species in addition to the Annual species which, with their numerous varieties, rank among our most popular garden plants. Suitable for many positions, in borders, as edging plants or in the rock garden, the ease with which they may be cultivated and the diversity of their beautiful shades of colour entitle them to a place in every collection of Annuals. Seeds sown during September in the open ground will produce splendid plants, flowering early the following summer, or sowings may be made any time from the middle of March to the end of May to flower the same summer. Plants succeed best when given a fairly good soil, rich in humus, and they should never be allowed to become overcrowded.

I. AMARA var. CORONARIA (*I. coronaria* of gardens). Rocket Candytuft. Numerous strains of the Common White Rocket, or White Spiral Candytuft, are at present on the market, and by selection very massive heads of large pure white flowers have been obtained. Height $1-1\frac{1}{2}$ ft. When grown in pots from autumn sowings, plants often reach a height of $2-2\frac{1}{2}$ ft., bearing handsome spikes of bloom.

The variety Little Prince is a dwarf spreading white-flowered form about 6 ins. in height, useful for edgings and carpeting or for filling up blank spaces in the rock garden.

I. CORONARIA see I. AMARA var. CORONARIA.

I. UMBELLATA. Common Candytuft. The type, from which many garden varieties have been derived, is a tall, rather sparsely-flowered plant bearing purplish flowers. It reaches a height of about $1\frac{1}{2}$ ft. and the modern improvements show a great advance in decorative value upon the wild form. These include both tall and dwarf types obtainable in a wide range of colours. Some of the best varieties are given below.

Tall forms, about 1 ft. in height: carmine, crimson, lilac, purple and white.

Dwarf Large-Flowered forms, about 9 ins. in height: brick-rose, crimson, lilac, rose and white. A low-growing form, Queen of Italy, not more than 6 ins. in height, is specially suitable for rock-work; the flowers are small and of a pale rose-pink colour.

ICE PLANT see MESEMBRYANTHEMUM CRYSTALLINUM.

ICELAND POPPY see PAPAVER NUDICAULE.

Impatiens (L. *impatiens* = impatient, in reference to the elasticity of the valves of the turgid seed pods which discharge the seeds violently if touched when ripe). Balsam. Touch-Me-Not. *Balsaminaceae*. 350 species; Tropical and Northern Temperate regions.

An interesting genus, containing several species which in cultivation have given rise to valuable forms of very definite garden merit. Seeds of the species described below as Hardy Annuals may be sown in the open ground during April and cultural directions are given for the other kinds at the foot of their respective paragraphs.

I. BALSAMINA. The Garden Balsam or Ladies' Slipper. One of the most beautiful tender Annuals, the Garden Balsam makes a valuable display as a bedding or border plant; several varieties are now in cultivation, and these are described below. The wild form bears large rose-coloured flowers and grows to a height of about $1\frac{1}{2}$ ft. Seeds of this species should be sown under glass in a temperature of about 70° during March or early April and the seedlings transplanted to their flowering positions in the open ground after all danger of frost is past in June. They are also suitable subjects for cultivation in pots for the cool greenhouse.

Among the varieties the following are noteworthy: Double or Rose-Flowered. Usually sold in mixture, this strain contains many shades of colour, but is not so effective for garden purposes as the following.

Camelliaeflora, Camellia-Flowered Balsam. This is a large-flowered very double form, free-flowering and most handsome for all types of bedding. Though never seen to better advantage than when grown in mixture, a wide range of separate colours which breed very true from seeds is obtainable, height $1\frac{1}{2}$ ft.; Dwarf Bush-Flowered, a new form which is more showy than the last, and its habit dwarfer and more compact; the plants, being less leafy, display the large double flowers to better advantage. Several separate colours of this strain are obtainable, notably blush-rose, rose-scarlet and white. This is definitely the best type for bedding. Height about 1 ft.

I. DELAVAYI. One of the finest of the annual species, it is very floriferous, the flowers being of a clear yellow richly marked with purple. As it is rather apt to bloom late in the year, seeds are best sown under glass during March and the seedlings transplanted during May, although in favourable seasons it will flower before the coming of the autumn frosts if sown in the open ground during May. Height 4–5 ft.

I. GLANDULIGERA see I. ROYLEI.

I. HOLSTII. A Half-Hardy Perennial often quite successfully treated as an Annual. It may be used either as a pot plant for the greenhouse or conservatory or for bedding out of doors. The plant grows to a height of about 2–3 ft., bearing numerous brilliant scarlet flowers 1–2 ins. in diameter. There are also hybrid forms in several shades of colour. For cultural instructions see *I. Balsamina*.

I. NOLI-TANGERE (*I. Noli-me-tangere*). Touch-Me-Not Balsam. An orange-spotted yellow-flowered hardy annual species, native to Great Britain, it is a showy plant for wild parts of the garden, although it may become a nuisance if allowed to seed itself freely. Height $1\frac{1}{2}$–2 ft.

I. ROYLEI (*I. glanduligera*). A strong-growing, rather coarse, hardy annual species which does well in shady borders. It will reach a height of about 4 ft. and bears a profusion of dark purple and white flowers. This is another species which establishes itself readily from self-sown seeds, and on this account is a good plant for the woodland garden. The variety White Queen (*I. glanduligera* var. White Queen) is a pure white form of the foregoing.

I. SULTANI. More useful for greenhouse work than for bedding purposes, this perennial species is sometimes grown as an Annual. The plant, about 1–2 ft. in height, bears rosy-carmine flowers in great profusion over a very long period. Hybrid forms with *I. Holstii* are also available, sold usually as a mixture of many beautiful shades of rose and scarlet. Cultivation is similar to that described for *I. Balsamina*, but the plants should be potted on in the greenhouse.

INDIAN CORN see ZEA, p. 43.

INDIAN CRESS see TROPAEOLUM MAJUS.

INDIAN PINK see DIANTHUS CHINENSIS.

INDIAN SHOT see CANNA.

Ionopsidium (Gr. *Ion* = a violet, *opsis* = appearance). *Cruciferae*. 1 species; Portugal.

I. ACAULE (*Cochlearia acaulis*). Violet Cress, Carpet Plant. A most useful little plant for sowing in empty corners of the rock garden or between crazy paving. It grows rapidly and forms a little carpet, not more than three inches in height, of tiny violet-blue flowers. Seeds may be sown at any time between the end of March and the middle of June in the open ground, preferably in a shady situation. It is also sometimes grown in pots for window boxes or in the conservatory. There is a white form rarely seen in gardens.

Ipomoea (Gr. *ips* = bindweed, *homoios* = like; according to Linnaeus, in reference to its resemblance to *Convolvulus*). *Convolvulaceae*. 400 species; Tropical and warm Temperate regions.

Some of the members of this large genus are cultivated in this country for their showy Convolvulus-like flowers, which are short-lived but exceedingly lovely; others, like *I. Batatas*, the Sweet Potato, and *I. Purga*, the jalap plant, are grown abroad for their edible tuberous roots. The decorative varieties in a favourable season will often climb to a height of 5–9 ft. and produce a succession of flowers from July to September. They are useful for all purposes where a fairly rapid-growing climber is required, such as covering trellises, walls, tree stumps and the like, or for growing upon pea sticks in small clumps at the back of a border. Seeds should be sown under glass during March or April and the seedlings potted on and planted out during June.

Considerable confusion exists about the names of Ipomoeas, as found in trade catalogues, but the list below includes those most commonly grown and of the greatest garden value.

I. ATROPURPUREA see I. PURPUREA.

I. BONA-NOX. A large blue-flowered species not very commonly grown.

I. HEDERACEA (*I. imperialis*). Japanese Morning Glory. Very beautiful forms of this species have been obtained in cultivation. They are usually sold under the name of *I. imperialis* in a mixture of many lovely shades of colour varying from light blue, rose, copper-red to white. They thrive best in a light soil and a fairly sunny position.

I. HUBERI var. VARIEGATA see I. PURPUREA var. HUBERI.

I. IMPERIALIS see I. HEDERACEA.

I. LEARI. A very beautiful blue-flowered greenhouse Perennial which may be flowered in its first year from seeds.

I. PURPUREA (*Convolvulus major*, *C. purpureus*, *Ipomoea atropurpurea*). Tall Morning Glory. Numerous separate shades of colour are now available of this popular species, including white, white spotted violet, flesh, rose, carmine, dark red, light blue, lilac and black blue. The type from which these have originated is a curious blending of purple and pink. In the double form *fl. pl.*, the flowers are bluish-white streaked with pink; also the variety *Huberi* (*I. Huberi* var. *variegata*), in which the colour of the flowers is variable, usually white margined and the leaves are curiously streaked with white. It is not often seen in gardens.

I. QUAMOCLIT. China Creeper, Cypress Vine. A greenhouse Annual, bearing very finely cut foliage and small scarlet flowers. This species and its white variety, *alba*, do not thrive in the open in this country, although in favourable seasons they will produce a few flowers. Its variety *cardinalis*, Cardinal Climber, bears very brilliant scarlet flowers.

I. RUBRO-CAERULEA. One of the most lovely of all annual climbing plants. The large sky-blue flowers, sometimes tinged with rose, are often 4 ins. across, and when the plant is doing well in a warm sunny position, in a favourable season, it is a sheer joy to behold.

There are two varieties worthy of note, namely: *grandi-flora*, which bears larger flowers which appear a little earlier in the season; and Heavenly Blue, a clear sky-blue form, similar to the last.

I. SETOSA (Brazilian Morning Glory). A vigorous climber, bearing large rosy-purple flowers often 3 ins. in diameter.

I. VERSICOLOR (*Mina lobata*). Usually grown and sold as *Mina lobata*, this plant, if given a warm sheltered position and favoured by congenial weather conditions, will produce a profusion of attractive flowers, scarlet in bud, opening a deep yellow and developing to a pale creamy-white.

IPOMOPSIS ELEGANS see GILIA AGGREGATA.

JACOBAEA see SENECIO.

JAPANESE PINK see DIANTHUS CHINENSIS.

Jasione (derivation doubtful, perhaps Gr. *iasis* = healing, and *ion* = violet, or *sios* = godly, referring to *Convolvulus Sepium* to which the name *Jasione* was applied in olden times). *Campanulaceae*. 5 species; Europe, Mediterranean regions.

J. MONTANA. Sheep's-bit. A pretty little annual or sometimes biennial plant, native to Great Britain, which is useful for edging or in rock gardens. It is easy to grow and the plant forms a rosette or tuft of leaves surmounted by pale-blue flowers borne on stems, which reach a height of about 1 ft. A useful plant for the wild garden. Seeds may be sown in the open ground during April to flower the same year, or in September to flower the following year.

JERUSALEM CHERRY see SOLANUM PSEUDOCAPSICUM.

JEWEL OF THE VELDT see URSINIA.

KAULFUSSIA see CHARIEIS HETEROPHYLLA.

KENILWORTH IVY SEE LINARIA CYMBALARIA.

Kochia (in honour of W. D. J. Koch, 1771–1849, a professor of botany at Erlangen). Summer Cypress. Broom

Cypress. *Chenopodiaceae.* 80 species; mostly in Australia, but also in Asia, North and South Africa and Western America.

K. TRICHOPHYLLA. Height 2–3 ft. An ornamental Annual of great value as a foliage plant. The flowers are of no importance, but the compact bush of pale green feathery foliage which the plant forms is an object of great beauty. When planted in groups it is extremely effective, especially in the autumn, when the leaves and stems begin gradually to change colour until a rich copper-red takes the place of the fresh pale green shade so cool and restful during the hot summer months. Seeds should be sown under glass during early April and the seedlings transplanted to their flowering positions in the open ground towards the end of May. Care must be taken never to water the pots from above when the seeds are germinating, but to immerse them in water up to the rim of the pot for a short time, as the young seedlings are very susceptible to damping-off. See p. 26.

The variety *Childsii*, height 2½ ft., is a more compact form which is a definite improvement for bedding purposes.

KÖNIGA see ALYSSUM.

KNOT-WEED see POLYGONUM.

LADIES' SLIPPER see IMPATIENS BALSAMINA.

LADY'S THUMB see POLYGONUM.

LAGENARIA see list of varieties on p. 44.

LARKSPUR see DELPHINIUM.

Lantana (old Italian name applied at one time to *Viburnum*). *Verbenaceae.* 60 species; Tropical and Sub-tropical regions.

L. CAMARA. These showy, dwarf, shrubby Perennials may be flowered during their first year from seeds, and the strain found in most seedsmen's catalogues under the name *L. hybrida nana* is a selection of the dwarf forms of this species.

It contains many brilliantly coloured varieties and is of a convenient size for bedding or pot culture, rarely exceeding 1 ft. in height. Seeds should be sown in a greenhouse during March and strong bottom heat given until they germinate; the young plants may be transplanted to their flowering positions in the open ground during June.

Lasthenia (in honour of a girl pupil of Plato). *Compositae*. 6 species; Western America.

L. GLABRATA (*L. californica, Hologymne glabrata*). A dwarf, attractive little Hardy Annual of spreading habit, which bears bright golden-yellow Daisy-like flowers. Seeds may be sown in September in the open ground to bloom early the following spring, or sowings may be made in March or April to produce flowering plants the same summer. Height 8 ins. to 1 ft.

Lathyrus (Gr. *Lathyros*, the old name of the Pea, used by Theophrastus). *Leguminosae*. 110 species; Northern Temperate regions and mountains of Tropical Africa and South America.

The popularity of the Sweet Pea continues unchallenged, and each year new varieties come, larger and more beautiful than ever; longer stems, new shades, colours that are fast to the sunlight, varieties which carry more flowers on a stem than of old—all these characteristics are carefully considered and fostered by the enthusiastic specialists, who labour to make this time-honoured garden favourite still more lovely. Seeds sown in the open ground during September will produce strong healthy plants flowering early the following summer, while sowings may also be made under glass during January or February or in the open ground during March or April. For further information on the cultivation of the Sweet Pea see pp. 20–21.

L. ODORATUS. Sweet Pea. Generally supposed to be a native of Italy, the pink and purple species which, with the pink and white form originally introduced from Ceylon, have given rise to the extraordinary number of varieties in commerce to-day, first appeared in gardens about 1700.

The varieties of Sweet Peas are so numerous and new-comers to the list are so constantly appearing, that it is only possible to give here a short selection of some of the most popular and meritorious varieties. These include: Ambition, deep lavender; Blue Bell, delphinium blue; Charming, bright cerise; Damask Rose, carmine-rose; Empire, rich cerise; Gigantic, pure white; Golden Star, salmon, flushed orange; Halo, lilac-pink; Highlander, rosy-lavender; Jack Hobbs, cream, flushed pink; Loch Lomond, deep maroon; Lochnagar, orange-vermilion, shaded cerise; Magnet, pink, cream ground; Mastercream, deep cream; Monty, deep cream-pink; Mrs. A. Searles, cerise, suffused salmon; Mrs. Robert Bolton, deep almond-pink, white ground; Patricia Unwin, salmon-pink; Pink Frills, salmon-pink, on cream; Powerscourt, rich rosy-lavender; Reconnaissance, cream ground picotee; Tell Tale, white with a picotee edge; The Admiral, dark blue; Toreador, scarlet, overlaid salmon; Welcome, scarlet; Youth, white ground, pink edge.

For cultivation under glass the Early Flowering Spencer varieties are most suitable.

Many people prefer to grow the old-fashioned smaller-flowered type of Sweet Pea known as *grandiflora*, as it is more strongly scented than the modern "Spencer or Waved Standard" varieties. This, however, is a matter of degree, and the modern Sweet Pea still retains a powerful and delicious scent.

The dwarf or Cupid type of Sweet Pea, which achieved at one time a passing popularity, is now seldom seen in gardens, although it is sometimes cultivated for bedding purposes.

L. SATIVUS var. AZUREUS. Chickling Vetch. Height 2–3 ft. A bright-blue-flowered Annual which possesses a certain charm, and is not unworthy of inclusion in a mixed border.

It is often sold for the famous "Lord Anson's Pea," which is a Perennial, and quite distinct from this plant. 1640.

L. TINGITANUS. Tangier Scarlet Pea. Height 2–3 ft. A rapid-growing Pea, bearing scarlet flowers, seldom seen in gardens, but sometimes used as a forage plant.

Lavatera (in honour of two brothers Lavater, Swiss physicians and naturalists of the eighteenth century). *Malvaceae*. 20 species; Mediterranean regions, Australia and Central Asia.

L. TRIMESTRIS (*L. rosea*). This species (and its varieties) is the only annual member of the genus commonly grown in gardens, and by reason of its flowering qualities and its easy cultivation may well claim to be numbered among our most popular Annuals. The type, from which the several varieties have been obtained, grows to a height of about 3 ft. and bears rosy-purple flowers. Seeds of this species and the varieties described below may be sown in the open ground where they are to flower at any time during April, but seeds sown in a warm sheltered spot during September, to flower the following year, often produce finer plants than those resulting from spring sowings.

Among the best varieties are: *alba splendens*, a large-flowered white form of the foregoing; *rosea splendens*, an improved form of the type, which bears larger flowers of a pure rose colour; *rosea splendens* Sunset or Loveliness, height 2–3 ft., the latest and most beautiful development. The flowers are larger, their colour is of a deeper, richer rose than the last variety, and the plant is slightly dwarfer, more compact and tidy. It is a splendid subject for a mixed border of Annuals and will provide a gay show over a long flowering period.

Layia (in honour of Thomas Lay, the naturalist on Beechey's voyage). Tidy-tips. *Compositae*. 14 species; North-Western America.

Although they have never achieved any great popularity,

certain members of this genus are of considerable worth as dwarf border plants. The species described below are annual, and seeds may be sown in the open ground during April or in favourable localities in September to flower the following summer.

L. CALLIGLOSSA (*Calliglossa Douglasii*). Height 1 ft. Not often seen in gardens, this species forms a dwarf low-growing plant which covers itself with pale yellow Daisy-like flowers.

L. ELEGANS. Height about 1 ft. The best of the genus, this plant bears large yellow, white-tipped flowers which contrast effectively with the grey-green rather hairy foliage. This species is most effective when grown massed in the front row of a mixed border. There is a pure white form, *alba*, rarely seen in gardens.

L. GLANDULOSA. Height 1–1½ ft. A showy and desirable plant, bearing large flowers with broad, usually pure white rays. Sometimes the ray florets are tinged with pink.

Other species not commonly cultivated are *L. Douglasii*, *L. gaillardioides* and *L. platyglossa*.

LEONOTIS HETEROPHYLLUS see p. 17.

LEPTOSIPHON see GILIA ANDROSACEA and G. MICRANTHA.

Leptosyne (Gr. *leptos* = thin, delicate, in reference to the foliage). *Compositae*. 5 species; California, Mexico.

The graceful foliage of these fine Daisy-flowered plants together with the bright cheerful colour of their flowers entitles them to a place in the mixed border. They are also useful for cutting. Seeds of the species described as Half-Hardy should be sown under glass in March, the seedlings being transplanted towards the end of May; seeds of the annual species and its variety, a recent introduction, may be sown in the open ground during April.

L. CALLIOPSIDEA (*Coreopsis calliopsidea*). Half-Hardy Annual, about 1½–2 ft. in height. The golden-yellow flowers are often 3 ins. in diameter.

L. Douglasii. Height 9–12 ins. A showy yellow-flowered half-hardy annual species, not often seen in gardens.

L. gigantea (*Coreopsis gigantea*). Height 3–5 ft. A biennial species which may be treated as a Half-Hardy Annual. The flowers, golden yellow in colour, are said to be sweet scented but are not so large as in some of the other more popular species. Seldom met with in gardens.

L. maritima (*Coreopsis maritima*). A Half-Hardy Biennial or Perennial, useful for a cool damp position. The plant grows to a height of about 2–3 ft. and produces large golden-yellow flowers.

L. stillmannii. Height 1½ ft., Hardy Annual. The most popular species, bearing large bright golden-yellow flowers often 2 ins. in diameter on long stems very suitable for cutting. Although it has been in cultivation since 1873, it is only recently that any varieties of special merit have made their appearance and the double form described below represents a noteworthy introduction.

The variety Golden Rosette is a double, butter-yellow-flowered form, newly introduced, which should prove valuable both in the garden and as a cut flower. It will begin flowering within ten weeks of sowing and continue for a considerable period during the summer months.

Lesquerella see p. 18.

Limnanthes (Gr. *limne* = a marsh, *anthos* = a flower). *Limnanthaceae*. 4 species; Pacific North America.

L. Douglasii. Height 6 ins. A low spreading plant very effective when massed and useful for all purposes where a dwarf free-flowering Annual of simple needs is required. The flowers are delightfully scented, about 1 in. in diameter and vary somewhat in colour, being usually bright yellow shading to white at the tips of the florets. Seeds may be sown in the open ground during September to flower the following year, or at any time from the end of March until late May, to flower the same summer. It thrives in a moist situation. There is a pure white garden variety, *alba*, also a garden form, *grandiflora*, sometimes met with, which has slightly larger flowers.

Linaria (L. *linum* = flax, in reference to the resemblance which the leaves of some species bear to this plant). Toad-flax. *Scrophulariaceae*. 100 species; Northern hemisphere and South America.

Recent years have seen the introduction of several splen-did varieties of this admirable garden plant. The wild Lin-arias, many of them in themselves charming and showy Annuals, have responded well to the efforts of the horti-culturist and there is now a choice of numerous decorative forms ideal for bedding and border purposes, also for pot culture. Cultivation is of the simplest. Seeds may be sown in the open ground during March or April. Sowings may also be made under glass during late February, the seedlings being transplanted during May; this method produces large handsome plants flowering early in the summer and should be adopted in particular for the half-hardy perennial species *L. triornithophora*.

L. ALPINA. A compact and elegant little plant 4–6 ins. in height, useful for rock-work, or the front row of a mixed border. It is a Hardy Perennial but may be flowered during its first year from seeds. The showy little flowers are violet with an orange palate and are freely produced. 1750. A mixture of several attractive shades of colour, hybrids or varieties, is available under the name *L. alpina hybrida*, and there is also a charming variety, *nana rosea*, bearing rosy-purple flowers with an orange palate.

L. ANTICARIA. Height 6 ins. An interesting dwarf yellow-flowered perennial species which may be successfully treated as an Annual.

L. APARINOIDES see L. HETEROPHYLLA.

13. NICOTIANA HYBRIDA VAR. SENSATION

14. PAPAVER NUDICAULE VAR. SUNBEAM

L. BIPARTITA. Height about 1 ft. An old-fashioned favourite, bearing lilac-purple flowers with a yellow palate. There are several garden varieties of this species, some of which are described below.

Among the varieties are: *alba*, a form with creamy-white flowers; *splendida*, a popular variety, in which the flowers are deep purple with a sharply contrasting yellow palate; *striata*, not often seen in gardens, has purple and yellow-striped flowers.

L. BROUSSONNETTII (*L. multipunctata*). Height 5–8 ins. A dwarf species useful for rock-work, bearing showy bright-orange, black-spotted flowers.

L. CYMBALARIA. Kenilworth Ivy. Mother of Thousands. A native of this country, where it generally grows in cracks of old walls. A perennial species usually grown as an Annual, it is a low-growing creeping plant bearing charming deep lilac flowers.

There are several varieties including: *alba*, a white-flowered form; *globosa*, a compact, bushy, lilac-flowered variety; *maxima*, a large pale lilac-flowered form; *rosea*, a variety with pale rose-coloured flowers.

L. FAUCICOLA. A pretty, large-flowered deep lavender-coloured annual species, height about 6 ins.

L. HETEROPHYLLA (*L. aparinoides*). Height 1 ft. An erect-growing annual species bearing straw-coloured flowers with a yellow palate. A mixture of many shades of colour ranging from pale yellow to violet-bronze is sometimes found in catalogues under the name of *L. aparinoides* var. *splendens*.

L. MAROCCANA. Height 1 ft. This fine annual species has given rise to numerous popular garden forms. The type is a handsome plant bearing dense spikes of bright violet-rose flowers, which are most effective for all forms of bedding or in mixed borders, also standing well in water when cut. 1815.

Among the splendid varieties are: *alba*, a pure white form, of which by constant selection a strain has been produced and is sold under the name of White Pearl, which is very large-flowered and of a glistening whiteness; *carminea*, a garden form which is brighter and more rosy in colour than the type—the latest development in this carmine section is *L.* Ruby King which is a deep blood-red variety, most colourful and handsome; Excelsior, a cheerful many-coloured mixture which shows a great advance upon the type in size of flower, and contains a great number of shades, including rose, carmine, crimson, yellow, blue, purple, salmon, beige and white; Fairy Bouquet, a new dwarf, compact and very floriferous strain containing all the shades of colour of Excelsior. It represents a notable achievement and has already done much to increase the already considerable popularity of the Annual Linarias. Two of the colour forms have been fixed and are available under the names Fairy Bride, pure white, and Fairy Bridesmaid, rich yellow. Diadem, an interesting variety, bears very large rich purple flowers, height about 6 ins.; Yellow Prince, a pure yellow variety, is of considerable garden worth, height 1 ft.

L. MULTIPUNCTATA see L. BROUSSONNETTII.

L. RETICULATA. Height 1–1½ ft. An old favourite, bearing purple flowers with a yellow palate. 1788. The variety *aureopurpurea* is more often seen in gardens than the type; the flowers, rich deep purple in colour with a deep golden-yellow palate, are strikingly handsome.

L. TRIORNITHOPHORA. Height 2 ft. A half-hardy perennial species which may be successfully treated as an Annual. This very handsome plant, which bears large violet-purple striped flowers with an orange palate, deserves to be seen more often in gardens because of its high decorative qualities.

L. TRISTIS. Height 1 ft. An interesting annual species, bearing yellow flowers with a bronze-purple palate. 1727.

Linum (L. *linum* = flax). Flax. *Linaceae*. 95 species; Temperate and Sub-tropical regions.

Few Annuals give such a generous return for a minimum of trouble as the members of this genus. Extremely free-flowering, they are among the best subjects for massing in mixed borders, and their cultivation is of the simplest, as seeds may be sown during April where the plants are to flower.

L. GRANDIFLORUM. Height 1–2 ft. A charming plant bearing flowers 1–2 ins. in diameter, bright red in colour. The varieties include: *alba*, a white form not very widely grown; *roseum*, a rose-coloured variety; *rubrum*, the most popular variety, bearing rich scarlet flowers.

L. USITATISSIMUM. Flax. Linseed Oil Plant. Height 2 ft. The small flowers of this species are pale blue in colour; it is from seeds of this plant that linseed oil is extracted, and the fibres provide commercial flax.

Loasa (native South American name). *Loasaceae.* 100 species; Mexico and South America.

A genus of annual and perennial plants of small garden merit, usually treated as Half-Hardy Annuals. The foliage inflicts a sharp sting, the effects of which often last for several days, and the flowers, although not large, are in several species quite colourful. Seeds may be sown under glass during April and the seedlings transplanted to a warm sheltered situation towards the end of May or early in June. A fairly light soil suits them best.

L. LATERITIA (*Blumenbachia lateritia, Cajophora lateritia*). A climbing species generally considered the most desirable of the genus. It attains a height of 4–5 ft. in a favourable season, but usually blooms at about 2–3 ft. The flowers are about 1 in. in diameter, bright orange in colour and are freely produced.

L. VULCANICA. A pretty, erect bushy species, usually about 2 ft. in height, bearing curious pure white flowers with a red and yellow centre.

The following species are not commonly grown but are said to be serviceable plants: *L. hispida* and *L. tricolor*.

Lobelia (in honour of Matthias de Lobel or L'Obel, 1538–1616, a Flemish botanist). *Lobeliaceae*. 220 species; Tropical and Temperate regions.

The dwarf types of this valuable genus have, after many years of selection, become recognized as the edging plant *par excellence*, and although almost invariably treated as Annuals they are really biennial or sometimes perennial. In addition to the compact varieties the genus has provided us with those trailing forms which are so much prized for growing in hanging baskets. Another species worthy of special mention is *L. tenuior*, a magnificent pot plant for the cool greenhouse, with flowers of an entrancing shade of blue.

Seeds of all the kinds described below should be sown in a greenhouse early in February, and the seedlings transplanted during June. Sowings may also be made of the varieties of *L. Erinus* during September or October and the plants kept in boxes in the greenhouse all the winter. This method, although entailing more trouble, has the advantage of producing large plants which will flower early the following summer.

L. ERINUS. A very variable species from which have been derived the many fine garden forms described below. The type is a small spreading plant, 6–12 ins. in height, bearing numerous light blue, white-throated flowers $\frac{1}{2}$–$\frac{3}{4}$ in. across. 1752.

Some of the best varieties are described below.

Compact blue-flowered varieties: Blue Gown, dark blue, very large-flowered, compact and shapely; Blue Wings, large-flowered ultramarine; Cambridge Blue, a fine variety; Celestial, clear sky-blue; Crystal Palace, a dark-leaved deep blue variety, exceedingly popular; Emperor William, clear light blue; Golden Queen, a curious golden-leaved form with deep blue flowers; Mrs. Clibran Improved, most effective, deep blue with conspicuous white eye.

Compact white-flowered varieties: Snowball, very compact and large-flowered; White Perfection, good pure white.

Trailing blue-flowered varieties: gracilis, a fine clear blue; *hybrida pendula coerulea,* a splendid light blue form; *hybrida pendula* Sapphire, the most showy of these trailing forms; the flowers are deep blue with a white eye.

Other interesting varieties sometimes grown but not so popular are: L. *Erinus* var. *flore pleno,* a double-flowered blue form; L. *Erinus* var. *kermesina oculata,* a compact crimson-purple form with a prominent white eye, and L. *Erinus* var. *marmorata,* in which the flowers are marbled blue and white.

L. GRACILIS (*L. trigonocaulis*). Height 9 ins. to 1 ft. The flowers are ½–¾ in. across, light blue with a white eye. Not widely grown in gardens.

L. TENUIOR (*L. ramosa*). Height 6 ins. to 1 ft. This large-flowered handsome species is one of the finest subjects for pot culture in the cool greenhouse, but usually produces indifferent results when grown in the open ground. The individual flowers are often 1½ ins. across in the selected strains now on the market. The plant forms a shapely little bush covered with intense blue flowers. The plant usually described in trade lists as L. *ramosa,* together with its white variety L. *ramosa* var. *alba,* is now referred to this species, although it is not such a desirable plant as the modern selected forms of L. *tenuior.*

L. TRIGONOCAULIS see L. GRACILIS.

LOBEL'S CATCHFLY see SILENE ARMERIA.

Lonas (derivation uncertain). *Compositae.* 1 species; South-Western Mediterranean regions.

L. INODORA (*Athanasia annua*). Height 1 ft. Of little garden value, this plant bears small clusters of yellow, papery flowers of the "everlasting" type. Seeds may be sown under glass in February or March, or in the open ground during April. 1686.

Lopezia (in honour of a Spanish botanist Thomas Lopez who wrote on the natural history of America). *Onagraceae.* 15 species; Central America.

L. CORONATA. Height 2–3 ft. A little-grown Annual which has never become popular as a garden plant. The small pink and white flowers are born in the axils of the leaves over a considerable period. Seeds may be sown under glass during March or in the open ground during April.

LOPHOSPERMUM see MAURANDIA SCANDENS.

LORD ANSON'S PEA see LATHYRUS SATIVUS var. AZUREUS.

LOVE-IN-A-MIST see NIGELLA.

LOVE-LIES-BLEEDING see AMARANTHUS CAUDATUS.

Lupinus (L. *lupus* = a wolf, as a crop of Lupines was supposed to destroy the fertility of the soil). Lupine. *Leguminosae.* 150 species; America and Mediterranean regions.

Colourful and showy, comprising several types and both tall and dwarf kinds, the annual Lupines should not be overlooked when planning a mixed border or bed. Their needs are simple and they will flourish almost anywhere; seeds may be sown during April in the open ground in the position where the plants are desired to flower. Certain perennial species which will flower during their first year from seeds are described below; seeds of these should be sown in a cold frame during January or February and the seedlings transplanted during April or May.

L. ALBUS. White Lupine. One of the rather coarse Lupines, generally grown as a fodder plant but quite useful in the garden. It bears large white flowers. Height 1½ ft. 1596.

L. AFFINIS. A deep-blue-flowered species growing to a height of about 1 ft. Often a rather coarse, rank-growing plant. 1848.

L. Cruckshanksii see L. mutabilis.

L. densiflorus (*L. Menziesii*). A fine garden plant, its handsome densely packed spikes of yellow flowers rise to a height of about 1½ ft. There is a white variety, *L. densiflorus* var. *lacteus*, of considerable garden value.

L. Douglasii. A tall handsome perennial species; flowers are borne in long spikes and their colour varies in shades of rosy purple and blue. Height 3 ft.

L. grandiflorus see L. polyphyllus.

L. Hartwegii. Height 2½–3 ft. One of the most popular of the annual Lupines, this species and its varieties are tall brightly coloured plants, splendid for the mixed border. The type bears dense spikes of sky-blue and white flowers which fade to a dull reddish-lilac shade. 1838.

There are several notable varieties and the best of these are: *albus*, a pure white form; *albo-coccineus*, a beautiful white and red bicoloured form; *coelestinus*, sky-blue and a great improvement on the type; *nigrescens*, a deep rich blue variety; *roseus*, soft rich pink, a very pretty shade; *superbus*, a striking combination of rosy purple and white; *Tom Thumb*, height 1½ ft., a dwarf mixture of many charming shades of colour.

L. hirsutissimus. A very effective species, 1½–2 ft. in height; the flowers, deep reddish-purple in colour, are large and freely produced.

L. hirsutus. Blue Lupine. Height 2–3 ft. A coarse species, similar in habit to *L. luteus* and *L. albus*, and grown sometimes as a fodder plant. The flowers are large and their colour varies in shades of violet and blue. There is a white variety, *albus*; also a variety *ruber*, bearing light rose flowers tinged with red.

L. hybridus albo-coccineus. Height 2½ ft. Of doubtful origin, this annual hybrid, which is rosy-red and white in colour, and its rosy-pink variety *roseus*, are serviceable plants.

L. leucophyllus see p. 18.

L. LONGIFOLIUS. Height 3 ft. A perennial species not very widely grown but valuable for its long spikes of light blue flowers.

L. LUTEUS. Yellow Lupine. A commonly-grown fodder plant used green or dried, but possessing a certain ornamental value. The golden-yellow flowers are large and fragrant. 1596. There is an improved, larger-flowered, deeper-coloured form named Romulus.

L. MENZIESII see L. DENSIFLORUS.

L. MICRANTHUS. A light graceful plant, about 9 ins. in height, carrying numerous short dense spikes of small violet flowers.

L. MUTABILIS. Height 4–5 ft. A bushy, tall-growing, annual species bearing attractive spikes of flowers, which are a combination of blue and white marked with yellow in the centre. There is a splendid form, *Cruckshanksii* (*L. Cruckshanksii*), which grows to a height of about 4 ft. and bears large fragrant flowers in which rose and yellow are attractively blended. As they age they assume a pale violet shade tinged with rose and yellow merging to deep lavender on fading.

L. NANUS. One of the most showy dwarf annual species, 6 ins. to 1 ft. in height, very floriferous; the colour of the flowers is blue and lilac, and the elegant, fine foliage greatly enhances the beauty of the plant. 1833. There is a white form, *albus*, which has been vastly improved; the variety Snow Queen is more compact and upright, and the flowers are of a glistening whiteness.

L. NOOTKATENSIS. Height 2–3 ft. An interesting perennial species, of considerable garden merit and naturalized in many places in Scotland. The flowers, which vary a little in colour, being usually deep blue variegated with rose and yellow, are carried in dense spikes and are very showy. This species, which is a native of North America, has escaped from gardens and is firmly established in certain parts of the country, being now included in the British Flora. 1794.

L. PILOSUS. Height 2–4 ft. A strong-growing annual species; the flowers are an attractive combination of rose and red.

L. POLYPHYLLUS (*L. grandiflorus*). Height 2–4 ft. The finest of all Lupines have been derived from this handsome perennial species. They may be very successfully flowered during their first year from seeds, and there are many fine strains obtainable which contain a delightful range of lovely shades of colour. The type is a noble plant, bearing long spikes of deep blue flowers. Of the many varieties available only those which may be relied upon to reproduce themselves fairly true from seeds are mentioned here. 1826. The following varieties are worthy of note: *albus*, pure white; *carmineus*, a pleasing shade of deep rosy-red; Lavender Queen, a charming light lavender form tinted pale rose; *luteus*, yellow, slightly variable in shade; *Moerheimii*, a splendid well-tried variety of compact habit; the flowers are a combination of rose and white; *salmoneus*, a recent introduction; this strain includes many lovely soft salmon and buff shades and is certain to find many admirers.

L. SUBCARNOSUS (*L. texensis*). Height 8–10 ins. A useful plant, of spreading habit; the flowers are generously produced and are deep blue in colour with a white spot in the centre. 1835.

L. SULPHUREUS. Height about 3 ft. A robust silky-leaved species bearing long spikes of sulphur-yellow flowers. It is a branching plant becoming rather bare and gaunt below.

L. TEXENSIS see L. SUBCARNOSUS.

Lychnis (Gr. *lychnos* = a lamp, probably in reference to the brilliant flowers). *Caryophyllaceae*. 10 species; Northern Temperate regions.

The genera *Agrostemma* and *Viscaria* are now referred by botanists to this genus although commonly grown and listed in seed catalogues under their old names. The production of new varieties, many of them plants of sterling merit both as border plants and cut flowers, has proceeded apace in recent years and some of these colourful and free-blooming forms should find a place in every garden. Seeds may be sown during late March or April in the open ground where the plants are to flower; certain kinds may also be used as pot plants for the cool greenhouse and for this purpose seeds should be sown under glass during February to flower about June or July.

L. COELI-ROSA (*Agrostemma Coeli-rosa, Coronaria Coeli-rosa*). Rose of Heaven. Height 1 ft. A popular Annual, free-flowering and continuing in bloom for a long period; the flowers are about 1 in. in diameter and rosy-red in colour. 1713. The white form, *alba*, is not much in evidence in gardens; *fimbriata kermesina* is an interesting form with delicately fringed carmine flowers. The variety *oculata* (*L. oculata, Viscaria oculata*) through many years of selection has produced several desirable garden forms usually described in catalogues as varieties of *Viscaria oculata*. The progenitor of these present-day forms bears large rosy-purple flowers with a dark eye. The following garden varieties are among the best: Blue Bouquet, an erect-growing columnar plant, very useful for cutting and border purposes with large flowers of a deep shade of blue enhanced by an almost black eye; Blue Pearl, somewhat resembling the last but the erect habit is not fixed, the flowers are pure lavender-blue without eye; *caerulea*, flowers of similar quality and colouring to *L.* Blue Bouquet, but of a more loose and branching habit; *candida*, a large-flowered pure white branching form; *cardinalis*, a brilliant crimson variety; Fire King, an improved form of *cardinalis*, the colour of the flowers is more vivid; *nobilis*, a pleasing chamois-rose-flowered variety; Tom Thumb Blue Gem, height about 6 ins., a compact blue-flowered plant suitable for bedding or the front row of a mixed border. The two following varieties are widely used for pot culture: Tomb Thumb Innocence, the white counterpart of the last; Tom Thumb Rosy Gem, a charming rosy-carmine-flowered plant of similar habit to the two last-mentioned varieties.

L. OCULATA see L. COELI-ROSA var. OCULATA.

L. VACCARIA see SAPONARIA VACCARIA.

MADARIA ELEGANS see MADIA ELEGANS.

Madia (from *Madi*, the Chilean name of the common species). *Compositae*. 15 species; Western America.

M. ELEGANS (*Madaria elegans*). Height 1-2 ft. A little-grown Annual seldom found in seed lists, but of value for its graceful habit and free-blooming qualities. The Daisy-like flowers are yellow, sometimes with a red spot at the base of the florets. Seeds may be sown in the open ground during April, a semi-shady sheltered position suiting the plant best.

MAIZE see ZEA, p. 43.

Malcomia (in honour of William Malcolm, a London horticulturist of the eighteenth century). Virginian Stock. *Cruciferae*. 35 species; Mediterranean region. Sometimes written *Malcolmia*.

M. MARITIMA. Virginian Stock. Ever popular, in constant demand for edgings or the front parts of mixed borders, the varieties of this pretty little plant are so easy to grow that it is small wonder they appear in almost every collection of Annuals. The type is a dwarf reddish-lilac-flowered plant, 3-4 ins. in height, from which several colour forms have been selected. Seeds are best sown in the open ground during September to produce large plants flowering early the following summer, or sowings may be made at intervals for a succession of bloom during March and April. 1713.

The varieties obtainable include *alba grandiflora*, large-flowered white; Crimson King, a richer-coloured form of the type; Fairy Queen, rosy-carmine; and a pale greenish sulphur-coloured form which passes under the name of *luteus* or in some catalogues, Yellow.

MALLOW see MALVA.

Malope (an old Greek name used by Pliny for a kind of Malva). *Malvaceae.* 3 species; Mediterranean region.

Familiar, old-fashioned Annuals of undeniable value as border plants. They thrive best in fairly rich soil, and when well-grown will make handsome very floriferous plants continuing in bloom over a long period during the summer months. Seeds should be sown in the open ground during April or May.

M. GRANDIFLORA see M. TRIFIDA.

M. MALACOIDES. Seldom seen in gardens, but a decorative violet-purple-flowered species growing to a height of about 2 ft. A rosy-red-flowered form is obtainable under the name *rosea*.

M. TRIFIDA. Height 2–3 ft. The large flowers, produced in great profusion, are rosy-purple in colour, and the varieties which have been derived from this species are among our most useful garden Annuals. 1710. The most popular variety is *grandiflora* (*M. grandiflora*); the flowers are larger than those of the type and are deep rosy-red in colour veined inside with red. A white-flowered variety *alba*, is not quite so large; the variety *rosea* is a charming shade of rosy-pink.

Malva (Latin name for Mallow. An alteration of the Greek name *Malache* derived from Gr. *malasso* = to soften, in reference to the emollient properties of the leaves). Mallow. *Malvaceae.* 30 species; Northern Temperate regions.

M. CRISPA. The Curled Mallow. This is the only annual species of any garden merit at present in cultivation. It is a tall plant of upright habit, reaching a height of 4–6 ft., sometimes grown as a foliage plant. The leaves are elegantly crisped and curled and are sometimes used for garnishing purposes. The flowers are small and pure white. 1573. Seeds may be sown under glass during March or April and the seedlings transplanted to the open ground during June.

M. MAURITIANA see p. 16.

MARGUERITE see CHRYSANTHEMUM FRUTESCENS.

MARIGOLD see TAGETES, also CALENDULA.

Martynia (in honour of Dr. John Martyn, 1699–1768, professor of botany at Cambridge). Unicorn Plant, Elephant's Trunk Plant. *Martyniaceae*. 8 species; Mexico.

A curious genus of Half-Hardy Annuals, usually cultivated in a cool greenhouse, but sometimes succeeding in a warm sunny border. The common names of the plant have arisen by reason of the strange fruits ending in a long curved horn, which splits into two as the pods ripen. These fruits are sometimes gathered when young and pickled like Cucumbers. Seeds may be sown in a greenhouse during March and the seedlings planted out in a sheltered position during June.

M. ANNUA see M. PROBOSCIDEA.

M. FRAGRANS. Height 2 ft. The most common species, bearing reddish-purple flowers 1–2 ins. long.

M. LOUISIANA, M. LOUISIANICA see M. PROBOSCIDEA.

M. LUTEA. Height 1½ ft. The flowers are produced sparingly, and are greenish-yellow outside, deep orange within. Not in general cultivation.

M. PROBOSCIDEA (*M. annua, M. louisiana, M. louisianica*). Not so commonly grown as *M. fragrans*, the flowers are large, creamy-white and mottled with purple and yellow spots within. The seed pods are large and the beak or horn is often 3 ins. in length.

MARVEL OF PERU see MIRABILIS.

Matricaria (L. *matrix* = womb). Certain varieties of the species mentioned below are useful bedding plants, as they produce an abundance of bloom over a considerable period. They are also employed as cut flowers in some localities. Seeds are best sown under glass during March and the seedlings transplanted during May.

M. CAPENSIS see M. PARTHENOIDES.

M. CHAMOMILLA. Height 1 ft. Wild Chamomile. A white-flowered annual species of little decorative value.

M. INODORA (*Chrysanthemum inodorum, Pyrethrum inodorum*). A floriferous branching Annual about 1½ ft. in height, bearing semi-double white flowers 1–2 ins. in diameter. The variety Bridal Robe is a dwarfer, more compact form in which the size and doubleness of the flowers have been much improved. The leaves of this species are practically free from the pungent scent common to most members of the genus.

M. PARTHENOIDES (*M. capensis* of gardens, *Chrysanthemum parthenoides*). About 2 ft. in height. The type, which has given rise to several attractive varieties, is usually treated as an Annual, although it will often persist for several seasons. The flowers, generously produced, are small, and in the wild form usually single.

The following are the varieties most popular for garden purposes: *eximia fl. pl.* A double-flowered white form which has been subjected to continued selection over many years, resulting in the appearance of a number of large-flowered strains sold in various degrees of quality by the trade; Double Yellow, a slightly dwarfer golden form of the last; Tom Thumb Double White, height about 8 ins., a compact floriferous white form very suitable for bedding; Tom Thumb Yellow, a deep yellow counterpart of the foregoing.

Matthiola (in honour of Piero Andrez Matthioli, 1500–1577, an Italian physician and botanist). Stock. Gilliflower. *Cruciferae.* 50 species; Mediterranean region, Europe, South Africa.

Indispensable, brightly coloured, a favourite of garden lovers, the sweetly-scented Stocks in their endless variety of form and cheerful colouring are unsurpassed as plants of all-round garden suitability. From early May until the coming of the autumn frosts it is possible to have a succession of bloom, ideal both for garden decoration and for cutting, while certain varieties respond willingly to treatment as pot plants. The species are now recognized, from which the modern Stocks have originated, *Matthiola incana*, *M. fenestralis* and *M. sinuata*, the first being responsible for most of the Ten Week varieties. The selection and hybridizing of different forms has proceeded for many years, and each season sees the introduction of still finer varieties, and as different strains are liable to vary in purity and doubleness, the advice given elsewhere in these pages is repeated here, namely to purchase only the best strains from reliable seedsmen.

Cultural directions are given for the various types at the end of their respective descriptions.

M. ANNUA see M. INCANA.

M. BICORNIS. Night-Scented Stock. Height 1 ft. A popular sweetly-scented low-growing single-flowered species; its pale lilac flowers, which remain closed during the daytime, open towards evening and give off their delicious perfume. Seeds may be sown during March or April where the plants are to flower.

M. FENESTRALIS. A biennial species native of Crete, which has given rise to varieties which will be found in the Brompton or Giant Cape Section below. The type is about 1 ft. in height and bears numerous light purple flowers. 1758.

M. INCANA (*M. annua*, *M. graeca*). The progenitor of most of the popular types of Stocks. The form hitherto known as *M. annua* has given rise to the Dwarf Bedding and Ten Week types, while that originally described as *M. graeca* has played an important part in the production of Biennial Brompton Stocks. As the original types are no longer grown in gardens, their detailed description is omitted, and the various sections, together with the cultivated varieties of the following species, are dealt with fully under the names they bear in the majority of trade catalogues.

M. SINUATA. A wild British plant from which originated the Intermediate Stocks and later the East Lothian Intermediate varieties now of such widespread popularity.

The garden types of Stocks are divided into two classes, those which are usually sown in spring to flower the same year, and those generally sown during the summer and autumn to flower the following spring, although they can all be flowered almost without exception during their first year from seed.

Stocks for Spring Sowing

Ten Week Column. A strain largely grown for cutting, producing one long densely flowered spike, often reaching a height of 2–2½ ft. Obtainable in a variety of colours ranging from rose, crimson, light and dark mauve to white.

Ten Week Dwarf Large-Flowering. An ideal type for bedding, about 1 ft. only in height; the plants are very floriferous and produce a mass of bloom when in full flower. All the colours mentioned in the preceding paragraph are available in this strain, also canary yellow.

Ten Week Dwarf Pyramidal. About 8 ins. in height, this type produces strong central and lateral spikes densely crowded with bloom. Obtainable in many shades of colour.

Ten Week Giant Perfection. A handsome type for both cutting and bedding purposes. The plants attain a height of about 2½ ft. and bear splendid spikes of bloom. A wide variety of pleasing colours is available, in particular Queen of the Belgians, a delightful shade of silvery lilac, and Princess Alice, pure white.

Mammoth, Beauty, Winter or Nice. Originates from the pale pink variety Beauty of Nice, at one time largely grown in the South of France; a splendid choice of fine varieties is now offered in this handsome type. In addition to providing useful bedding plants or cut flowers from spring sowings, they may be successfully grown as pot plants for winter

15. PAPAVER RHOEAS VAR. THE SHIRLEY

16. PETUNIA

decoration in the cool greenhouse if sown during August. Some of the best named varieties are: Almond Blossom; Crimson King; Heatham Beauty, a rosy-mauve shaded terra-cotta; Nuit d'Eté or Summer Night, intense dark violet; Queen Alexandra, rosy-lilac; and Snowdrift, the finest white.

Stock All the Year Round. A distinct Wallflower-leaved variety bearing massive spikes of large white flowers. It is one of the best for pot culture or for cutting, and may be sown either in spring or autumn.

The cultivation of the above-mentioned types presents no difficulty to those of moderate experience in raising plants from seeds; the seeds should be sown during March in a greenhouse of temperature 60° and the seedlings transplanted to the open ground as soon as they are large enough, usually during May.

Stocks for Summer and Autumn Sowing

Brompton or Queen. The old-fashioned Biennial Brompton Stocks, which are a familiar sight in cottage gardens, and revel in the mild seaside conditions on the South Coast, grow to a height of about 1½–2 ft., and, although not productive of so many double flowers as the Ten Week types, are nevertheless most handsome and desirable plants. The large single flowers are also attractive and, indeed, preferred by many people to the doubles, for use as a cut flower. These old-world Stocks are obtainable in crimson, purple and white, and the varieties Carmine King, Cottager's Scarlet and Cottager's White, Crimson Beauty and Pink Beauty are worthy of mention. The latest introduction in this massive robust section is the variety Dawn of Day, which produces immense showy spikes of a pleasing shade of lilac-pink.

Brompton or Giant Cape. A biennial type dwarfer and

more branching than the former, available in several bright and attractive colours, which include crimson, bright rose, purple and white.

Brompton Hybrid Early Flowering Harbinger. The appearance of this valuble race of Stocks a few years ago has proved an event of considerable importance, as these hybrids between the old-fashioned Brompton type and the Mammoth or Beauty type combine the strong robust habit of the former with the high percentage of doubleness and beautiful colourings of the latter. A wide selection of lovely shades is now available ranging from crimson, rose-crimson, rich rose, pale rose-pink, cream-pink, salmon, canary-yellow, to white. There is no finer Stock for sowing in the late summer to flower the following spring.

Brompton Hybrid Monarch, or late Harbinger. A similar choice of colours is obtainable in this strain which resembles the foregoing but blooms about a month later.

East Lothian Intermediate. A distinct, very floriferous type, dwarf and showy. The choice of colours includes brilliant rose, crimson, lavender, pink, purple, scarlet and white.

The types of Stocks described in the above class, although they may all, with the exception of the Brompton hybrid Monarch varieties, be flowered as Annuals, give of their best when treated as Biennials and sown towards the end of August. The seeds may be sown in a greenhouse or cold frame and when large enough pricked off into boxes. Later they should be moved into small pots, and placed in a cold frame, where they should remain until all danger of frost is past in May of the following year.

In sheltered positions in favourable localities, successful results may often be achieved by sowing in the end of July and planting the seedlings in the open ground in September. This practice, however, is attended by the risk of losing the plants in a severe or wet cold winter, but if conditions are suitable the plants so obtained are in every way far finer than those planted out in the spring.

Maurandia (in honour of Dr. Maurandy, a professor of botany at Cartagena). *Scrophulariaceae*. 6 species; Mexico.

A genus of climbing Perennials which, owing to their tenderness, are usually grown as Half-Hardy Annuals, although they are sometimes employed for greenhouse decoration and allowed to form large plants which will produce a show of bloom during the winter months. They will rapidly form a decorative covering if allowed to ramble over trellises, arbours and the like, but must be planted in a warm, sunny, sheltered position. Seeds may be sown during March in a greenhouse, and the seedlings moved into small pots as soon as they are large enough, being transplanted to the open ground during June.

M. BARCLAIANA (usually, but not originally, written *M. Barclayana*). This species has given rise to several varieties; the type bears large purple flowers somewhat resembling those of a Foxglove. A mixture of the various shades of colours which have appeared in cultivation is available. 1825. The varieties generally cultivated are: *albiflora*, a white-flowered form; *purpurea grandiflora*, a deep violet-purple garden form; *rosea*, a lilac-rose garden form.

M. ERUBESCENS. The flowers of this species, which is not widely grown in gardens, are about 3 ins. long and rosy pink in colour. 1830.

M. SCANDENS (*Lophospermum scandens*). A fairly popular species bearing rosy lilac flowers.

MECONOPSIS HETEROPHYLLA see STYLOMECON HETEROPHYLLA.

Mentzelia (in honour of Christian Mentzel, 1622–1701, a German botanist). *Loasaceae*. 50 species; warmer parts of America.

An attractive genus bearing flowers of unusual beauty; of

the two annual species in general cultivation *M. Lindleyi* is useful for border purposes, and *M. gronoviaefolia* is a splendid plant for the cool greenhouse.

M. GRONOVIAEFOLIA (*M. bartonioides, Microsperma bartonioides, Eucnide bartonioides*). Height 1½ ft. Usually listed under the name of *Eucnide bartonioides*, this most attractive plant is not seen so frequently as it deserves. An ideal pot plant for greenhouse or conservatory, it produces a profusion of large golden-yellow flowers with a tuft of golden stamens that greatly enhances their beauty. Seeds should be sown in a greenhouse during February and the seedlings potted on as soon as they are large enough. Plants may also be grown outdoors in a warm sheltered spot and should be planted out towards the end of May. A selected form, possibly a shade deeper in colour, is sold under the varietal name of Golden Tassel. 1849.

M. LINDLEYI (*Bartonia aurea*). Height 1½ ft. Usually grown and sold as *Bartonia aurea*, the large golden-yellow flowers of this species, often 2½ ins. in diameter, are extremely effective in borders; seeds may be sown in the open ground during April. 1834.

Mesembryanthemum (Gr. *mesembria* = midday, *anthemon* = a flower, the flowers usually opening in sunshine but remaining closed on sunless days). *Aizoaceae*. 350 species; South Africa.

The species described below are the only members of this large genus commonly cultivated as Annuals in gardens. They are ideal for use in rock gardens, and some of the species, if planted in dry sunny positions, will produce a profusion of bloom. Seeds should be sown in a greenhouse during March and the seedlings transplanted to their flowering positions during June.

M. CORDIFOLIUM. A perennial species sometimes treated as an annual plant and bearing reddish-lilac flowers. A

variety, obtainable under the name *variegatum*, has variegated foliage and rosy-purple flowers.

M. CRINIFLORUM. A low-growing, spreading plant, not
more than 4 ins. in height. The large brilliantly coloured
flowers are often 1–1½ ins. across and many colours and
combinations of colour are to be found among seedlings of
this remarkable plant. White, tinged or edged with crimson,
pink or buff, and self-coloured forms in delightful shades of
rose, golden-yellow, apricot and crimson are some of the
colours included in the range. A useful plant for all rock-
work or for edging and most happy in poor stony soils.

M. CRYSTALLINUM. Ice Plant. Cultivated rather for its
curious ample foliage than for the somewhat insignificant
white flowers. It forms a spreading plant about 6 ins. in
height, and the leaves are covered with glistening bladder-
shaped hairs. 1775.

M. PYROPEUM (*M. tricolor*). Height 3–4 ins. A pretty low-
growing species useful for hot dry parts of the rock garden.
The flowers vary in colour from self-coloured rose-red and
white, to light pink with a red centre, and white with a purple
centre. About 1780.

M. TRICOLOR see M. PYROPEUM.

MEXICAN FIRE PLANT see EUPHORBIA HETEROPHYLLA.

MEXICAN POPPY see ARGEMONE.

MEXICAN SUNFLOWER see TITHONIA.

MEXICAN TULIP POPPY see HUNNEMANNIA.

MICROSPERMA see MENTZELIA.

MILKWORT see POLYGALA.

Mimulus (L. *mimulus* = a little mimic, in allusion to the
grinning flowers). Monkey Flower. *Scrophulariaceae*. 80
species; Cosmopolitan.

A genus of attractive annual and perennial plants, many
of the latter being successfully flowered in their first year

from seed. They all have a certain decorative value, and are eminently suitable for shady borders and for planting near water. Seeds should be sown in a greenhouse during March and the seedlings planted out towards the end of May or in June.

M. BREVIPES. Yellow Monkey Flower. Height 1 ft. A useful annual species, bearing canary-yellow flowers 1½–2 ins. long.

M. BREWERI. Height 6 ins. A low-growing plant, showy and attractive; the flowers are small, varying in colour from pale pink to red, but the form offered by the trade is generally deep rosy-red.

M. CARDINALIS. Height 1½ ft. A handsome plant, its flowers are freely produced in varying shades of orange and scarlet. There is a garden form, *grandiflorus*, bearing rather larger flowers.

M. CUPREUS (*M. luteus* var. *cupreus*). Height 6 ins. A dwarf tufted plant of considerable merit. The shapely flowers open a deep yellow, becoming copper-red when fully expanded. There are several garden varieties of which seeds are obtainable. Some of the best of these are the following: Bee's Dazzler, a crimson-flowered variety, particularly brilliant; Leopard, slightly more robust than the other varieties, a showy form bearing yellow flowers quaintly marked with brown spots; Red Emperor, one of the latest introductions, the flowers are produced in abundance and their colour is bright crimson-scarlet; Whitecroft's Scarlet, a form which has become deservedly popular; the flowers, very freely produced, are of an intense shade of bright scarlet.

M. FREMONTII. Pink Monkey Flower. Height 6–12 ins. The flowers are large and very attractive, deep rose-pink in colour; they are enhanced by the darker markings on the throat. It is found in dry, sandy open places, and is common in desert regions of California.

M. IMPLEXUS see M. TILINGII.

M. LEWISII. Height 1–2 ft. A splendid species, somewhat

resembling *M. cardinalis* in habit, but of a more slender appearance. The large flowers are a soft shade of rose and are produced in profusion.

M. LUTEUS. Monkey Flower. Height 1–2 ft. The flowers are often 1½–2 ins. long, yellow-blotched, crimson within. There are many fine colour forms and also a number of hybrids which have been obtained mainly by crossing with *M. cupreus*; several plants listed in the trade catalogues as varieties of this species have now been referred to other species such as *cupreus* (see *M. cupreus*). Among the best varieties are: Bonfire, which has large vivid crimson-scarlet flowers; *guttatus* see *rivularis*; Queen's Prize, the most attractive and strikingly beautiful large-flowered strain on the market, the mixture of both blotched and self-coloured forms including many shades of crimson, rose-pink, salmon-pink and yellow; *rivularis* (*M. luteus* var. *guttatus*), a dwarf variety 6–9 ins. in height which bears sweetly-scented yellow flowers, spotted with red in the throat; *variegatus*, a variable form 6–12 ins. in height, the flowers of the wild form being usually yellow, tinged pink at the edges, the throat spotted with small red markings; the garden strains have been encouraged to produce many handsome variations of colour and markings.

M. MOSCHATUS. Musk. Height 6–9 ins. The well-known creeping, small yellow-flowered species. Useful for a damp shady position and often seen planted under greenhouse staging.

M. PALMERI. Height 9–12 ins. One of the most handsome annual species, but not in general cultivation. The flowers are large, deep reddish-purple in the throat, with a large yellow patch, streaked with red, forming a striking contrast.

M. TILINGII (*M. implexus*). This extremely free-flowering, creeping species has recently become quite a favourite. The small golden-yellow flowers appear in great profusion and cover the plant with bloom.

MINA LOBATA see IPOMOEA VERSICOLOR.

Mirabilis (L. *mirabilis* = to be admired or wondered at; the old name *Admirabilis* was shortened by Linnaeus to *Mirabilis*). Marvel of Peru, Four o'Clock, Belle de Nuit. *Nyctaginaceae.* 25 species; Tropical America.

An interesting genus of Tropical Perennials usually treated as Annuals. Given a warm sheltered position they will often form large ornamental bushy plants 2–3 ft. in height and bear a profusion of flowers which, except in the case of *M. multiflora*, only open on cloudy days or in the late afternoon, a peculiarity which has given rise to the common name "Four o'Clock."

Seeds should be sown under glass during February or March, the seedlings being transplanted towards the end of May or in June.

M. JALAPA. Marvel of Peru, Four o'Clock. Height 2–3 ft. The most common species; the colour of the long tubular funnel-shaped flowers varies from white, rose and red to yellow, striped forms also being common. W. Indies, 1596.

M. LONGIFLORA. Height 2–3 ft. The flowers, very fragrant in the evening, are white with a rose or carmine centre. Not frequently met with in gardens, but at one time fairly widely grown. Hybrids with *M. Jalapa* have been recorded. 1759.

M. MULTIFLORA. Not in general cultivation; this species has very long tubular flowers in shades of rose and purple. They are borne in clusters of about 6 and are less prone to remain closed in sunny weather than those of the last species. 1876.

MONKEY FLOWER see MIMULUS.

MONSONIA see p. 19.

MORNA see WAITZIA ODONTOLEPIS.

MOTHER OF THOUSANDS see LINARIA CYMBALARIA.

MULLEIN see VERBASCUM.

MUSK see MIMULUS MOSCHATUS.

NAMAQUALAND DAISY see DIMORPHOTHECA AURANTIACA.

NASTURTIUM see TROPAEOLUM.

Nemesia (a name used by Dioscorides for some allied plant). *Scrophulariaceae*. 50 species; South Africa.

During the past few years the Nemesias have achieved outstanding popularity as garden Annuals. Their wide range of brilliant colourings and wealth of bloom make them suitable for many purposes—in the mixed annual border, in pots for the cool greenhouse, or the newer dwarf compact varieties even as edging plants. A complaint is frequently heard that the seeds are difficult to germinate, but this trouble will be entirely avoided if they are sown in pots in a cold frame during April and not in a greenhouse, as is often recommended. The seedlings may be planted out towards the end of May; in very favourable seasons it is sometimes possible to obtain good flowering plants from sowings made in the open ground during May, but this practice is attended by risk of failure.

N. BARBATA. Height 1 ft. An uncommon species bearing rich purple and white flowers.

N. FLORIBUNDA. Height 6–12 ins. A little-grown species bearing small yellow-throated, creamy-white flowers.

N. LILACINA. Height about 1 ft. A much-branched narrow-leaved species with small lilac flowers marked with yellow on the palate and white on the spur. S.W. Africa.

N. STRUMOSA. Height 1–1½ ft. It is from this popular species that the present-day garden varieties have been derived. The flowers of the wild plant vary in shades of yellow, purple or white and are large by comparison with those of the other species. Some of the best garden varieties are:

Compacta, a shapely, dwarf bushy form, 6–9 ins. in height, which presents a mass of bloom when in full flower; many shades of colour are to be found in the mixture; *compacta* Blue Gem, a splendid plant bearing beautiful, brilliant blue flowers; *compacta* Fire King, brilliant flowers of an intense shade of scarlet; *compacta* Orange Prince, one of the finest varieties of all for bedding purposes, the flowers are extremely large and rich deep orange in colour; Triumph, the best dwarf compact strain in existence, ideal for bedding; the individual flowers are very large and the variety of colours and combinations of colour is surprising; *Suttonii*, a mixture of large-flowered varieties, about 1 ft. in height, including many attractive shades of colour, some of which, such as blue, carmine, orange, pale pink, scarlet, and white, may be obtained separately; *Suttonii reticulata*, a showy strain in which the flowers are all curiously mottled and marked, usually with golden yellow.

N. VERSICOLOR. Height 1 ft. A sulphur-yellow-flowered species of rather untidy habit.

Nemophila (Gr. *nemos* = a grove, *philos* = loving, in reference to the habitat of certain species). Californian Blue-Bell. *Hydrophyllaceae*. 20 species; North America.

Pretty Annuals, of low compact or trailing habit, producing an abundance of their bright bell-shaped flowers over a long period in the summer months; the Nemophilas are in great demand for all types of border work or massing in beds. Seeds may be sown in the open ground where the plants are to bloom during September for flowering the following year, or during March or April to flower the same year. They thrive in a cool moist situation.

N. ATOMARIA see N. MENZIESII.

N. AURITA. A trailing species, which occasionally appears in trade lists. The flowers, about 1 in. across, are deep violet in colour.

N. DISCOIDALIS see N. MENZIESII.

N. INSIGNIS. Baby Blue Eyes. Considered by some authors to be a sub-species of *N. Menziesii*, this is the most showy and popular member of the genus. The clear blue flowers are often 1 in. across and are produced in great numbers.

Several garden varieties have sprung from this ornamental plant, some of which are: *alba*, a pure white form; *grandiflora*, a fine large-flowered variety, clear sky-blue in colour; *marginata*, flowers clear blue edged with white; *purpurea-rubra*, claret-coloured flowers, not so effective as the foregoing varieties.

N. MACULATA. This species is not common in gardens, but is quite attractive. The white flowers are large and embellished by dark purple blotches.

N. MENZIESII (*N. atomaria, N. discoidalis, N. modista*). This species and its varieties, although not so popular as *N. insignis*, are sometimes met with in gardens. The flowers are usually very pale blue or white and are marked with dark brown spots. Certain forms have a dark eye. Some of the following varieties are obtainable; *discoidalis*, distinguished by a large brownish-purple eye; *elegans* (*N. atomaria elegans*), pure white flowers with a deep chocolate centre; *oculata*, white flowers with a contrasting purple centre; *vittata*, velvety-black flowers edged with white.

N. MODISTA see N. MENZIESII.

N. PHACELIOIDES. Height 1–2 ft. A species not widely grown; the flowers are pale blue with a white centre

Nicandra (in honour of Nicander, poet of Colophon, who wrote on medicine and botany in 100 B.C.). *Solanaceae*. 1 species; Peru.

N. PHYSALOIDES. Apple of Peru. Height 3–4 ft. An old-fashioned, strong-growing, spreading Annual, somewhat resembling Physalis or Winter Cherry. The showy blue flowers are valuable for the border, and the curious fruits are sometimes used for winter decoration. Seeds may be sown in the open ground during late March or April or under glass earlier in March.

Nicotiana (in honour of Jean Nicot, 1530–1600, French Ambassador to Portugal, who presented tobacco obtained from merchants in Flanders to the Portuguese Court and to Queen Catherine de Medici). Tobacco Plant. *Solanaceae.* 45 species; America, Polynesia, and 1 in Australia.

The varieties of the ornamental Tobacco Plant have taken their place among the most valuable features of the annual border. Their delightful fragrance in the evening, when the flowers of most of the members of the genus open, more than compensates for their rather sad and unbecoming appearance during the daytime. Although the genus includes annual, biennial and perennial species, those commonly cultivated as garden plants are almost invariably treated as Annuals. Seeds should be sown under glass during late March or in April and the seedlings planted out towards the end of May.

N. AFFINIS see N. ALATA var. GRANDIFLORA.

N. ALATA. An erect-growing herbaceous Perennial, this species has given rise to several varieties and garden forms. The true plant is probably not in cultivation, the forms found in gardens being varieties. The type attains a height of 2–3 ft., and bears flowers 2 ins. across, white within and tinged pale violet on the outer side.

N. ALATA var. GRANDIFLORA (*N. affinis*). Commonly grown and sold as *N. affinis*, the variety *grandiflora* bears very large creamy-white flowers, very sweetly scented. It is an established favourite as a border plant and is decidedly handsome when given plenty of room. Several colour forms of this plant are available in mixture, usually under the name of *N. affinis* hybrids: the dwarf free-flowering variety Crimson Bedder grows to a height of 1½ ft., with large flowers, deep crimson in colour, and the habit of the plant renders it most suitable for bedding purposes; Crimson Bedder is the dwarf

form of the old-established favourite Crimson King, which
is similar in colour but taller and more loosely branching,
attaining a height of about 2½ ft.

N. ATROPURPUREA see N. TABACUM.

N. COLOSSEA see N. TOMENTOSA.

N. HYBRIDA DAYLIGHT. An outstanding introduction resulting from a cross between N. Langsdorffii and N. alatum.
The flowers are pure white, scented and, unlike all other
garden Nicotianas, they do not close up during the daytime.
A mixture of various colours derived from the same cross
and having the same unique characteristic is obtainable
under the name Sensation.

N. MACROPHYLLA see N. TABACUM.

N. RUBRA see N. TABACUM.

N. SANDERAE. A hybrid between *N. alata* and *N. For-
getiana*, the latter an unimportant species rarely grown as a
garden plant. The plant is usually about 3 ft. in height and
the colour of the large flowers varies from deep rosy-carmine
to rosy-red. A mixture of colour forms of this type, probably
obtained by crossing it with different forms of *N. alata*, is
sold under the name of *N. Sanderae* Hybrids. These include
shades of crimson, mauve, pink and white.

N. SILVESTRIS. Height 3 ft. A striking species; its long
drooping white flowers somewhat similar in shape to those
of *N. alata* are carried in short panicles and are most effective
at evening, when they give off a very sweet scent.

N. SUAVEOLENS. Height 1½–2 ft. Splendid for the conservatory, but not so valuable for the garden as some of the
other species. It forms a handsome much-branched plant
when grown in pots and produces an abundance of pure-
white flowers about 1½ ins. across and very sweetly scented.

N. TABACUM (*N. atropurpurea, N. macrophylla, N. rubra*),
the species from which have been obtained the forms grown
for commercial purposes. It is a handsome garden plant, and
several of the varieties are sometimes used as decorative

plants. These include *virginica*, a showy narrow-leaved plant about 3 ft. in height, bearing rosy-purple flowers; *macrophylla* (*N. macrophylla*), a large-leaved form bearing red flowers which has produced several garden varieties usually known as *N. atropurpurea*, *N. atropurpurea* var. *grandiflora* and *N. rubra*.

N. TOMENTOSA (*N. colossea*). Of giant proportions, this rapid-growing perennial species will reach a height of 5–6 ft. in its first year and produce numbers of pale pink flowers. A form with mottled and margined leaves is obtainable under the name *variegata*.

N. WIGANDIOIDES. Height 5–6 ft. A large robust plant with ample foliage; the flowers are creamy-white. 1874.

Nierembergia (in honour of John E. Nieremberg, 1595–1658, a Spanish Jesuit and first professor of natural history at Madrid). *Solanaceae*. 20 *species*; Tropical and Subtropical America.

The species of this beautiful genus described below, although perennial, may be very successfully cultivated as Annuals. Their narrow foliage and attractive salver-shaped flowers entitle them to a place in every garden. Seeds should be sown under glass during February, and the seedlings planted out towards the end of May. For pot culture they are ideal and will provide a bold display for many months in the cool greenhouse or conservatory.

N. CAERULEA. Height 1 ft. This splendid species has achieved widespread popularity under the name *N. hippomanica* which was applied to it in error at its introduction a few years ago. Ideal for bedding and as a pot plant, it is more compact than *N. frutescens* and forms a little bush, the narrow green foliage being almost hidden by the profusion of large deep-lilac flowers. It is ideal for the groundwork of bedding schemes, massed in a mixed border, or planted in small groups on the rock garden. A sterling plant for all purposes.

N. FRUTESCENS (*N. fruticosa*). Height 1–2 ft. A graceful plant; the flowers are white, delicately tinged with lilac. It is exceedingly pretty when cut and arranged among other flowers. It is best to sow early in the autumn to obtain large plants for the following year, although it will flower during the first twelve months from spring sowings.

N. HIPPOMANICA see N. CAERULEA.

N. INTERMEDIA see p. 17.

Nigella (L. *nigellus*, the diminutive of *niger*, black, in reference to the colour of the seeds). Love-in-a-Mist, Fennel Flower, Devil-in-the-Bush, Lady-in-the-Bower. *Ranunculaceae*. 16 species; Europe and Mediterranean regions.

The ever-popular Love-in-a-Mist is one of the most delicately beautiful plants for cutting or for massing in borders. The feathery, light green foliage, the strange shape of the flowers and later the attractive seed pods lend these pretty Annuals a charm and distinction possessed by few garden plants. The best plants are obtained by sowing the seed in the open ground towards the end of September for flowering early the following summer; spring sowings made in the open ground in March will flower about July of the same year.

N. DAMASCENA. Height 1–2 ft. The flowers of the type are pale blue or white. 1570. Various garden forms are in cultivation. There is a dwarf large-flowered variety, *nana*, sometimes met with in gardens; Miss Jekyll, the most popular of all the Nigellas, bears large semi-double flowers of a most beautiful shade of blue; Miss Jekyll Dark Blue is a much deeper coloured form and becoming deservedly popular; Miss Jekyll White is not so attractive to most people as the blue form, but useful for contrasting effect.

N. FONTANESIANA see N. HISPANICA.

N. HISPANICA. The flowers are large, of a paler blue than the last species, but the seed pods are larger and often used for winter decoration, either in their natural state or sprayed with metallic paint. 1629. Among the varieties available are: *alba*, the white-flowered form; *atropurpurea*, with violet-red flowers and quite effective in a mixed border; *Fontanesiana* (*N. Fontanesiana*), a variety seldom grown in gardens, but said to be earlier-flowering than the type.

N. INTEGRIFOLIA. In this species the leaves are not so finely divided as in the foregoing species. The flowers are blue but are bell-shaped. Not often grown in gardens.

N. ORIENTALIS. Height about 1½ ft. Seldom seen in gardens, this species bears small pale yellow flowers and is quite pretty.

N. SATIVA. A pale greenish-yellow-flowered species grown in some countries for its aromatic seeds. It is said to be the Fitches mentioned in Isaiah xxviii. 25 and 27. 1548.

NIGHTSHADE see SOLANUM.

NIGHT-SCENTED STOCK see MATTHIOLA BICORNIS.

Nolana (L. *nola* = a little bell, in reference to the shape of the corolla). Chilian Bellflower. *Nolanaceae*. 20 species; Chili and Peru.

Good blue-flowered Annuals are always to be desired, as the number of really bright shades of blue is somewhat limited in this class of plants. The Nolanas, with their decorative Convolvulus-like flowers, are serviceable plants either for the border or in pots for the conservatory. Seeds should be sown under glass, either in September for flowering the following spring, or during March to flower in the summer of the same year.

N. ATRIPLICIFOLIA (*N. grandiflora*). Height 4–6 ins. Of trailing habit, this attractive species bears numerous lilac-blue flowers with contrasting white and yellow centres. 1834. There is a white variety, *alba*, not often seen in gardens.

N. GRANDIFLORA see N. ATRIPLICIFOLIA.

N. LANCEOLATA. One of the finest of all, this species has recently been re-introduced to cultivation. Its flowers are

17. PRIMULA OBCONICA

Left: The Type   *Right*: Rose Queen

18. SILENE PENDULA VAR. PEACH BLOSSOM

large, clear sky-blue and enhanced by showy white and yellow centres. 1862. The variety Blue Ensign is deeper coloured and larger flowered.

N. PARADOXA. Height 1 ft. The large blue flowers are similar to those of *N. atriplicifolia.* They are often 2 ins. in diameter. 1824.

N. PROSTRATA. Height 3–6 ins. A very low-growing species, producing an abundance of deep blue flowers veined with purple in the throat. A showy plant but not in general cultivation. 1761.

N. TENELLA. Apparently not in cultivation, this species is distinguished from *N. paradoxa,* to which it bears a close resemblance, by the hairiness of its stems and leaves. The flowers are violet-blue with a white throat. 1824.

NYCTERINIA see ZALUZIANSKYA.

Oenothera (Gr. *oinos* = wine, *thera* = wild beasts; the name was originally applied to *Epilobium hirsutum*, plants of which, sprinkled with wine, were alleged to tame wild animals). Evening Primrose. *Onagraceae.* 50 species; America.

Several members of this charming genus may be successfully flowered during their first year from seeds. Their delightful scent at evening makes them valuable plants for grouping in a mixed border. Seeds should be sown under glass during March and the seedlings planted out towards the end of May.

O. ACAULIS (*O. taraxacifolia*). Height about 6 ins. A handsome trailing species with finely-cut foliage, bearing large pure white flowers shading to pink with age. The variety *aurea* has bright yellow flowers.

O. BIENNIS. Height 2–4 ft. The popular lemon-yellow-flowered species; it bears its large strongly-scented flowers very freely. There is a dwarfer, larger-flowered variety, *Lamarckiana* (*O. Lamarckiana*).

A.—M

O. BISTORTA. Height 1–2 ft. The deep yellow flowers of this species are about 1½–2 ins. across and are produced in abundance. The variety *Veitchiana* is the most popular form, being a little richer in colour and slightly more compact.

O. CAESPITOSA (*O. marginata*). A very handsome species bearing large pure white flowers often 3 ins. across.

O. DRUMMONDII. Height about 1 ft. A showy species bearing large light yellow flowers, often 2–3 ins. across.

O. LAMARCKIANA see O. BIENNIS.

O. MARGINATA see O. CAESPITOSA.

O. ODORATA. Height about 2 ft. A graceful, slender species, bearing deep yellow flowers. The variety *sulphurea* produces pale sulphur-yellow flowers.

O. ROSEA. Height 1–2 ft. The flowers of this species, rose or rosy-purple in colour, are small but quite attractive.

O. TARAXACIFOLIA see O. ACAULIS.

O. TRICHOCALYX. Height 1–2 ft. One of the best species for treatment as an Annual. The shapely plant bears numerous large pure white sweetly-scented flowers which remain open during the daytime.

O. WHITNEYI see GODETIA GRANDIFLORA.

Omphalodes (Gr. *omphalos* = the navel, *eidos* = form, in reference to the shape of the seed). Venus's Navelwort. *Boraginaceae*. 24 species; Europe, Asia and Mexico.

O. LINIFOLIA (*Cynoglossum linifolium*). Height about 9 ins. A pretty blue-flowered Annual not so widely grown as it deserves to be; the foliage is greyish-green and the small white flowers, which resemble those of Myosotis, are freely produced. A patch, planted fairly close in a mixed border, or a group in the rock garden, is most effective. Seeds may be sown in the open ground at any time between the end of March and June.

OPIUM POPPY see PAPAVER SOMNIFERUM.

Orthocarpus (Gr. *orthos* = straight, *carpos* = fruit). *Scrophulariaceae.* 30 species; Western America.

O. PURPURASCENS. Height 1 ft. A curious, showy Annual bearing pretty spikes or clusters of rosy-purple flowers. It is a useful plant in a mixed border of Annuals. Seeds may be sown in the open ground during April.

Oxalis (Gr. *oxis* = acid, in reference to the taste of the leaves). Wood Sorrel. *Oxalidaceae.* 300 species; cosmopolitan, chiefly South Africa and America.

A genus of Annual or creeping bulbous or tuberous perennial plants, of which several species are easily flowered during their first year from seeds. Their attractive foliage and small but pretty flowers make them effective subjects for rock-work, planting on old walls or between large crazy paving. Seeds should be sown in the open ground during March or April in a fairly warm situation. A well-drained position in a fairly porous soil suits them best; they may also be successfully treated as pot plants for the house.

O. CORNICULATA. Height about 6 ins. A yellow-flowered species, native of Great Britain. There is an interesting crimson-leaved variety, *atropurpurea* (*O. tropaeoloides*).

O. ROSEA. Height 6 ins. A graceful species sometimes used for pot work; the flowers, freely produced, are deep rosy purple. Chili, 1826. There is also a white variety, *alba.*

'O. SIMSII. Similar to *O. rosea*, but the foliage is more delicate and the flowers are a rich shade of deep red.

O. TROPAEOLOIDES see O. CORNICULATA var. ATROPURPUREA.

O. VALDIVIENSIS (*O. valdiviana*). Height 6 ins. A common species, bearing small yellow flowers lightly veined with red. Chili, 1862.

PALAFOXIA HOOKERIANIA see p. 17.

Palaua (in honour of Anton Palau y Verdera, professor of botany at Madrid in the latter half of the eighteenth century). *Malvaceae.* 5 species; Chili and Peru.

P. DISSECTA (*P. flexuosa*). Height about 1 ft. A free-flowering graceful Annual; the flowers, about 1 in. in diameter, are lilac with a white centre and crimson stamens. Seeds should be sown in a greenhouse during March and the seedlings planted out towards the end of May. 1866.

P. FLEXUOSA see P. DISSECTA.

P. RHOMBIFOLIA, see p. 17.

PALMA CHRISTI see RICINUS.

PANSY see VIOLA.

Papaver (old Latin name, of Greek origin, derivation doubtful). Poppy. *Papaveraceae.* 110 species; Europe, Asia, America, South Africa and Australia.

Few plants can claim so universal an appeal as the Poppies. The tiny alpine species of exquisite form and beauty; the graceful, taller kinds; the Iceland and Shirley Poppies, in whose range are found such delicate shades of almost every lovely colour; the more flamboyant types, barbaric in their splendour—all of them rank among the glories of the garden. Their flowers, although short-lived, succeed each other with such diligent rapidity that the corner of the annual border devoted to Poppies is a source of constant joy for many weeks. It is regrettable that flowers so light and colourful are of such small service for cutting. Though the flowers of certain kinds, if cut when very young, will expand and last a short while in water, they are more at home in the garden, where their own particular charm can be appreciated to the full.

Cultivation of the Annual Poppies presents no difficulty. Seeds of all the kinds described below may be sown in the open ground during March or April, while the varieties of *P. Rhoeas* may be sown in the open ground towards the end of September, the resulting plants flowering well early in the following summer. *P. nudicaule* and its many varieties will produce large handsome plants if seeds are sown in a cold frame towards the end of July, the seedlings being planted out in September where they are to flower the following year.

P. ALPINUM see P. NUDICAULE.

P. ARENARIUM. Height about 1 ft. A biennial species which may be treated as an Annual. Seldom seen in gardens, this is one of the most beautiful of Poppies; the flowers are of the most dazzling scarlet, and the petals are marked with a large indigo-blue spot. Caucasus, 1828.

P. CAUCASICUM. Height 1–1½ ft. A beautiful biennial species which may be flowered in its first year from seeds. The foliage is blue-grey and the handsome flowers are orange-scarlet in colour.

P. COMMUTATUM see P. RHOEAS.

P. DUBIUM. Height 1–2 ft. Of little consequence as a garden plant, it bears rosy-red flowers varying to rose or pale pink.

P. GLAUCUM. Tulip Poppy. Height 2 ft. The brilliant crimson flowers of this species bear a striking resemblance to those of a Tulip, the inner petals being almost surrounded by the outer ones, forming a cup within a cup. Syria to Persia.

P. MACROSTOMUM. Height 1 ft. A showy species, the semi-double scarlet flowers are enhanced by a shining black centre.

P. NUDICAULE. Iceland Poppy. One of the most graceful and popular of all the species, it has produced many garden varieties in which the range of beautiful shades of colour is remarkable. Although biennial or sometimes perennial, it is easily grown as an Annual and is a plant of undeniable merit. The type is usually bright yellow and the flowers are borne singly on long naked stems. Among the varieties of this splendid species is *alpinum* (*P. alpinum*), the alpine Poppy which is now considered by botanists merely to be a dwarfed form of *P. nudicaule*. It is possible to flower it during the first year from seed, although it is generally treated as biennial or perennial. The range of colours includes pale rose-pink, orange, yellow and white, and the plants form tufted rosettes of greyish-green leaves most attractive in the rock garden. Seeds may also be had of separate colours, under the names *album, roseum, coccineum* and Chamois.

Of the tall Iceland Poppies there are numerous varieties and selected strains in mixture, including *album*, pure white; *album fl. pl.*, a double-flowered form of the foregoing, of which several selections, under trade names, are available, one of the best being White Swan; Coonara, a strain containing a great variety of lovely shades, including rich orange, rose, pink, yellow and white; Coonara Pinks, a mixture of similar type and habit to the last from which the yellow, white and orange shades have been eliminated; Excelsior, one of the most beautiful strains, containing an almost infinite variety of shades; Gartref, a unique strain, in that it is principally composed of flowers whose petals are edged a deeper shade, the range of colours is very wide; *miniatum*, the old orange variety, now surpassed in size and depth of colour by improved forms; Red Cardinal, crimson scarlet; Sunbeam, the flowers of selected strains of this mixture, which includes white, orange, yellow and shades of rose-pink, are the largest of all Iceland Poppies; Tangerine, a large orange-flowered variety very strong-growing and handsome.

P. PAEONIAEFLORUM see P. SOMNIFERUM.

P. PAVONINUM. Peacock Poppy. Height 1–1½ ft. The flowers, about 1 in. across, are bright scarlet, with a greyish centre and a black zone.

P. PILOSUM. Height 2 ft. A perennial species sometimes grown as an Annual. The flowers are large, often 2 ins. across, and brick-red in colour. Bithynia.

P. RHOEAS (*P. commutatum*). Corn Poppy. Height 1–2 ft. This is the common field Poppy whose scarlet, black-blotched flowers are a familiar sight in the cornfields. It has given rise to numerous garden varieties both single and double which have, by selection, been encouraged to vary into a surprising number of beautiful colours. Some of the best are:

Begonia-flowered, aptly named, as the flowers bear a striking resemblance to those of a double Begonia; the range of colours in this delightful strain includes white, rose, pink, salmon-pink and brick-red; Celeste, a curious form of the Shirley Poppy described below, containing a number of lavender-blue shades; Dazzler, a vivid scarlet selection of the Ryburgh Hybrid strain described below; Fairy, a free-flowering double strain containing many lovely shades; French Dwarf, a dwarf mixture of double-flowered varieties in shades of red, ranging to white; Japanese Pompon, dwarf, double-flowered, in great variety of colour; Little Gem, resembling the Shirley varieties described below in type of flower, is a dwarf bushy very free-flowering pink form, most attractive and ornamental; Ryburgh Hybrids, of recent introduction this fine strain is outstanding by reason of its large double flowers which are found in every possible shade ranging from rose, salmon-pink, scarlet, to white; Ranunculus-flowered, similar in type to the French Dwarf form described above; Shirley, the Shirley Poppies are too well known to need description; many of the shades and bicoloured forms may be obtained separately but they are never more lovely than when grown in mixture. We owe this beautiful strain to the late Rev. Wilks of Shirley, who introduced it about 50 years ago. He described how he obtained it in the *Journal* of the Royal Horticultural Society, vol. 25, p. 161, in the following words: "In 1880 I noticed in a waste corner of my garden abutting on the fields, a patch of the common wild Poppy of cornfields—Papaver Rhoeas—one solitary flower of which had a very narrow white edging to the four petals. This one flower I marked and saved the seed of it alone. Next year, out of perhaps 200 plants, I had four or five on which *all the flowers* were white-edged. The best of these were marked and the seed saved, and so on for several years, the flowers all the while getting a larger infusion of white to tone down the red, until they arrived at quite a pale pink, and one plant absolutely pure white in the petals. I then set myself to change the black central portions of the flowers, the anthers, stigmatic surface, and pollen, from black to yellow or white, and succeeded at last in obtaining a strain with petals varying from the brightest scarlet to pure white, with all shades of pink in between, and with all possible varieties of flakes and edged flowers, and having golden or white stamens, anthers, stigmatic surface, and pollen, and a white base to each petal."

Similar to the wild Corn Poppy is the variety *umbrosum* (*P. umbrosum*); it differs from it in being dwarfer and the flowers are a deeper shade of scarlet with black markings on the petals.

P. SOMNIFERUM. Opium Poppy. Height about 3 ft. The type, which has given rise to so many garden varieties, is a large plant with greyish-green (glaucous) foliage and flowers 4–5 ins. across, varying in colour from pink, rose and purple to white. Various garden forms were cultivated as early as 1613, when several were figured in *Hortus Eystettensis*. A selection of some of the most popular varieties is given below. It is from the milky juice which oozes from cuts made in the young capsules of this Poppy that opium is made and it has been grown for many centuries on this account. Among the many fine single-flowered varieties are: Admiral, white with a broad band of brilliant scarlet; Charles Darwin, rich dark amaranth; Dainty Lady, pale lilac; Danebrog, sometimes known as Danish Flag, Danish Cross or Victoria Cross, a striking variety in which the base of each petal is marked with a large white blotch which together form a cross in the centre of the flower; King Edward, deep scarlet; The Bride, pure white.

The double-flowered varieties include: Carnation-flowered, a robust, very double form, obtainable in a mixture of many shades, several of which are sold separately. Dwarf forms of this variety are also to be had in separate colours, the best of which are Cardinal, rich scarlet fringed flowers; Chamois Rose, a delicate shade; Rosy Pink, a fine variety; White Swan, a large pure white form; *Mursellii fl. pl.*, a snowy white and red-flowered variety; Mikado, similar to the last, the flowers are white, margined wine-red; Paeony-flowered (*P. paeoniaeflorum*), a serviceable form available in several colours. A range of separate colours may be obtained in the dwarf Paeony-flowered group, which includes Fireball, bright scarlet; Salmon Pink, and Snowball, pure white.

P. UMBROSUM see P. RHOEAS var. UMBROSUM.

PARIS DAISY see CHRYSANTHEMUM FRUTESCENS.

Penstemon (Gr. *pente* = five, *stemon* = stamen). Beard Tongue. *Scrophulariaceae.* 150 species; North America, Eastern Asia.

Several members of this genus, which is composed of perennial plants, may be flowered during their first year from seed, as well as a hybrid form sometimes known as Annual Penstemon. Seeds should be sown in a greenhouse in February or early March and the seedlings planted out towards the end of May.

P. HARTWEGII. Height $2\frac{1}{2}$ ft. This species, and its varieties, are the most suitable for treatment as Annuals. A wide range of colours is now obtainable and the flowers are large and bright. For a late summer show they are particularly valuable. There is a white variety, *albus*, and a large scarlet and white-flowered form, Scarlet Queen.

P. MURRAYANUS. Height about 2 ft. A deep scarlet, rather small-flowered species of considerable merit.

Perezia (in honour of Lazarus Perez, an apothecary of Toledo who wrote in the sixteenth century a history of drugs). *Compositae.* 75 species; Texas to Patagonia.

P. MULTIFLORA. Height about 3 ft. A rather coarse Biennial which may be treated as an Annual. The flowers, carried in large clusters, are about 1½ ins. across and are a clear shade of porcelain blue. Seeds may be sown in the open ground in April, or under glass in March, and the seedlings planted out during May. A useful plant for the wild garden or for a large border.

Perilla (generally supposed to be from a native Indian name). Beefsteak-plant. *Labiatae.* 3 species; India to Japan.

Useful though sombre foliage plants, the Perillas were at one time very popular for bedding purposes. Seeds should be sown in a greenhouse during February or March and the seedlings planted out towards the end of May or in June.

P. ARGUTA var. ATROPURPUREA (*P. nankinensis*). Known in the trade as *P. nankinensis*, this is a very dark-foliaged plant with broad leaves, not so crinkled as the variety *laciniata* (*P. nankinensis* var. *foliis atropurpureis laciniatis*) which is similar in the colour of its rich dark foliage, but the leaves are cut almost to the middle and are very crisped and crinkled. Another interesting variety is *macrophylla* (*P. nankinensis* var. *macrophylla compacta*) a compact plant with very large leaves.

P. NANKINENSIS see P. ARGUTA.

PERSICARIA see POLYGONUM.

Petunia (South American native name *Petun*, said to mean tobacco, a closely related genus). *Solanaceae.* 30 species; South and warmer regions of North America.

The modern varieties of Petunia rank among our most useful bedding plants. For pot culture and garden decoration alike they have won well-deserved popularity, while for hanging baskets and window-boxes they are unsurpassed. Seeds should be sown in a greenhouse during February or March and the seedlings planted out during June. They are plants which revel in a hot dry summer, and a warm sunny situation will encourage them to give of their best.

P. HYBRIDA. Probably the result of hybridization between two species both native of South America. The group of garden Petunias contains many different and serviceable forms, in numerous shades of attractive colours. Some of the best of these are grouped below under the classification usually found in seedsmen's catalogues.

P. HYBRIDA GRANDIFLORA. Admiration, very large deep violet flowers, blotched with white; *alba*, a fine large pure white; Carmine Glory, of recent introduction, the colour of the flowers is an exceptionally brilliant shade of carmine rose; Hender's Striped and Blotched, a showy strain containing many curiously marked forms; Ideal, a dwarf strain about 1 ft. in height, containing a wide range of beautiful shades.

P. HYBRIDA GRANDIFLORA SUPERBISSIMA. A splendid strain in which the large flowers are delicately veined in the throat. *Alba*, pure white, tinted yellow in the throat, and beautifully fringed; Giants of California, a very large-flowered strain in great variety of colour; Prince of Wurttemberg, a striking deep purple variety with a dark veined throat.

P. HYBRIDA GRANDIFLORA FL. PL. Large-flowered Double. The best of the double-flowered forms is the new "All Double" strain which throws no single flowers. It is very large and obtainable in mixture as well as in separate colours. All Double Mammoth Paeony-flowered; the flowers are often 5 ins. across, and are very double. The range of colours includes rose, pink, rosy-purple and white; *fimbriata* All Double, a form with delicately fringed flowers which includes in its range all the colours of the last; *fimbriata* All

Double, Dwarf, similar to the last but about 1 ft. in height, ideal for pot culture; *fimbriata* All Double Dwarf Rosy Carmine, one of the most lovely of all Petunias, the colour is a rich attractive shade.

P. HYBRIDA PENDULA, BALCONY. A useful type for window-boxes and the like, also for pot work in the conservatory. Several separate colours are available, including *alba*, pure white; *rosea*, lilac-pink; Star, red striped white; and *violacea*, deep purple.

Bedding varieties. Height 1–1½ ft.

Blue Bedder, a fine bright lavender blue; Delight, large rose-pink flowers; Flaming Velvet, rich velvety scarlet; Gottfried Michaelis, a deep reddish-purple variety, with beautifully fringed flowers; Lace Veil, a lovely pure white fringed variety; Ruby Red, a rich warm shade; Setting Sun, most attractive, the delicately fringed flowers are of a striking shade of brilliant rose-pink.

P. NANA var. COMPACTA. Height 1 ft. Adonis, carmine rosy with a showy white throat; Alderman, a splendid dwarf large rich violet-flowered variety in great demand for bedding; Lavender Queen, pale lilac, large-flowered and very pretty; Rose Queen, one of the finest dwarf bedding varieties, the colour is rich deep rosy-carmine; Snow Queen, the large flowers are of the purest white; Violet Queen, erect compact habit with large deep violet flowers.

Phacelia (Gr. *phakelos* = a cluster, in reference to the crowded flower clusters). *Hydrophyllaceae.* 114 species; mostly in North America but 2 in Africa, 1 in the Sandwich Isles, and another in Northern Asia.

A genus of hardy annual and perennial plants which, by reason of their showy flowers, usually freely produced and either blue or lavender in colour, are of great service in the annual border. Seeds of the following kinds may be sown in the open ground in late September for flowering the following year, or during April, to flower in the summer of the same year.

P. CAMPANULARIA. Height 9 ins. The most popular species, ideal for edging, its large, brilliant blue flowers are produced in abundance. The plant is dwarf and shapely and the greyish-green leaves, tinted with red, are almost hidden by the profusion of bloom.

P. CILIATA. Height about 1 ft. A sweetly-scented lavender-blue-flowered species of considerable garden value.

P. CONGESTA (*P. conferta*). Height 1 ft. The flowers of this species are lavender-blue and are carried in large clusters.

P. DIVARICATA (*Eutoca divaricata, E. mexicana*). Height 1 ft. A spreading species with large bright-blue flowers. *Wrangeliana* (*Eutoca Wrangeliana*) is the variety usually found in trade catalogues, which differs from the type mainly by having leaves inclined to be three-lobed. 1835.

P. GRANDIFLORA see P. WHITLAVIA.

P. LONGIPES. Height 1 ft. An interesting species bearing clusters of large creamy-white flowers.

P. PARRYI. Height about 1 ft. The deep violet flowers of this species with their white anthers are particularly showy and they are usually marked with five spots, one on each lobe, 1885.

P. TANACETIFOLIA. Height 1–1½ ft. A species largely cultivated for bees; the flowers carried in large clusters are small and bright blue in colour. 1832.

P. VISCIDA (*Eutoca viscida*). Height 1–2 ft. The flowers are ½–1 in. in diameter, deep blue in colour with a purple or sometimes whitish centre. The foliage is hairy at the base and covered with minute glandular hairs above. 1835.

P. WHITLAVIA (*P. grandiflora*). Height about 1–1½ ft. Although generally known in the trade as *Whitlavia grandiflora*, this plant is now referred to *Phacelia*; its flowers, violet-blue in colour, are very large, often 1 in. long and of

similar diameter. A fine plant for the mixed border. 1902.
Two varieties are sometimes seen in gardens: *alba*, the white
form, and *gloxinioides* (*Whitlavia gloxinioides*), which is a
handsome plant bearing blue-centred white flowers.

PHEASANT'S EYE see ADONIS AUTUMNALIS.

Phlox (Gr. *phlox* = a flame, in reference to the brilliance
of the flowers). *Polemoniaceae*. 60 species; North America
and Siberia.

P. DRUMMONDII. Height 1–1½ ft. The type from which all
the varieties now in cultivation have been derived was col-
lected in Texas in 1835 by Drummond, who sent home seeds
in that year. It is a showy plant, bearing numerous light-
purple crimson-eyed flowers, the outer side being a pale
blush. Seeds should be sown under glass during March or
April and the seedlings planted out towards the end of May
or in June.

There are numerous attractive varieties, among which
some of the best are: *alba*, pure white; *alba oculata*, pure
white with a dark eye; Brilliant, deep rose with a dark eye;
carnea, pale blush; Chamois-Rose, a very attractive shade;
cinnabarina, vermilion red; *coccinea cuspidata*, a mixture of
star-shaped flowers in many shades of colour; Isabellina,
pale yellow; *Leopoldii*, deep rose with a white eye; Lilac
White Centre, a pretty combination; Purple, a deep rich
colour; *Radowitzii*, rose and white striped; *stellata splendens*,
vivid red with a white eye.

A splendid bedding form, 9 ins. only in height, is also
available under the name *nana compacta* in a mixture of
many lovely shades. An improved form of this mixture is
known as Cecily, while the following separate colours are
noteworthy: *caerulea stellata*, light blue with a white star-
shaped centre; *carminea*, brilliant carmine; Chamois-Rose,
a delicate shade; *cinnabarina*, vermilion; Fireball, dazzling
scarlet; Purple; Rose Cardinal, a splendid deep carmine-

rose variety; Scarlet; Surprise, vermilion, white centre; Snowball, pure white.

PIMPERNEL see ANAGALLIS.

PINCUSHION FLOWER see SCABIOSA.

PINK see DIANTHUS.

PINK MONKEY FLOWER see MIMULUS FREMONTII.

Platystemon (Gr. *platys* = broad, *stemon* = a stamen, in reference to the expanded filaments). Cream Cups. Californian Poppy. *Papaveraceae.* 60 species; Western North America.

P. CALIFORNICUS (*P. leiocarpus*). A delightful little Poppy-like plant bearing numerous light-yellow or cream-coloured flowers, which, against the glaucous, grey-green foliage, are extremely showy. It is a dwarf shapely plant about 6–9 ins. in height and ideal for massing towards the front of a border, or for planting here and there in the rock garden. Seeds may be sown in the open ground during April. 1833.

P. LEIOCARPUS see P. CALIFORNICUS.

POINSETTIA, ANNUAL see EUPHORBIA HETEROPHYLLA.

Polygala (Gr. *polu* = much, *gala* = milk, in reference to its reputed quality of promoting the secretion of milk). Milkwort. *Polygalaceae.* 475 species; cosmopolitan, but not in New Zealand, Polynesia nor the Arctic Zone.

P. LUTEA. Height about 9 ins. An annual species remarkable for its clusters of brilliant orange flowers and its long flowering period; it is a useful plant for the mixed border. Seeds may be sown in the open ground during April.

Other annual species, not in general cultivation, include *P. cruciata, P. cymosa, P. ramosa* and *P. viridescens.*

Polygonum (Gr. *polus* = many, *gonu* = a knee, in allusion to the numerous joints of the stem). Including *Persicaria*; Knot-weed; Prince's Feather; Lady's Thumb.

Several members of this genus are useful annual plants,

and employed for a background to borders or for screening walls or fences. They are admirable for planting in small groups in the wild parts of the garden, and for this purpose seeds may be sown in the open ground during April.

P. ARENARIUM (*P. elegans*). A dwarf species bearing multitudes of little creamy-white flowers in small clusters. Useful for the rock garden.

P. ELEGANS see P. ARENARIUM.

P. ORIENTALE (*Persicaria orientalis*). Prince's Feather. A tall old-fashioned plant often 4–5 ft. in height. The short spikes of crimson flowers, borne in long drooping panicles, are extremely pretty. 1707. There are several garden varieties, notably: *album*, with creamy-white flowers; *pumilum*, a dwarf crimson-flowered plant about 2–3 ft. in height, and *variegatum*, in which the leaves are marked with yellowish-white.

P. PERSICARIA. Lady's Thumb. About 1–2 ft. in height; the leaves of this attractive plant have a crescent-shaped spot near their centre, whence the name Lady's Thumb. The flowers, carried in short spikes, vary from pink to greenish-purple.

POPPY see PAPAVER, ARGEMONE, ESCHSCHOLZIA, GLAUCIUM, PLATYSTEMON and ROEMERIA.

POPPY MALLOW see CALLIRHOË.

POT MARIGOLD see CALENDULA.

PRETTY BETSY see CENTRANTHUS RUBER.

PRICKLY POPPY see ARGEMONE.

Primula (L. *primus* = first, in reference to the early flowering qualities of some of the species). *Primulaceae*. 250 species; Northern Hemisphere, a few elsewhere.

Although perennial, several members of this lovely genus, together with their many splendid varieties, are usually

19. TAGETES PATULA VAR. HARMONY

20. URSINIA PULCHRA

grown to flower during their first year from seed. As pot plants for the house, in the cool greenhouse or conservatory, they have established themselves in the forefront of public favour, providing a show of blooms for many weeks at a time when flowers are none too plentiful. Brief cultural directions are given for the different types below.

P. CHINENSIS see P. SINENSIS.

P. FLORIBUNDA. Buttercup Primrose. Height 5–8 ins. A splendid pot plant for winter flowering, this species bears whorls of small fragrant golden-yellow flowers. The two varieties most often grown are *grandiflora*, with considerably larger flowers, and Isabellina, which produces its sulphur-yellow flowers more freely than the type. For cultural directions see *P. obconica*.

P. KEWENSIS. A hybrid between *P. floribunda* and *P. verticillata*, which appeared in one of the houses at Kew in 1897. It most resembles P. *floribunda* but has retained some of the mealiness of its other parent and is a robust handsome plant growing to a height of about 1 ft. The flowers, carried in several whorls, are about ¾ in. across, delicately fragrant and bright yellow in colour. A variety, *farinosa*, is remarkable for the silvery-white powder which covers the stems and foliage. It is treated in the same manner as that described under *P. obconica* below.

P. MALACOIDES. Fairy Primrose. This delicately graceful species has given rise to many beautiful varieties which rank among the finest of our greenhouse plants. The type grows to a height of about 1 ft.; the foliage is pale green above, often slightly mealy underneath, and generally covered with small white hairs. The flowers, carried in numerous whorls, are about ½ in. across and pale lilac-pink in colour.

Foremost among the many varieties are: *alba*, pure white; *alba fl. pl.*, a splendid double white-flowered kind; Brightness, deep glistening rose; Dawkins' Carmine Pink, rich carmine pink, of striking habit; Dawn, a new departure in colour, being a clear shade of bright salmon-pink, from which the pale lilac-pink characteristic of the type is completely eliminated; Duchess of Kent, large-flowered, clear pink; Eclipse, large-flowered deep lavender-pink, with a large deep yellow eye; *fimbriata*, a form having delicately fringed pale pink flowers; *flore pleno*, a double-flowered form of the type; *flore pleno* Rosella, double, rich pink; Mauve Queen, large flowered; Melody, large flowers, pure rose; Pink Beauty, a delightful shade of rose pink; Pink Sensation, clear pink; Princess Mary, deep rose; Rose Queen, brilliant deep rose; Snow Queen, the best large-flowered white variety; Spring, large mauve flowers enhanced by a paler eye; True Rose, a remarkable pink with no touch of mauve.

Seeds should be sown during April to flower in the following January, or in July to flower in March. It is grown in a similar manner to *P. obconica* but requires little or no shading after the seedling stage is past; it should be kept fairly cool, however, and given plenty of water.

P. OBCONICA. There are few greenhouse plants which provide such continuity of bloom as this fine Primula and its modern varieties. The type attains a height of about 10 ins., and bears numerous umbels of small lilac flowers. The foliage of this species and its varieties is covered with minute sharp hairs which, when handled by some people, cause an irritation of the skin. The finest of the large-flowered varieties now obtainable are usually classified in catalogues under the descriptive heading *grandiflora gigantea* and include: *alba*, pure white; *caerulea*, a fine clear blue; Chenies' Giant Hybrids, a mixture of many lovely shades; Crimson King, a very large-flowered crimson; Eureka, rosy-carmine, yellow-eyed flowers, borne in large umbels; Müller's Rosea, large rose-pink flowers; Mohnstein's Red, a rich shade; Red Chief, the deepest crimson of all; Rivoirei, very large carmine flowers; Rose Queen, a very lovely rosy-carmine variety; Salmon, a distinct shade of salmon-rose.

The cultivation of these Primulas is not difficult providing a little effort is made to understand their requirements. Seeds of the foregoing may be sown towards the end of January in a temperature of about 65°. After germination, the seedlings should be pricked off into boxes and later moved into small pots. They may then be placed in a shaded cold frame, and kept well watered until they are ready for potting into 5-in. pots, in which they will flower. They are usually sufficiently advanced for this move by the middle of July. They may then be brought into the greenhouse or conservatory at any time up to the end of September and will provide a show of bloom for many weeks. For further details regarding potting composts, etc., see the chapter on Cultivation, pp. 20–27.

P. SINENSIS (*P. chinensis*). Chinese Primrose. As a winter-flowering greenhouse plant this species and its lovely varieties are widely grown and deservedly popular. The type grows to a height of about 9 ins. and bears its flowers, variable in colour and about $1\frac{1}{4}$ ins. across, in large umbels. Some of the best varieties are described below under the classification usually adopted in most seedsmen's catalogues.

Single Fringed, or fimbriata, a form having single flowers delicately cut or fringed: Bright Rose, a splendid shade with dark green fern-like foliage; The Czar, a rich dark shade; Crimson King, a striking shade of deep crimson-scarlet; Dazzler, a recent novelty, the flowers are the brightest scarlet yet introduced; The Duchess, a striking pure white variety with a rosy-carmine zone and a clear yellow eye; Orange King, rich orange in bud, becoming salmon-orange when fully expanded; Pink Beauty, delicate rose-pink with a zone of deeper colour; Royal Blue, a rich dark shade; Ruby Queen, a large flower of good substance; The Pearl, a splendid pure white; True Blue a fine clear shade.

Giant-fringed, or fimbriata gigantea. The flowers are larger and of a more solid texture, and the plant is a little taller and more robust: Coral Red, a distinct shade; Magnifica Blue, a fine rich light blue; Prince George, a striking combination, the bright cerise flowers are enhanced by a deep yellow eye; Prince of Wales, bright crimson-scarlet; Queen Alexandra, pure white flowers of great size; Queen Mary, clear rose-pink; The Emperor, rich terra-cotta; Excelsior Mixture, contains a wide range of beautiful shades.

Star, or *stellata*, a free-blooming form about 1 ft. in height, bearing attractive star-shaped flowers: Blue Star, delicate porcelain-blue; Crimson Star, a rich deep shade; Dark Blue Star, a fine colour; Double Crimson Star, large double flowers of a rich shade; Giant White Star, large pure white flowers; King of the Stars, rich carmine-crimson; Miss Irene, salmon-pink; Princess Marina, deep coral-pink; Rosy Star, rosy-mauve.

Double Fringed, or *fimbriata fl. pl.*, a popular form obtainable in several separate shades, usually sold under the descriptive colour names: Blue, Crimson, Rosy Pink, Salmon Pink, Scarlet and White. A double form of the variety Dazzler mentioned above was introduced but it proved to be practically sterile and is now unobtainable from the trade.

Sowings may be made from March to June for flowering the following winter. The seeds should be sown thinly in pans or pots and allowed to germinate in a temperature of 60–65°. The seedlings should be given plenty of air in their growing stages to ensure sturdy plants which will flower well and freely. The young plants should be moved, when large enough, into 3-in. pots and finally into 5-in. pots, in which they are allowed to flower.

PRINCE'S FEATHER see AMARANTHUS HYPOCHONDRIACUS, also POLYGONUM.

PROPHET'S FLOWER see ARNEBIA.

PURPLE HORNED POPPY see ROEMERIA.

PURSLANE see CALANDRINIA and CLAYTONIA.

PYRETHRUM see CHRYSANTHEMUM PARTHENIUM also MATRI-
    CARIA INODORA.

QUEEN STOCK see MATTHIOLA SINUATA.

RED CAMOMILE see ADONIS AUTUMNALIS.

RED MOROCCO see ADONIS AUTUMNALIS.

RED VALERIAN see CENTRANTHUS RUBER.

Reseda (L. *resedo* = I calm, in reference to its supposed
quality of allaying pain when applied externally to bruises,
etc.). Mignonette. *Resedaceae.* 55 species; Mediterranean
regions, Europe.

Few flowers possess a fragrance so delightful and so dis-
tinctive as the ever-popular Mignonette, *Reseda odorata.*
Bereft of its powerful scent the plant would probably never
have attracted the attention of the plant selectors, but during
the past 150 years it has been encouraged to produce varieties whose spikes of flower in several shades of colour are
far larger than the wild type. Seeds may be sown in the open
ground during April, or in pots during March, the seedlings
being transplanted in May. Certain varieties, as indicated
below, are especially suitable for flowering in pots.

    R. ALBA. White Upright Mignonette. Height 1–2 ft. Some-
times grown as an ornamental plant in a mixed border; the
flowers, carried on short spikes, freely produced, are pure
white, but their scent is neither powerful nor pleasing.

    R. CRYSTALLINA. Somewhat similar to the last, the flowers
are deep yellow. Canary Islands.

    R. GLAUCA. Seldom seen in gardens, this species is said to
be a useful plant for a dry border. The flowers are creamy-
white.

    R. ODORATA. Height 1–1½ ft. The species from which the
modern massive-spiked varieties have been obtained. The
type bears rather loosely arranged spikes of creamy-white
fragrant flowers. North Africa, 1752.

Among the best of the garden varieties are: Crimson Giant, an improved pale red-flowered form of the type; Golden Queen, dwarf and compact with golden-yellow flowers; Machet Giant, this and the following varieties of similar type are the best for pot culture; the flowers are pale red, borne in massive spikes; Machet Goliath Golden, large handsome spikes of deep yellow flowers; Machet Orange Queen, a splendid orange-red; Machet Rubin, copper-scarlet; Machet White Pearl, unusual and attractive; Red Monarch, a fine shade of deep red.

RHODANTHE see HELIPTERUM MANGLESII.

Ricinus (L. *ricinus* = a tick, in reference to the supposed resemblance of the seeds to this insect). Castor Oil Plant, Palma Christi. *Euphorbiaceae.* 1 species; Tropical Africa.

R. COMMUNIS. This plant, which forms a small tree in the tropics, is cultivated abroad, chiefly in India and the United States, for the oil which is extracted from its seeds and used for medicinal purposes, and in some places in the preparation of food. In this country it is often grown as an Annual for its foliage, which, when contrasted with other plants, is extremely effective. The type grows to a height of 5–7 ft. when treated in this way, and the varieties commonly cultivated are mostly of similar height. Seeds may be sown under glass during March and the seedlings planted out towards the end of May. Among the popular varieties the following are notable: *africanus*, the whole plant is glaucous green, and very attractive; *borboniensis arboreus*, a rapid-growing plant often reaching a height of 10 ft., the foliage is bronze-green with red stems; *cambodgensis*, the whole plant is black-purple; *Gibsonii*, slightly dwarfer than the last, the foliage and stems deep red; *lacinatus*, foliage glaucous-green, finely cut and most attractive; *sanguineus*, foliage reddish-purple; Scarlet Queen, a showy variety with deep maroon foliage and scarlet flowers; *zanzibariensis*, a handsome large-leaved form, usually sold in a mixture of many fine shades, varying from green to reddish-purple.

RICOTIA LUNARIA see p. 18.

ROCCARDIA see HELIPTERUM.

ROCK PURSLANE see CALANDRINIA.

ROCKET LARKSPUR see DELPHINIUM AJACIS.

Roemeria (in honour of J. J. Roemer, 1763–1819, professor of botany at Zurich). Purple Horned Poppy, Wind Rose. *Papaveraceae.* 10 species; Mediterranean to Afghanistan; one species native to Britain.

These interesting Annuals are well worth including in a mixed border, and seeds may be sown during April where the plants are to flower.

R. HYBRIDA see R. VIOLACEA.

R. REFRACTA. A showy Poppy-like plant, growing to a height of about 2 ft., bearing bright scarlet flowers, the base of each petal enhanced by a white blotch.

R. VIOLACEA (*R. hybrida*). A pretty violet-blue-flowered species about 1 ft. in height. At one time quite popular, but apparently not now in general cultivation. It is a rare weed in cornfields in south-eastern England.

ROSE OF HEAVEN see LYCHNIS COELI-ROSA.

Rudbeckia (in honour of Professor Rudbec, 1630–1702, of Upsala). Black-Eyed Susan. *Compositae.* 35 species; North America.

The species and varieties of *Rudbeckia* described below are of great value in the annual border, and last extremely well in water when cut. Seeds should be sown in March under glass and the seedlings planted out towards the end of May.

R. BICOLOR. An annual species, 1–1½ ft. in height, bearing numerous showy flowers. The rays are generally yellow, marked at the base with blackish-purple, and the disc is black. Among the best garden varieties are: Kelvedon Star, a mixture of double and semi-double forms, the yellow flowers being enhanced by a broad brown zone; *semi-plena*, similar to the foregoing.

R. HIRTA. Black-Eyed Susan. A variable biennial species, which can be successfully treated as an Annual. In the wild the rays of the flowers are yellow, sometimes tinged with orange at the base. It is a troublesome weed in parts of North America. In cultivation, various colour forms have appeared, including bronze-yellow, deep rich crimson, pure deep yellow, and forms in which the flowers are beautifully zoned with a deeper shade. It is this bright and attractive mixture which is usually sold by seedsmen.

Other varieties worthy of note are: Mon Plaisir (My Joy), a handsome very free-blooming plant bearing rich golden flowers often 4 ins. across, the rays being very broad and without markings of any kind; *vomerensis*; similar to the last, but varying slightly in shades of yellow.

Sabbatia (in honour of L. Sabbati, an Italian botanist of the eighteenth century). *Gentianaceae*. 12 species; North America.

Included in this genus of uncommon but very pretty plants, are the two species described below, which are suitable for cultivation as Annuals. Seeds should be sown in a greenhouse during February or March and the seedlings planted out early in June. A light sweet soil suits them best. They may also be successfully flowered in pots in the cool greenhouse.

S. CAMPESTRIS. Height 9–12 ins. The flowers of this attractive species are generously produced, and are about 1½–2 ins. across. Their colour is deep rose-pink with a bright yellow star-shaped centre. 1855.

S. STELLARIS. Height 1 ft. More often seen in gardens than

the foregoing, this species bears bright rosy-pink flowers
with a yellow eye. 1827.

SAGE see SALVIA.

Salpiglossis (Gr. *salpinx* = a tube, *glossa* = a tongue,
in reference to the tongue-shaped style in the mouth of the
tubular flower). *Solanaceae.* 8 species; South America.

S. SINUATA (*S. variabilis, S. grandiflora, S. hybrida*). It is
from this species that the modern varieties of Salpiglossis,
in all the splendour of their lovely colourings, have been
obtained. Few plants have been favoured with flowers at
once so colourful and so delicately marked as the rich trumpet-shaped blooms of this aristocrat among the Annuals.
The type is a rather loosely-branched plant about 2 ft. in
height, the colour of its flowers ranging from pale yellow
to scarlet, purple and blue, variously striped and marked.
Seeds sown in a greenhouse early in March will produce
plants ready for planting out early in June, which will give
a good show in beds or borders for many weeks during the
summer. As a cut flower they are elegant and most decorative, while for use as pot plants in the cool greenhouse they
are unsurpassed. Larger plants will be obtained from
autumn sowings made in early September, the plants being
potted on and kept in a greenhouse through the winter to be
planted out towards the end of May.

The varieties may be roughly divided into two sections,
the *grandiflora*, and the *superbissima* or Emperor types.
The latter are rather more erect-growing, larger-flowered
and definitely more valuable for garden purposes. Mixtures
of both these types are available in a great variety of shades
and markings and many of the colours can be had separately. In the *superbissima* section the following are notable:
crimson, light blue, primrose, rose and gold, scarlet and
gold.

S. VARIABILIS see S. SINUATA.

Salvia (L. *salvo* = I heal, in reference to the supposed medicinal properties of some of the species). Clary, Sage. *Labiatae*; 550 species; Tropical and Temperate regions.

Of this very large genus, several species are annual, and certain others, while perennial, are easily flowered during their first year from seed. With the exception of *S. carduacea* and *S. Horminum*, seeds of which may be sown in the open ground during April, all the kinds described below will give of their best only if sowings are made early in the year. Seeds should be sown in a greenhouse during January or early February and the seedlings potted as soon as they are large enough They will be ready for planting out early in June, and will flower freely throughout the summer until the coming of the autumn frosts.

S. CARDUACEA. Height 1 ft. An interesting annual species, not often seen in gardens. The plant forms a rosette of downy thistle-like leaves, and the lavender-coloured flowers are carried in a compact head on long stems. California, 1854.

S. COCCINEA. Height about $2\frac{1}{2}$ ft. A perennial species usually treated as an Annual; the flowers, deep scarlet in colour, are borne rather sparingly on long spikes. 1772.

S. FARINACEA. Height $2\frac{1}{2}$ ft. A lovely perennial species, which will produce long spikes of violet-blue flowers in its first year from seed. Texas, 1847. Of this handsome plant there is a white-flowered garden variety, *alba*, and a splendid form, Blue Bedder, which is dwarfer and more compact than the type, and bears spikes more densely packed with flowers of a deeper and richer blue.

S. GRAHAMII. Height $2\frac{1}{2}$ ft. Apparently not in general cultivation, this species bears long racemes of deep crimson flowers, becoming purple with age. Although perennial it is usually treated as an Annual. Mexico, 1829.

S. HORMINUM. Clary. Height $1-1\frac{1}{2}$ ft. An annual species which has given rise to several well-known varieties. The plant is grown for its brightly-coloured floral leaves which terminate the upright stems. In the type these floral leaves vary in colour; usually they are purple or pale lavender-pink. There are several varieties which differ in the colour of their floral bracts; *alba*, white; Oxford Blue, a deep rich colour; *purpurea* (*S. Horminum* var. *rubra*), varying from carmine-red to brilliant purple-red; and *violacea*, light violet-blue. S. Europe, 1596.

S. PATENS. Height 2 ft. Easily grown as an Annual, this beautiful perennial species bears large flowers of an intense shade of blue. The foliage is deep green covered with small rough hairs. There are two varieties, *alba*, pure white, and a recent introduction, Cambridge Blue, a very popular and attractive shade.

S. ROEMERIANA. Perennial, but usually cultivated as an Annual, this species grows to a height of about 1½ ft. and bears its deep scarlet flowers sparingly in long rather loose racemes. Texas, 1852.

S. SPLENDENS. Scarlet Sage. Height 2–3 ft. From this superb perennial species have sprung numerous garden varieties, which, treated as Annuals, have taken their place in the forefront of our most popular bedding plants. The vivid scarlet flowers are carried freely in racemes 6 ins. or more in length, and when massed are brilliantly effective. Mexico, 1822. Among the varieties are: *alba*, creamy white; Bonfire, scarlet, erect and compact; Coral, a recent introduction with closely packed spikes of deep coral-pink flowers, a bright and attractive plant; Dwarf Gem, a very dwarf compact plant suitable for edging, scarlet flowers; Fireball, an early-flowering scarlet variety, compact and free blooming; Harbinger, the most popular of all; the flowers appearing very early in the season are vivid scarlet, carried in dense spikes, freely produced—a noteworthy variety; Rocket, a distinct variety, with very dense spikes of deep scarlet flowers and foliage a rather darker shade of green than most of the foregoing; *violacea*, a deep violet variety, which blooms rather late in this country, but is a distinct and interesting plant.

SAND VERBENA see ABRONIA.

Sanvitalia (in honour of the noble Italian family San-vitali). *Compositae*. 8 species; warm parts of America.

S. PROCUMBENS. Height about 6 ins. This free-flowering Annual of trailing habit could be more generally employed for the front parts of mixed borders or for planting here and there in the rock garden. The flowers, about 1 in. across, resemble those of *Rudbeckia*, the disc being dark purple and the rays bright yellow. A double yellow form, *flore pleno*, possessing considerably more value as an ornamental plant, reproduces itself true from seed. Seeds may be sown in the open ground during September to flower early the following summer or during April to flower the same year.

Saponaria (L. *sapo* = soap, in reference to the mucilaginous juice which makes a lather with water). Fuller's Herb. Soapwort. *Caryophyllaceae*. 20 species; Northern Temperate regions, chiefly Mediterranean.

Useful in mixed borders, the Saponarias described below are quite hardy and seeds may be sown in the open ground during September to flower the following summer, or in April to flower the same year.

S. CALABRICA (*S. multiflora*). Height 6–9 ins. A low-growing plant which covers itself with showy deep rose-coloured flowers. Massed in the front parts of a border it is quite effective. 1830. There is a white variety, *alba*; a dwarf form, *compacta* (*pumila*), which bears flowers of a similar colour to those of the type; and a brilliant scarlet variety, Scarlet Queen, which is a very serviceable plant.

S. MULTIFLORA see S. CALABRICA.

S. VACCARIA (*Lychnis Vaccaria, Vaccaria vulgaris*). Of graceful habit, this species is much in demand for cutting.

It grows to a height of about 2½ ft. and bears numerous large deep pink flowers. 1596. The variety *alba* is a pure white counterpart of the type.

Saxifraga (L. *saxum* = a rock, *frango* = I break, allusion uncertain; by some considered to refer to the fact that they generally grow in stony places, or possibly in reference to the supposition that certain species would cure stone in the gall bladder). Saxifrage. *Saxifragaceae*. 325 species; Northern Temperate and Arctic regions and the Andes.

Of this large genus only a few species are annual; those described below are useful for planting in moist places on the rock garden or beside running water.

S. CYMBALARIA. Height about 6 ins. A pretty, deep yellow-flowered species; the foliage is a glossy green, becoming striped with brown as the plant ages. Caucasus and Asia Minor.

S. HUETIANA. Height 4–6 ins. This low-growing plant, which bears numerous small bright yellow flowers, is frequently sold under the name of *S. Cymbalaria*, from which it differs principally in its less upright, dwarfer habit. Asia Minor.

Scabiosa (L. *scabies* = itch, in reference to the common species' supposed properties of curing this disease). Scabious, Sweet Scabious, Pincushion Flower. *Dipsacaceae*. 60 species; Europe and Mediterranean regions.

Whether for massing in a mixed border or for use as a cut flower, the varieties of the annual Sweet Scabious have become firm favourites; for indoor decoration their long wiry stems and large handsome flowers, which last well in water, recommend them to every gardener. Seeds may be sown under glass during late March or in April to flower the same year; sowings made in the open ground during April will produce plants flowering late in the summer.

S. ATROPURPUREA (*S. major*, *S. maritima*). Height 2 ft.

From this species the many fine garden varieties now in cultivation have been obtained. It is said to be biennial in certain places but is usually considered to be an Annual and is generally treated as such. The flowers of the type, small by comparison with the modern varieties, are variable in colour, ranging from dark purple to rose and white. 1629. Among the best tall large-flowered varieties are: Azure Fairy, a lovely shade of deep lavender-blue; Blue Cockade, similar, but of a slightly deeper shade; Coral Pink, a rich pleasing colour; Fire King, intense rosy-crimson; King of the Blacks, very dark purple; Peach Blossom, a delicate shade of pink; Shasta, the finest pure white variety.

There is also a small-flowered tall yellow form, Golden Yellow, and a dwarf type, *nana*, or Tom Thumb, about 9 ins., suitable for bedding, which is obtainable in mixture or in the following separate varieties: Coral Rose, a rich shade; Dark Purple, a very deep colour; Fiery Scarlet, glowing rosy-crimson; Flesh, a delicate shade; Sky Blue, a pleasing pale lavender; and Yellow (*S. minor* var. *aurea flore pleno*), a small-flowered yellow variety.

S. MAJOR see S. ATROPURPUREA.

S. MARITIMA see S. ATROPURPUREA.

S. MINOR var. AUREA FLORE PLENO see S. ATROPURPUREA.

S. PROLIFERA. Height 9 ins. A dwarf species useful for planting in odd corners of the rock garden or in the front of a mixed border. The flowers, freely produced, are pure white.

S. STELLATA. Height $1\frac{1}{2}$ ft. A little-grown annual species bearing pale blue flowers sometimes varying to pale lavender-pink. 1823.

SCARLET FLAX see LINUM GRANDIFLORUM var. RUBRUM.

Schizanthus (Gr. *schizo* = I cut, *anthos* = a flower, in reference to the deeply incised corolla). Butterfly Flower. *Solanaceae*. 15 species; Chili.

Splendid pot plants for the cool greenhouse or conservatory, the varieties of *Schizanthus* will also succeed in the open border from sowings made under glass during March or early April. For cultivation in pots seeds should be sown in a greenhouse during August or early in September, the seedlings being potted on and placed in a well-ventilated cold frame until the end of the year, when they may be taken into the greenhouse. To obtain strong healthy plants it is essential to give them plenty of air and guard against them becoming drawn and spindly in their young stages.

S. GRAHAMII. Height 2 ft. The flowers of this species vary from lilac to rose, with a prominent orange marking. 1831. The garden varieties include: *albus*, white and orange; *carmineus*, carmine-pink and orange; *carneus*, pale flesh-pink with orange; *lilacinus*, lilac and orange; *niveus*, pure white; and *roseus*, deep rose and orange.

S. PINNATUS (*S. porrigens*). Height 2 ft. The flowers of this variable species are usually violet or lilac, the upper lip being paler than the lower and the centre segment marked at the base with a large yellow or orange blotch. 1822.

There are several varieties, some of which are described below, and also the various fine garden forms—usually listed under the names *hybridus* or *grandiflorus*—which have probably been obtained by hybridization with this and other species.

The variety *albus* has creamy-white and orange flowers; Brilliance, a rich glowing carmine-crimson, very showy; Dr. Badger's Hybrids, a splendid mixture of many beautiful colours, ranging from deep purple to carmine, rose, lilac, yellow and white; Pansy-flowered, a large-flowered many-coloured strain, in which the characteristic gold markings of the flowers have been almost entirely eliminated; *papilionaceus*, purple flowers, dotted and blotched with dark spots, and a yellow base to the middle segment of the upper lip; *oculatus* (*S. grandiflorus* var. *oculatus*) similar to the last, but the flowers are laced with various shades of colour; *roseus*, a deep rose and orange variety.

S. PORRIGENS see S. PINNATUS.

S. RETUSUS. Height 2 ft. A deep rose-coloured species, the large middle segment of the upper lip being rich orange, shading to brown. 1831.

The varieties include *albus*, white and orange; Pink Beauty, a beautiful shade of rose-pink; Rosamond, rosy-lilac and yellow; *trimaculatus*, an interesting variety, having purple flowers marked with three golden spots surrounded with bright purple.

S. WISETONENSIS. Height 1 ft. A hybrid between *S. pinnatus* and *S. Grahamii*, this magnificent strain is now widely cultivated for pot work in the cool greenhouse. The plants are dwarf and shapely, and a wide range of lovely shades of white, pink and crimson are included in the mixture. Among the varieties are: Bridal Veil, pure white; Excelsior, an improvement on the type, being dwarfer and more compact and containing a greater number of shades of colour; Pink Pearl, a pretty and attractive variety, having white flowers delicately margined with rosy-pink; Snowflake, the finest white variety, bearing large fringed flowers.

Schizopetalon (Gr. *schizo* = I cut, *petalon* = a petal, in reference to the divided or incised petals). *Cruciferae.* 5 species; Chili.

S. WALKERI. Height 1–1½ ft. The deeply cut white flowers of this useful annual are delicately scented in the evening, and a few patches of it are well worth including in a mixed annual border. 1822. Seeds should be sown under glass during March and the seedlings transplanted towards the end of May. Satisfactory results are obtainable from sowings made in the open ground during April.

SEA LAVENDER see STATICE.

SEA POPPY see GLAUCIUM.

21. VERBENA AUBLETIA

Sedum (L. *sedeo* = I sit, in reference to the manner in which the plants fix themselves to rocks or walls), Stonecrop. *Crassulaceae.* 150 species; predominantly in Northern Temperate regions, but with small outliers in South America and Tropical Africa.

S. CAERULEUM. Height 2–3 ins. A charming little pale-blue-flowered species, which is very pretty in the rock garden or for carpeting purposes. Seeds may be sown in the open ground during April. 1822.

Senecio (L. *senex* = an old man, in allusion to the hoary white pappus). *Compositae.* 1450 species; cosmopolitan.

The popular Annual *Senecio*, commonly listed in trade catalogues under its old name, *Jacobaea*, is a useful plant for massing in a mixed border, while many people find the colourful Daisy-like flowers attractive for cutting. Seeds of *S. elegans* and its varieties may be sown under glass during March and the seedlings planted out towards the end of May or sowings made in the open ground during April will produce fine plants flowering later in the summer. Seeds of *S. multibracteatus* should be sown in a greenhouse during February and the seedlings potted on as they become large enough.

S. ELEGANS (*S. purpureus, Jacobaea elegans*). The type from which several varieties have been derived grows to a height of about 1½ ft.; the rays of the numerous flowers are deep purple and the disc yellow. South Africa, 1700.

The following varieties are notable: *albus*, pure white; *albus fl. pl.*, double-flowered white; *purpureus fl. pl.*, a double-flowered form of the type; *roseus*, a brilliant rose single variety; *roseus fl. pl.*, double-flowered rose. There is also a dwarf form about 9 ins. in height, usually grown in mixture.

S. MULTIBRACTEATUS. Height 1–1½ ft. A very pretty species often cultivated in pots for the cool greenhouse, although it may be planted out during the summer months. The flowers, carried in large loose heads, are bright rosy-mauve in colour with a yellow disc. South Africa, 1872.

S. PURPUREUS see S. ELEGANS.

SHEEP'S BIT see JASIONE MONTANA.

SHIRLEY POPPY see PAPAVER RHOEAS.

SIBERIAN PURSLANE see CLAYTONIA SIBIRICA.

Silene (L. *Silenus* = a Greek mythological deity; or possibly from Gr. *sialon* = saliva, in allusion to the sticky substance exuded by the stems of certain species). Catchfly. *Caryophyllaceae.* 320 species; Northern Temperate regions.

Included in this genus are several annual species and biennial or perennial species which can be successfully flowered during their first year from seed. The dwarf kinds are useful for the front of borders, edgings, and also for filling gaps in the rock garden. Seeds should be sown under glass during April and the seedlings transplanted towards the end of May, or if required for spring bedding, sowings may be made either in a cold frame or in the open ground during August and September.

S. ARMERIA. Lobel's Catchfly, Sweet William Catchfly. Height 1–1½ ft. This old-fashioned annual plant bears dense clusters of deep rose-pink flowers and is quite colourful when massed in a border. There is a white-flowered variety, *alba*.

S. ASTERIAS. A perennial species which may be flowered during its first year from seed. The plant grows to a height of about 2 ft. and bears numerous purple flowers. The variety *grandiflora* produces large ball-shaped heads of crimson-scarlet flowers and is very effective.

S. PENDULA (*S. rosea*). This species and its varieties, both double- and single-flowered, are cheerful Annuals of simple cultivation. The type grows to a height of about 8 ins. and bears loose racemes of pale rose-coloured flowers. 1731.

Among the best varieties are: *alba*, pure white; *alba fl. pl.*, double-flowered white; Bijou, with deep salmon-coloured double flowers; *Bonnettii*, rosy-magenta; *Bonnettii fl. pl.*, a double-flowered counterpart of the last; *carnea*, pale flesh-pink; *flore pleno*, the double-flowered form of the type; *ruberrima*, deep purple-rose; and *ruberrima fl. pl.*, a double-flowered form of it. There is also a dwarf rose-coloured form, *compacta*, very useful for bedding, available in the following varieties: *flore pleno*, double rose; Dwarf Queen, double-flowered rosy-magenta; Peach Blossom, double-flowered, a very pretty shade; *ruberrima fl. pl.*, double deep rosy-crimson; and Snow King, a fine double white-flowered variety.

S. ROSEA see S. PENDULA.

SLIPPERWORT see CALCEOLARIA.

SNAPDRAGON see ANTIRRHINUM.

SOAPWORT see SAPONARIA.

Solanum (possibly from L. *solor* = I solace, in reference to the sedative qualities of certain species). Nightshade. *Solanaceae*. 1225 species; Tropical and Temperate regions.

There are several species of this large genus which produce bright and handsome fruits, and are largely used for conservatory work or as pot plants for the house. While these are perennial, and give of their best during their second year, a good show can be had during their first year if seeds are sown in a greenhouse during January or February. The seedlings should then be potted on and placed outside until the fruits are beginning to form towards the end of the summer, when they may be brought inside again for winter decoration.

S. CAPSICASTRUM. Height 1–2 ft. A small shrub which bears numerous round orange-red cherry-like fruits. A dwarf compact variety is available under the name *nanum* also a form, *variegatum*, which has variegated leaves.

S. MELONGENA (*S. insanum*). Egg Plant. A handsome species bearing large egg-shaped purple and white fruits.

S. PSEUDOCAPSICUM. Jerusalem Cherry. Height about 3 ft. The fruits of this species are globe-shaped, usually deep orange-red. There is a dwarf compact variety, *nanum*, and a hybrid form with pointed orange-red fruits, *Weatherillii*, usually known as Weatherill's Hybrids.

Specularia (L. *Speculum Veneris* = Venus's Looking Glass, the early name given to the common species, in reference to the resemblance of the flowers to a looking-glass with a straight handle). Venus's Looking Glass. *Campanulaceae*. 10 species; Northern Temperate regions and South America.

Interesting little plants resembling *Campanula*, which are useful for massing in borders or planting here and there in the rock garden. Seeds may be sown where the plants are to flower in the open ground in late March or April.

S. PENTAGONIA. Similar in most respects to the following, but bearing slightly larger flowers, deep purple in colour, with a dark-blue centre. 1686.

S. SPECULUM. Height about 9 ins. An erect-growing Annual, bearing numerous violet-blue flowers about 1 in. across with a pronounced deeper centre. 1596. The following varieties are recorded, but are seldom seen in gardens : *alba*, a pure white form; *grandiflora*, large-flowered; also *grandiflora fl. pl.*, a double-flowered form; *procumbens*, dwarf and more compact.

SPHENOGYNE see URSINIA.

SPIDER-FLOWER see CLEOME.

SPRING BEAUTY see CLAYTONIA.

SPURGE see EUPHORBIA.

Statice (L. *sto* = I stand or stop, in reference to its astringent qualities). Sea Lavender. *Plumbaginaceae*. 130 species; cosmopolitan.

The Sea Lavender ranks among our most popular "everlasting" flowers. The bright and cheerful colours now available of these showy Annuals are valuable in the gay patchwork of the mixed border, while the flowers, if cut when fully expanded and dried for winter decoration, are very welcome during the dark months when fresh flowers are scarce and expensive. Certain kinds, notably *S. Suworowii*, are useful for cultivation in pots for the cool greenhouse or conservatory; seeds of this species should be sown in September and the plants wintered in pots, although it will flower quite well from early spring sowings. Seeds of the other kinds mentioned below should be sown in a greenhouse during February or early in March and the seedlings planted out during May.

S. BONDUELLI. Resembling *S. sinuata* in habit and the shape of its flowers, this species grows to a height of about 2 ft. The bracts and the flowers, carried in large heads, are deep yellow. 1859.

S. PUBERULA. Height 1–2 ft. A shrubby perennial species which will flower during the first year from seed. It is specially suitable for cultivation in pots, and bears large manyflowered heads of a deep shade of rosy-purple. 1830.

S. SINENSIS. A perennial species easily flowered in its first year from seed. The flowers, borne in graceful sprays, are pale sulphur-yellow, and the showy bracts, white or creamy-yellow. 1845.

S. SINUATA. Height 1–1½ ft. This popular rose-mauve-coloured species has given rise to several varieties of great merit, notably Blue Perfection, a very strong, robust, large-headed, rich blue variety; Lavender Queen, a delightful shade of clear lavender; *rosea superba*, deep rich rose; White, a fine sturdy variety; and Tom Thumb Hybrids, a dwarf bushy selection 6–9 ins. in height in many shades of colour, suitable for bedding or pot culture.

S. SUWOROWII. A striking and extremely effective species;

the long densely flowered spikes of rose-pink flowers are of great value for interior decoration. It is a splendid pot plant for the cool greenhouse or conservatory, and will also flower well in the open border. 1883. A white variety, *alba*, was at one time in widespread cultivation but now seems to have completely disappeared.

Other species suitable for cultivation as Annuals are *S. spicata* and *S. Thounii*, but these are not often met with in gardens.

Stevia (in honour of P. J. Esteve, professor of botany at Valencia in the sixteenth century). *Compositae*. 110 species; Tropical and Sub-tropical America.

The two members of this genus described below, although perennial, are often grown as Annuals for cutting. Seeds should be sown under glass during February or March and the seedlings planted out during May.

S. PURPUREA. A useful species, growing to a height of about 1–1½ ft. and bearing heads of purple flowers. 1812.

S. SERRATA. Attaining a height of about 1½ ft., this plant bears large heads of small white sweet-scented flowers. 1827.

STOCK see MATTHIOLA.

STONECROP see SEDUM.

Streptocarpus (Gr. *streptos* = twisted, *karpos* = a fruit, in reference to the spirally twisted capsule). Cape Primrose. *Gesneriaceae*. 30 species; Africa and Madagascar.

These lovely greenhouse Perennials may be flowered during their first year from seed. Sowings made during January or February will produce plants which will bear a few flowers towards the end of August, but which will be finer the following year. Of the strains and varieties of *S. hybridus* now available, the following will be found satisfactory: Blue Shades, medium-sized flowers of several beautiful shades of blue, and delicately marked and striped; Caritus, snow white, large-flowered; Cirrhus, pure white, blotched with violet; Princess Mary, a delightful shade of rose; Tyrian Purple, a fine deep violet shade with a pronounced yellow throat; and Veitch's Giant Hybrids, a mixture of many lovely shades of colour and different markings.

Stylomecon (Gr. *stylos* = style, *mecon* = poppy). *Papaveraceae.* 1 species; California.

S. HETEROPHYLLA. Usually described in catalogues under the name *Meconopsis heterophylla*, this annual plant is now referred to the monotypic genus *Stylomecon*. It is a desirable Poppy-like plant about 1½ ft. in height, producing brilliant orange flowers, the base of each petal being marked with a maroon blotch. Seeds should be sown under glass during February or March and the seedlings planted out in May.

SUMMER ADONIS see ADONIS AESTIVALIS.

SUMMER CYPRESS see KOCHIA.

SUNFLOWER see HELIANTHUS.

SWAN RIVER DAISY see BRACHYCOME.

SWEET ALYSSUM see ALYSSUM.

SWEET PEA see LATHYRUS.

SWEET SCABIOUS see SCABIOSA.

SWEET SULTAN see CENTAUREA MOSCHATA.

SWEET WIVELSFIELD see DIANTHUS HYBRIDUS SWEET WIVELSFIELD.

Tagetes (L. *Tages*, an Etruscan deity). Marigold. *Compositae.* 20 species; warm America.

In view of the fact that all the known species of *Tagetes* are confined to America, it is difficult to account for the terms African and French, which have been used for over a century to describe the varieties of the two popular species. The name French Marigold, applied to the varieties of *T.*

patula, probably originated through this species being introduced to France from its native Mexico. Among the many varieties of Marigold are some of our finest bedding plants, and from the range of different types and colourings it is possible to find kinds suitable for use in almost any border or bedding arrangement. Until recently all the double-flowered varieties produced a percentage of single flowers, but now, in addition to the older strains, there are several newcomers which produce only semi-double or double flowers, without any singles. Seeds of all the species and varieties described below should be sown in a greenhouse during late February or in March and the seedlings planted out towards the end of May or in June. Sowings may also be made with some degree of success in the open ground during May.

T. ERECTA. African Marigold. The type, which grows to a height of about 2½ ft., bears lemon-yellow flowers. 1596.

The following varieties are among the best: Collarette Crown of Gold, golden-orange, incurved centre with a collar of flat broad rays, odourless foliage; Guinea Gold, a Marigold of great merit, the plant is of pyramidal habit, about 1½ ft. in height and bears numerous large semi-double rich golden-orange flowers; Lemon Prize Strain, a fine selection of the familiar lemon-yellow African Marigold; Mexican Harvest Gold, an all-double golden-yellow variety, most effective when massed; Mexican Dwarf Orange, about 1 ft. in height, a bushy form with large orange double and single flowers; Mexican Semi-dwarf Harvest Gold, 1½–2 ft., bright golden orange; Mexican Semi-dwarf Orange Queen, 1½–2 ft., light orange; Orange Prince, a dwarf form of the following; Orange Prize Strain, a large handsome strain of the orange African Marigold; Sunbeam, a pale golden variety resembling in habit and type of flower the variety Guinea Gold described above; Tom Thumb Golden Crown, one of the most outstanding introductions of recent years, this plant, ideal for bedding work, is in all respects a dwarf form of the variety Guinea Gold already described; Yellow Supreme, large sulphur-yellow flowers, most attractive.

T. LUCIDA. Height 1½-2 ft. Sometimes described as the Sweet-Scented Marigold; the flowers of this perennial plant are less pungently scented than those of the other species and are orange in colour.

T. PATULA. French Marigold. The flowers of this species vary considerably in colour, ranging from almost pure yellow to chestnut red. It forms a compact bushy plant about 1 ft. in height, bearing its flowers very freely. 1573. Among the many varieties now obtainable some of the best are: Fire Cross, single deep orange-red flowers, very showy; Golden Ball, produces double golden-orange flowers and a small percentage of singles; *grandiflora*, a splendid double chestnut-red variety, the flowers striped and marked with golden-yellow; the percentage of single flowers is very small; Harmony, a striking variety of recent introduction, the flowers are all semi-double, the outer rays being deep chestnut-red, and those in the centre of the flower quilled and deep orange in colour; Legion of Honour, the showy single flowers are golden-yellow, marked with a broad zone of chestnut-red; Tall Australian Tree, a late-blooming giant variety, often 4-5 ft. in height, bearing golden-yellow flowers zoned with red; Tall Scotch Gold Striped, about 3 ft. in height; this variety produces double rich chestnut-red flowers, striped and marked with golden-yellow, and a small percentage of singles.

T. SIGNATA. A branching species about 9 ins. in height, bearing small flowers, the rays of which are bright yellow with a deep red blotch at their base. The variety *pumila* is dwarfer and more compact than the type; a further improvement in habit and size of flower has been achieved in the variety Golden Gem.

TANGIER SCARLET PEA see LATHYRUS TINGITANUS.

Tare see Vicia.

Tassel Flower see Emilia.

Ten Week Stock see Matthiola.

Thorn Apple see Datura.

Thunbergia (in honour of Karl Thunberg, 1743–1822, professor of botany at Upsala). *Acanthaceae.* 150 species; tropical regions of the Old World.

T. ALATA. Black-Eyed Susan. This greenhouse perennial climber and its varieties are sometimes grown as Half-Hardy Annuals. It bears creamy-buff flowers with a dark purple centre, which are most effective on a well-flowered plant. Seeds should be sown in a greenhouse during February or March and the seedlings planted out during June.

There are several varieties, including: *alba*, white flowers with a deep purple centre; *aurantiaca*, bright orange with deep purple centre; *Doddsii*, a variegated form of the type; *Fryeri*, pale orange flowers with a pure white centre; *lutea*, with self-coloured yellow flowers; and *sulphurea*, pale yellow with dark centre.

Tickseed see Coreopsis.

Tidy-Tips see Layia.

Tithonia (of mythological derivation, from *Tithonus*, a favourite of Aurora). Mexican Sunflower. *Compositae.* 10 species; Central America and Cuba.

These robust Half-Hardy Annuals are sometimes grown in mixed borders, where their large Sunflower-like flowers are quite decorative. Seeds should be sown under glass during March and the seedlings planted out towards the end of May.

T. DIVERSIFOLIA. Height about 4 ft. A strong-growing shrubby plant bearing orange flowers 4–6 ins. across; not in general cultivation.

T. SPECIOSA. Height 3–4 ft. The most commonly grown

species, it bears orange-scarlet flowers about 3 ins. in diameter. 1833.

TOADFLAX see LINARIA.

TOBACCO PLANT see NICOTIANA.

TOUCH-ME-NOT see IMPATIENS.

Trachelium (Gr. *trachelos* = the neck, in reference to its supposed properties of curing diseases of the throat). *Campanulaceae.* 7 species; Mediterranean regions.

T. CAERULEUM. Usually grown as a pot plant for the cool greenhouse, this perennial species may also be treated as an Annual for planting in groups in the open border. It grows to a height of about 1 ft. and bears large dense heads of small deep lavender-blue flowers. A most attractive plant when well grown. 1640. There is a white-flowered variety, *album*, seldom met with in gardens. Seeds should be sown during March, and the seedlings potted on for flowering under glass or transplanted to the open ground towards the end of May.

Trachymene (Gr. *trachys* = rough, *hymen* = a membrane, in reference to the channels of the fruits). *Umbelliferae.* 14 species; Australia to Borneo.

T. CAERULEA (*Didiscus caeruleus*). Blue Lace Flower. Height 1½ ft. A dainty Half-Hardy Annual, bearing large clusters of small delicate pale blue flowers. It is a useful plant for pot cultivation in the cool greenhouse or conservatory, or for planting in groups in a sunny border. Seeds should be sown under glass during March and the seedlings planted out towards the end of May.

Tropaeolum (Gr. *tropaion* = a trophy, in allusion to the shield-shaped leaves). Nasturtium. *Tropaeolaceae.* 50 species; South America and Mexico.

The Nasturtiums have long enjoyed a widespread popularity which has during the past few years received an added

impetus by the introduction of the double-flowered varieties. The genus contains both climbing and dwarf sorts
which can be put to many uses in the garden. Thriving in
poor stony soil, which tends to make them produce their
flowers in greater profusion and to discourage excessive
leafiness, the dwarf varieties are ideal for bedding and edging,
while the tall climbers rapidly transform a wall or tree stump
with their attractive flowers and foliage. Seed should be
sown during April in the open ground where the plants are
to flower.

T. ADUNCUM see T. PEREGRINUM.

T. CANARIENSIS see T. PEREGRINUM.

T. MAJUS. Nasturtium or Indian Cress. This type which
has produced many splendid varieties is a strong-growing
climbing Annual, and bears large showy flowers varying in
shades of yellow and orange. 1686. The varieties may be
divided into three main sections, Tall, Double and Dwarf.

Of the tall forms some of the best are: Bronze, an old
favourite; Dark Crimson, a rich shade; Dunnett's Golden
Yellow, the best tall yellow variety; Pearl, creamy-white;
Queen Alexandra, blood-red with varigated foliage; Queen
Crimson Beauty, a fine colour with variegated leaves; Queen
of the North, sulphur-yellow with variegated leaves; Queen
Scarlet Beauty, vivid scarlet with variegated leaves; Scarlet,
a vivid colour; *Shillingii*, yellow flowers spotted with brown;
Vesuvius, rich deep apricot with dark foliage.

The new double-flowered varieties may be classed in two
groups, the Gleam or semi-dwarf type, and the Globe or
dwarf form.

Of the Gleam varieties, which have all received descriptive names, some of the best now available are: Golden
Gleam, Orange Gleam, Primrose Gleam, Scarlet Gleam, and
the many-shaded mixture usually catalogued as Gleam
Hybrids.

The Tom Thumb Double Globe varieties, which form

compact little ball-shaped plants covered with flowers, include: Firebrand, Golden Globe, Primrose Globe and Scarlet Globe. These dwarf double forms are exceptionally fine for bedding and edging.

The dwarf *nanum* or Tom Thumb single-flowered forms are very numerous, and some of the outstanding varieties are: Beauty of Malvern, a fine orange-scarlet; Empress of India, an intense crimson with very dark foliage; Feltham Beauty, vivid scarlet, very free-flowering; Fireball, brilliant orange-scarlet, dark foliage; King Golden, golden-yellow, dark foliage; Pearl, creamy-white; Queen of Tom Thumbs, bright crimson, variegated foliage; Silver Queen, creamy-white, flaked with rosy-scarlet variegated foliage; Terra-Cotta, salmon terra-cotta.

T. MINUS. A dwarf annual species with small foliage and deep yellow flowers streaked with orange and red.

T. PEREGRINUM (*T. aduncum*, *T. canariensis*). Canary Creeper, Fringed Canary Flower. Of rapid growth, this is a splendid plant for covering walls, fences or trellises. The foliage is small and elegant, and the pale yellow flowers, although small, are extremely showy. 1810.

TULIP POPPY see PAPAVER GLAUCUM.

UNICORN PLANT see MARTYNIA.

Ursinia (in honour of John Ursinius of Regensburg, 1608–1666, author of *Arboretum Biblicum*). Jewel of the Veldt. 60 species; South Africa and Abyssinia. Including *Sphenogyne*.

Although there is still considerable disagreement among botanists regarding the nomenclature of this genus, some preferring to style it *Sphenogyne*, it is here described as *Ursinia*, under which name the species and varieties mentioned below are sold and grown all over the world. The introduction and re-introduction during recent years of several species have done much to enrich our store of these lovely Annuals, which are becoming increasingly popular for all kinds of bedding work as well as for pot cultivation. Their delightfully graceful foliage and the abundance of their Daisy-like flowers have assured them a lasting place in our gardens. Seeds should be sown under glass during March or April and the seedlings planted out towards the end of May, although satisfactory results may often be obtained from sowings made in the open ground in late April or May.

U. ANETHOIDES. Height 1–1½ ft. A splendid species, bearing its large rich orange flowers, often 2–3 ins. across, on stiff wiry stems well above the foliage. The flowers are enhanced by a deep red zone near the base of the rays, which are each marked with a showy black blotch, and are quite suitable for cutting, lasting well in water. A new variety, Sunstar, has larger flowers of a richer shade of orange.

U. ANTHEMOIDES (*U. speciosa*). A rather variable species, growing to a height of about 1 ft. The flowers are not quite so large as those of the foregoing nor so richly coloured, but being produced in great abundance, they are very attractive in the mass. They are lemon-yellow, and the base of the rays is marked with a broad purple blotch. The variety *versicolor* is similar in habit, and the colour of the flowers varies in shades of yellow and light orange.

U. CAKILEFOLIA. Height about 1 ft. A showy plant bearing flowers about 1½ ins. across, deep apricot in colour, often zoned with a deeper shade.

U. PULCHRA. Height about 9 ins. One of the most handsome dwarf species, it forms a little bushy plant, covering itself with its bright rich orange flowers, enhanced by a jet-black zone at the base of the rays. It is ideal for pot culture, edging or massing in the front of a mixed border. A variety, possibly a hybrid between this species and *U. anethoides*, has recently appeared under the name Aurora. It is about 1 ft. in height and the orange flowers are zoned with a broad band of bronze-red.

U. PYGMAEA. A very dwarf rather spreading species about

6 ins. only in height, which is a splendid plant for filling gaps in the rock garden or for planting near the front of a border. The flowers, very freely produced, are deep rich orange, without zone or marking of any kind.

U. SPECIOSA see U. ANTHEMOIDES.

VACCARIA VULGARIS see SAPONARIA VACCARIA.

VALERIAN see CENTRANTHUS.

VALERIANELLA CONGESTA see p. 18.

VENICE MALLOW see HIBISCUS TRIONUM.

Venidium (no explanation of the name given by its author). *Compositae*. 18 species; South Africa.

Several members of this lovely genus of South African Daisy-flowered plants undoubtedly rank among our most brilliant Annuals. The individual flowers are strikingly handsome and when massed in a border most effective. Seeds are best sown under glass early in April and the seedlings planted out towards the end of May. Venidiums prefer a light soil because, especially with *V. fastuosum*, a soil too rich or heavily manured tends to produce fasciated imperfectly shaped flowers.

V. DECURRENS. Height 1–2 ft. This species is seldom met with in gardens, but its variety, *calendulaceum* (*V. calendulaceum*), is quite a popular border plant. It bears numerous large golden-yellow flowers embellished by a black disc, which close up during dull weather.

V. FASTUOSUM (*V. Weyleyi*). Height 2–2½ ft. The finest cultivated species, this plant is one of the most vividly striking of all Annuals. The foliage is covered with white downy hairs and the flowers are often 4–5 ins. across. The large disc is shining black, contrasting effectively with the long deep-orange rays, each of which is enhanced by a brown marking at the base. A mixture of colour forms, possibly obtained by hybridization, has recently appeared under

the name *V. fastuosum* Hybrids. These include several
shades, varying from orange, buff, yellow to white, the
flowers variously zoned and marked. In general, the flowers
of this strain are not quite so large as those of the type.

V. MACROCEPHALUM. Height about 2–3 ft. A desirable
species, not often seen in cultivation. The large flowers are
of a delicate shade of lemon-yellow, enhanced by a dark disc.

V. WEYLEYI see V. FASTUOSUM.

The following species, which are not in general cultivation
nor readily obtainable, are said to be serviceable plants:
V. fugax and *V. hirsutum*.

VENUS'S LOOKING GLASS see SPECULARIA.

VENUS'S NAVELWORT see OMPHALODES.

Verbascum (old Latin name used by Pliny—supposed to
have been altered from L. *Barbascum*—from L. *barba* = a
beard, in reference to the pubescent foliage). Mullein.
Scrophulariaceae. 210 species; Northern Temperate regions,
6 in Britain.

Of the many perennial and biennial Verbascums the two
species described below may be treated as Annuals and are
useful for grouping in a mixed border. Seeds may be sown
under glass during March and the seedlings planted out
during May, or sowings may be made during April in the
open ground, where the plants are to flower.

V. BOERHAVII. Height 2 ft. The handsome foliage is
covered with snow-white hairs, and the flowers carried in a
long erect spike are pure yellow in colour.

V. PHOENICEUM (*V. ferrugineum*). A showy species, bearing
spikes of purple or reddish-purple flowers. It prefers a fairly
shady situation away from the heat of the midday sun. A
mixture of colour forms which includes pink, salmon, purple,
rosy-purple and white is usually sold by the trade under this
name. There is also a white variety, *album*, sometimes obtainable separately.

Verbena (old Latin name used by Pliny of the common species). Vervain. *Verbenaceae.* 100 species; Tropical and Temperate regions.

The Verbenas are splendid plants for all kinds of bedding and border purposes as well as for growing in window-boxes and the like. Some of the dwarf and small-flowered trailing kinds are useful plants for placing here and there in the rock garden to fill up gaps where perennial plants have died. Although Perennials, treated as Annuals they produce an abundance of their bright flower-heads over a long period in summer and early autumn and revel in a hot sunny position. The modern large-flowered colourful varieties have been derived principally by hybridization between *V. chamaedry-folia,* *V. phlogiflora,* *V. incisa* and *V. teucrioides*; these species are not cultivated in gardens. Their hybrid forms are described below under *V. hybrida.* the name used in most seedsmen's catalogues. Seeds should be sown in a green-house during January or early February and the seedlings planted out during the end of May or in June.

V. AUBLETIA (*V. canadensis, V. Drummondii, V. Lambertii, V. montana*). Height about 1 ft. A valuable species, bearing large heads of rose-lilac flowers, which has recently returned to a certain popularity. 1774. There are two varieties obtainable: *grandiflora,* a larger-flowered improvement upon the type, and *purpureo-carminea,* a deeper-coloured form.

V. CANADENSIS see V. AUBLETIA.

V. DRUMMONDII see V. AUBLETIA.

V. ERINOIDES. Moss Verbena. A low-growing species with attractive narrow foliage and numerous clusters of small deep lilac flowers. There is a pure white variety, *alba.*

V. HYBRIDA. Height about 1 ft. The varieties of colour and habit now obtainable among these popular garden forms become yearly more numerous. They are usually grouped into three classes, the ordinary small-flowered hybrid forms,

Mammoth or Giant-flowered, and *compacta* or dwarf, bushy forms.

Among the old well-tried varieties are: Auricula-Eyed, a mixture of various colours, the flowers all possessing a prominent white eye; *caerulea*, blue with white eye; *candidissima*, pure white; Dark Blue, a deep rich shade; Defiance, brilliant scarlet; *lutea*, small-flowered, amber-yellow; *rosea*, deep rose-pink; Royal Bouquet, an erect-growing mixture of many fine shades, splendid for bedding or pot culture; *striata*, an interesting mixture of many colours, the flowers being all curiously striped and marked.

Of the Mammoth varieties the following are noteworthy: Cerise Queen, a pleasing shade of salmon-cerise; *colossea*, a mixture of very large-flowered varieties; Etna, fiery red with a creamy-white eye, most effective; Ellen Willmott, a beautiful variety, the colour of the flowers is a delicate shade of bright salmon-rose with a pronounced white eye; *monstrosa* Auricula-Eyed, a fine large-flowered mixture of many shades, each flower having a white or creamy eye; Rose Queen, delicate rose, a most attractive variety; Royale, one of the most handsome of all, the royal blue flowers are enhanced by a sharply contrasting creamy-yellow eye; Scarlet Queen, brilliant scarlet with white eye; Snow Queen, the largest white-flowered variety; Spectrum Red, brilliant red. In addition to these named varieties there are many mixtures sold under various names which give very pleasing results, massed in beds or borders.

The dwarf or *compacta* varieties, which grow to about the same height as the foregoing but form more bushy shapely plants, include: Carmine Ball, a bright shade of carmine; Crown Prince, deep blood-red; Danebrog, brilliant scarlet with a white eye; Fireball, a splendid pure bright scarlet variety; *violacea*, dark violet; White Ball, a fine pure white.

V. Lambertii see V. Aubletia.

V. montana see V. Aubletia.

V. VENOSA. Height about 1 ft. A useful species for edging or carpeting purposes as well as for grouping in mixed borders. The flower-heads are small, very freely produced, and deep lilac-blue in colour. There is a white form, *alba*, and a pale lavender-blue variety recently introduced under the name *lilacina*.

VERVAIN see VERBENA.

VETCH see VICIA.

Vicia (old Latin name used by Virgil). Tare, Vetch. *Leguminosae.* 150 species; Northern Temperate regions and South America, 10 in Britain.

Some of the Vetches are occasionally used as annual ornamental climbing plants; although in general their flowers are rather inconspicuous, their narrow foliage is not without some decorative effect. Seeds may be sown in the open ground during April.

V. CRACCA. Height 3–4 ft. The flowers are rose-purple, about ½ in. long, carried in dense racemes. Native of Great Britain.

V. GERARDI. Height about 4 ft. Described by some authors as a variety of the foregoing species, this plant bears short racemes of violet-blue flowers.

V. HYBRIDA SNOWDRIFT. Of uncertain parentage this plant bears pure white flowers produced very freely.

Viola (old Latin name used by Virgil). Pansy, Hearts-ease. *Violaceae.* 250 species; cosmopolitan.

The ever-popular Pansies and Violas are so well known that it is not necessary to emphasize their value as garden plants. While practically all the species and varieties are perennial, many of them are successfully flowered during their first year from seed. Sowings may be made in the open ground in early April to produce flowers the same year. To obtain large free-flowering plants for the following year, sowings may be made in the open during July or August, but many gardeners prefer to make their summer sowings in a cold frame rather than in the open ground, thus ensuring strong healthy seedlings for transplanting towards the end of September.

V. BIFLORA. Height about 2 ins. A charming little plant, the flowers are yellow streaked with black on the tip. Europe to Siberia, 1752.

V. BOSNIACA. Height about 3 ins. An interesting little species bearing numerous small rosy-magenta flowers. Ideal for the rock garden.

V. CORNUTA. Height about 6 ins. A fine species for bedding, carpeting or for planting in small groups in rock gardens. The elegant flowers are pale violet in colour, and the petals are widely separated. Switzerland, Pyrenees, 1776. There are many varieties and some hybrids of this charming species, some of the best of which are: Alannah, a hybrid with *V. declinata*, the flowers are lilac-magenta; *alba*, pure white; Blue Beauty, a splendid dwarf early-flowering bright blue variety; Blue Gem, compact, deep violet-blue; Lavender Gem, similar in habit to the last, with pale lavender flowers; Little Gem, a dainty small-flowered violet variety, ideal for the rock garden; Papilio, the large violet flowers are enhanced by a showy dark eye; Rose Queen, delicate rose-mauve; Spring Messenger, early-flowering, rich purple flowers; W. H. Woodgate, dark violet.

V. DELPHINIFOLIA. Height about 6 ins. A handsome species with large finely cut leaves, which produces its pure white sweetly-scented flowers in great profusion. This species should not be confused with *V. delphinantha*, which is a plant impatient of cultivation and of far less general garden merit.

V. EIZANENSIS. Height about 6 ins. A species recently introduced to cultivation which is a splendid plant for the rock garden. The large leaves are very finely cut, and the pure white flowers are delightfully scented. Japan.

V. GRACILIS. Height 6 ins. A violet-flowered species notable for its profusion of bloom; its habit is dwarf and compact, rendering it highly suitable for rock-work. The following are among the best varieties: *alba*, pure white; Black Knight, almost black flowers; Lord Nelson, a dwarf plant bearing a profusion of deep violet-purple flowers—one of the best; *lutea*, pure yellow; Purple Robe, large deep purple flowers.

V. HYBRIDA. The origin of the modern hybrid Violas is very uncertain and several species have probably been used in their development. Although the varieties described below reproduce themselves fairly true from seed, some variation in colour must be expected. Seeds of the following varieties may be obtained: Arkwright's Ruby, deep ruby-crimson flowers with a large black blotch; Chantryland, a recent introduction, in which the flowers are pure apricot; Crimson Beauty, bright crimson; Enid, rosy-mauve, streaked pale lavender; Jackanapes, a curious combination of yellow and chocolate-maroon.

The following varieties are of the large-flowered bedding-type usually described in catalogues as *grandiflora*: Admiration, rich purple; Archie Grant, deep blue; Ardwell Gem, pure yellow; Avalanche, pure white; David Simpson, lavender streaked with crimson; Maggie Mott, lavender-blue; Primrose Dame, pale yellow; Purple King, a rich deep shade.

V. LUTEA. A small yellow-flowered species growing to a height of about 6 ins. Native of Britain. There is a larger-flowered variety *grandiflora*.

V. TRICOLOR. Pansy. Height 6 ins. It is from this species, the common field Pansy or Heartsease of this country, that the splendid modern large-flowered Pansies have been derived. The type is a weedy plant whose flowers are a combination of yellow, purple and black. The large-flowered varieties, usually described under the name *V. tricolor* var.

maxima, are legion, and a selection of some of the best is given below under the classification usually adopted in seedsmen's catalogues.

Bedding varieties. Height about 6 ins. Apricot Queen, rich apricot, black centre; Fairy Queen, azure blue, white edge; Gipsy Queen, terra-cotta and bronze; Lord Beaconsfield, lilac merging to rich blue in the centre; Psyche, violet-blue with a broad white edge; Pure White, without blotch or eye; Purple, a rich colour; Ullswater, a rich clear blue with black blotch.

In addition to the foregoing separate varieties there are numerous strains which include a wide range of shades. Some of the best of these are Bath's Empress, Heath's Strain, Matchless, and Non Plus Ultra.

Trimardeau or Giant varieties. Goliath, Golden Queen, deep yellow with a black blotch; Madame Perret, a mixture of wine shades; Pure Yellow, without blotch or eye; Roggli Alpine Glow, a large rich crimson with black blotch; Roggli Berna, large flowers of dark velvety purple. Of these large-flowered Giant varieties there are several fine mixed strains, including Engelmann's Giant; Roggli Giant, a splendid range of colours; and Triumph of the Giants.

Winter Flowering. A type of Pansy growing to a height of about 6 ins., which flowers extremely early in the year: Celestial Queen, sky blue; Helios, pure yellow, a fine variety; Ice King, white with dark blotch; March Beauty, dark purple; North Pole, pure white; Winter Sun, golden-yellow, black blotch.

VIOLET CRESS see IONOPSIDIUM.

VIPER'S BUGLOSS see ECHIUM.

VIRGINIAN STOCK see MALCOMIA.

VISCARIA see LYCHNIS.

Waitzia (in honour of F. M. Waitz, state physician at Samarang in Java, writer about Javanese plants). *Com-*

positae. 6 species; Southern and Western Temperate Australia.

It is to be regretted that these showy "everlasting" flowers have practically disappeared from cultivation, although they achieved at one time a fair measure of popularity, being used for grouping in mixed borders. They are mostly Half-Hardy Annuals and carry their flowers in terminal clusters. Seeds should be sown under glass during March or April, the seedlings being planted out in a sunny position early in June.

W. ACUMINATA see W. CORYMBOSA.

W. AUREA. Height 1–1½ ft. A bright golden-yellow species, very showy and of a fairly robust habit. 1836.

W. CITRINA see W. STEETZIANA.

W. CORYMBOSA (*W. acuminata*). Height 1–2 ft. The colour of the flowers varies from pale yellow to white or pale pink. 1864.

W. GRANDIFLORA. Height 1½ ft. A large-flowered yellow species, described by some authors as the best of the genus. 1863.

W. ODONTOLEPIS (*W. nivea, Morna nivea*). Height 1½ ft. The flowers of this species are generally pure white, although pink and yellow forms are recorded. 1836.

W. STEETZIANA (*W. citrina, W. tenella*). Height 6–12 ins. Similar to the last, this species bears pure white flowers, sometimes varying to pale yellow. 1861.

W. TENELLA see W. STEETZIANA.

WALLFLOWER see CHEIRANTHUS.

WHITE SNAKEROOT see EUPATORIUM AGERATOIDES.

WHITLAVIA see PHACELIA WHITLAVIA.

WIND ROSE see ROEMERIA.

WINGED-STALKED EVERLASTING see AMMOBIUM.

WINTER PURSLANE see CLAYTONIA PERFOLIATA.

WOODRUFF see ASPERULA.

WOOD SORREL see OXALIS.

WORMSKIOLDIA see p. 19.

Xeranthemum (Gr. *xeros* = dry, *anthemon* = a flower, in reference to the dry, papery flowers). Everlasting. *Compositae.* 6 species; Mediterranean regions and the Orient.

X. ANNUUM. Height about 2 ft. This is the only species in general cultivation, and several serviceable varieties have been derived from it. The type is an erect-growing showy plant, bearing numerous purple, papery, "everlasting" flowers about 1–2 ins. in diameter. It is extremely attractive massed in a mixed border and has the advantage of remaining colourful over a long period. The flowers are also valuable for cutting for winter decoration.

The following varieties are obtainable: *ligulosum* (*X. imperiale*), a semi-double purple form; *ligulosum alba* (*X. imperiale* var. *alba*), semi-double white; *perligulosum album* (*X. superbissimum* var. *album*), very full double white flowers; *perligulosum roseum* (*X. superbissimum* var. *roseum*), full double rose-coloured flowers; *perligulosum purpureum* (*X. superbissimum* var. *purpureum*), full double purple flowers.

X. IMPERIALE see X. ANNUUM.

X. SUPERBISSIMUM see X. ANNUUM.

YELLOW THISTLE see ARGEMONE.

YOUTH-AND-OLD-AGE see ZINNIA.

Zaluzianskya (in honour of Adam Žaluziansky, of Prague, who wrote *Methodus Herbariae* in 1592). Including *Nycterinia. Scrophulariaceae.* 20 species; South Africa.

These useful and dainty little Annuals are usually sold under their old name of *Nycterinia.* They are dwarf compact-growing plants covering themselves with a multitude of small flowers, which remain closed during the day, and are useful for a mixed border or grouping here and there in the rock garden. Seeds should be sown under glass during March and the seedlings planted out towards the end of May, or sowings may be made in the open ground during May.

Z. CAPENSIS (*Nycterinia capensis*). Height about 1 ft. The flowers are pure white and sweetly scented.

Z. LYCHNIDEA (*Nycterinia lychnidea*). Height 1–1½ ft. This species, which is not widely grown in gardens, bears large flowers yellowish-white inside, reddish-purple outside. 1776.

Z. SELAGINOIDES (*Nycterinia selaginoides*). Height 3–6 ins. The flowers, which are delicately fragrant, especially at night, are white, becoming lilac with age, and enriched by a showy orange centre. 1854.

ZEA see p. 43.

Zinnia (in honour of Johann Gottfried Zinn, 1727–1759, professor of medicine at Göttingen). Youth-and-Old-Age. *Compositae.* 12 species; North America.

The popularity of the Zinnias grows with each successive season. The wide choice of types and brilliantly coloured varieties which the efforts of the plant selectors have now made possible provides material for all kinds of border and bedding work; while for cutting purposes, although rather stiff and formal, the long firm stems and bright cheerful colourings of the giant varieties have won them many admirers. Seeds should be sown in a greenhouse, temperature about 60°, during April. The seedlings may then be potted on, or pricked off into boxes and transplanted to their flowering positions during June. For the best results it is advisable to plant in ground which has received a liberal dressing of manure.

Z. ELEGANS. Height about 1 ft. This type, which has produced most of the modern varieties, bears pale rose-purple single flowers about 1 in. in diameter. It has been encouraged in cultivation to produce many variations in the colour of its flowers, and the strains usually sold by the trade consist of a mixture of many shades ranging from white, yellow, red and crimson to purple. 1796.

Some of the best varieties are described below under the classification generally adopted in most seedsmen's catalogues.

Robusta grandiflora. Height about 2 ft., with large double flowers, obtainable in the following colours: crimson, flesh, golden, purple, scarlet, sulphur and white. There is also a mixture of striped varieties in which the flowers are all curiously streaked and marked, and a form with curled and twisted rays, Achievement, usually grown in a many-coloured mixture.

Scabious-flowered. Height about 1½ ft. A strange form with a tight, quilled centre and a collar of broad flat rays, sold in a mixture of various shades.

Dahlia-flowered. Height about 2½ ft., a very handsome large-flowered type, of which the following varieties are among the best: Canary Bird, primrose yellow; Crimson Monarch, crimson scarlet; Exquisite, light rose, shaded deeper towards the base of the rays; Golden Dawn, pure golden-yellow; Golden State, rich orange; Meteor, deep red; Oriole, orange and gold; Polar Bear, white; Scarlet Flame, vivid scarlet.

Giant Mammoth. Height about 2½ ft. The flowers are as large as the foregoing but rather flatter and more shapely. Cerise Queen, scarlet-cerise; Enchantress, deep rose-pink; Golden King, rich golden-yellow; Lemon Queen, pale yellow; Rose Queen, bright rose-pink; Scarlet Gem, a vivid shade.

Lilliput. Height 1 ft. A small double-flowered type but producing an abundance of bloom, available in the following colours: golden, lilac, orange, salmon, scarlet and white.

Z. HAAGEANA (*Z. mexicana*). Height about 9 ins. A dwarf bushy species, bearing numerous deep orange flowers. There are several varieties, notably *aureola*, in which the rays are enriched by a broad zone of chocolate-maroon at their base; *flore pleno*, double orange flowers; and a mixture of several shades of colour, *hybrida flore pleno* Perfection.

Z. LINEARIS. Height about 9 ins. Somewhat resembling the last species in habit, this plant bears small orange flowers, marked with a broad maroon zone at the base of the rays.

Z. MEXICANA see Z. HAAGEANA.

INDEX

NOTE: *As Part II is arranged alphabetically, the plants mentioned therein are not included in this index.*